To Dr. Robert Swanson
with best salaams

UNKNOWN OMAN

UNKNOWN OMAN

WENDELL PHILLIPS

DAVID McKAY COMPANY, INC.

NEW YORK

UNKNOWN OMAN

In Honour of His Majesty

SULTAN SAID BIN TAIMUR ALBU SAID

King of Oman and Dependencies

CONTENTS

ILLUSTRATIONS

ACKNOWLEDGEMENTS

Unknown Oman is based on my own travels, explorations and excavations in Oman. It was written concurrently with my *Oman: A History*, which is scheduled for publication shortly, and the research for the two books was inextricably bound together. I drew upon the world's leading Near Eastern scholars, Orientalists, Arabists, and Arabian military and political specialists. It has become impossible to distinguish the help thus received in writing this present volume from that received in writing the history. I therefore do not hesitate to express to the following my appreciation for their generous aid in the making of both books.

To His Majesty Sultan Said bin Taimur, always a king and a scholar for his unfailing support, ever generous assistance and royal patronage; to Professor William F. Albright, the dean of Biblical Archaeologists and supreme Orientalist for reading this manuscript and making available his profound scholarship.

And to the following:

Iman Haj Ahmed	Professor A. M. Honeyman
Paul Aiken	Colonel Frank Hough
Major St John Armitage	Dr Albert Jamme
Professor Charles F. Beckingham	Colonel Eric Johnson
Dr Jerry Beavan	Hal Knudson
Reverend Laurence P. Byers	Dr Louis Krause
British Museum Library	Dr B. M. Luben
Colonel Hugh Boustead	Wing-Commander Eric Macro
Dr Ray L. Cleveland	Wing-Commander Alfred Marsack
Keith and Huda Collins	Dr Bradford G. Martin
Canon Kenneth Cragg	Colonel Colin Maxwell
Dr Thomas Crosby	Dr Mohamed Mazhar
Brian Doe	Alastair J. McIntosh
Dr G. S. P. Freeman-Grenville	Professor Alexander Melamid
Foreign Office Library	John Meier
Ahmed Jama Galaal	Lee Mortimer
Robert J. Gavin	Major Sir Berkeley Ormerod
Reverend Richard E. Hanna	H. St John B. Philby
Laurie J. Hobson	Horace Phillips

Merilyn Phillips

Sunshine Phillips

Richard M. Preece

Samuel F. Pryor

Royal Asiatic Society

Royal Central Asian Society

Royal Geographical Society

Saiyid Qaboos bin Said

T. F. T. Al Said
  (Former Sultan Taimur)

Dr Lewis Scudder

Professor Robert Serjeant

Major T. E. (Jock) Snell

Saiyid Tariq bin Taimur

William and Gladys Terry

Wilfred Thesiger

Lowell Thomas

Dr Wells and Beth Thoms

Dr Gus Van Beek

Mrs John Van Ess

Brigadier Pat Waterfield

Arthur S. Watts

Sir Evelyn Wrench

Alec Wight

Willis Kingsley Wing

A special word of thanks goes to my secretaries, Eileen Salama, Jan Imerman, Jackie Grant, Zelma Rogers, Helen Jackson, Margaret Deering, Beth Morgan and Irene Castaneda, for their patience over a period of eight years in typing and re-typing this manuscript as it slowly evolved into *Unknown Oman*.

Thanks are also due to the following for permission to reproduce copyright material:

The Clarendon Press for Material from *Portuguese off the Southern Coast of Arabia* by R. B. Sergeant, Longmans, Green & Co. Ltd. for material from *Arabian Sands* by Wilfred Thesiger; Methuen & Co. Ltd. for material from *Sheba's Daughters* by H. St. J. Philby, and the author's agents for material from *Forty Years in the Wilderness* and *The Heart of Arabia* by H. St. J. Philby, published by Robert Hale Ltd.

Note on Arabic Transcription and Usages

The problem of spelling Arabic names and words in English is one which can easily drive a writer to despair. Lawrence of Arabia despaired of system and spelled them variously as he felt inclined at a given moment. The author of this book has adopted, except for a very few names, as simple a system as devisable to give the reader an idea of approximate pronounciation. It is hoped that the extensive imposition of the system chosen will not be regarded as too strict and harsh, in spite of the fact that it does lead to spellings which in some cases appear rather different from those usually seen in the press.

In the system of spelling used, only three vowels are employed (except where popular spellings are retained), as in Classical Arabic. For approximation, *a* should be pronounced as in *father*, *i* as *ee* in *feet*, and *u* as *oo* in *food*. The consonantal combination *dh*, not normally found in English is to be pronounced as *th* in *the* (in contrast to *th* in *thing*), while *gh* and *kh* for convenience may be pronounced as *g* in *good* and as *k* in *kind* respectively. Although in Arabic it is a distinct sound (not found in English), *q* may be pronounced the same as *k*. The special mark (') represents a guttural sound not found in English or other European languages; it is distinct from the glottal catch, which is represented by the mark ('). The former sound in fact occurs in the name of the Sultan, i.e., Sa'id, and in the name of the country, i.e., 'Oman (both of these names are accented on the final syllable), but typographical expediency has made it necessary to omit the symbol. The macron and other diacritical marks of interest to specialists have also been omitted.

The word for 'son' is pronounced in two ways in Arabic; *bin*, normal in Arabia itself, especially South Arabia and Oman, is usually employed here, though *ibn* is a more literate pronounciation. (*Bin* is pronounced approximately as the English word *bin*). Said bin Taimur means 'Said the son of Taimur'; thus the normal Arabic usage is to append the father's name, and sometimes the paternal grandfather's name, to identify a person. Women's names are subject to exactly the same usage, with the replacement of *bin* by *bint*, 'daughter (of)'.

The Arabic title *sultan* (pronounced with the accent on the final syllable) has the same meaning as the English word 'king' for all practical purposes. Sometimes 'king' is used in reference to the ruler of Oman, sometimes 'sultan'. The reader need not be confused by this alternation – nor by the fact that 'Sultan' is also used by Arabs as a personal name.

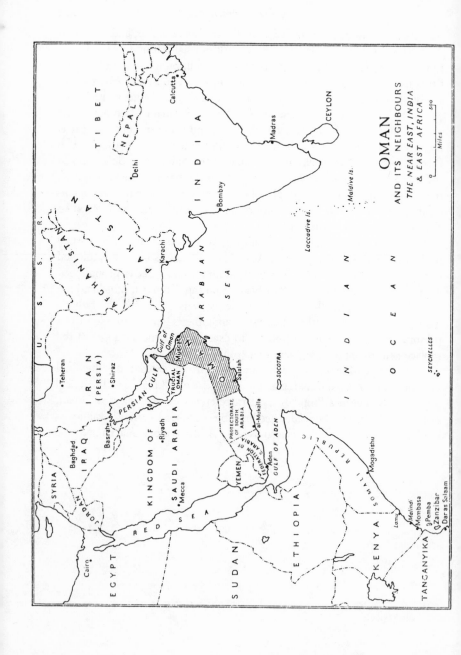

OMAN

AND ITS NEIGHBOURS

THE NEAR EAST, INDIA
& EAST AFRICA

Miles
500

I

AKHDHAR AND MUSCAT

Flying into Oman – The Green Mountain – 'Torrid' Muscat
Dining with the Sultan – An ancient inscription
The Sultan's person and family

> And wit well, that the realm of Arabia is a full great country,
> but therein is overmuch desert. And no man may dwell
> there in that desert for default of water, for the land is all
> gravelly and full of sand. And it is dry and no thing fruitful,
> because that it hath no moisture; and therefor is there so
> much desert.
>
> *Sir John Mandeville*

The Southern Cross was still visible; the sky grew redder, then changed to gold; the sun emerged from the sapphire blue of the sea and so another day began just as our wheels lifted from the rough runway. That day was Thursday, 2 January 1958, and our Dakota (DC–3) had just taken off from the runway on the inland side of the coconut-laden palms of Salalah, which was the two-thirds-of-the-way mark on our journey from Aden to Muscat. After crossing the Qara Mountains we flew north-east for the next three hours over reddish-yellow, empty, featureless sand. Eventually the red changed to rough blue as we passed over a gravel plain; then came a series of 'hog's backs' with high mountains looming up in the distance. On the right glimmered a beautiful green oasis with small dark grey houses clustered around glistening pools of water shining like mirrors. Beyond this, still on the right at an elevation of 1,900 feet, was a little town nestled against the mountains near a winding *wadi* bed. This was Nazwa; only a few months earlier this isolated spot had been featured throughout the world during the abortive revolt against the Sultan or King of Oman.

Right outside the window and almost touching our wing was a sheer wall of stone reaching straight up. On the other side a peak rose over us as well, for we were exploring the great Jabal Akhdhar, 'The Green Mountain', a grand gigantic pile of desolate nakedness, towering to a massive height of 10,000 feet and forming the central backbone of Oman.

The greenish cast of the great mountain was no illusion, for the rock which forms it is of a dark green colour, as green as ancient bronze. The mountain is thus a mass of rock, with grass and thorn only at widely spaced intervals. Ahead I could see a huge jagged peak coming closer. The side facing us was practically perpendicular. It almost seemed as if our wing tip might scrape the sharp knife-like edge. The other side was almost as bold and abrupt. The views we beheld constituted a fantastic panorama of cliffs and peaks cut by geologically youthful vertical canyons, of precipitous green escarpments, stupendous crags and weirdly shaped domes. The deep yawning chasms were strange and unreal, because their sides were so steep – like deep narrow pockets. The ravines were filled with cascading streams and the walls covered with maidenhair ferns. Sustained by heavy rain in winter and showers throughout most of the year, agriculture thrives. On the lower half of the mountain garlic is grown while higher up wild olive and cedar trees abound. An elaborate system of artificial watercourses irrigates the plots of land which are in tiers cut into the steep canyons below the plateau, and water from large storage tanks of locally made cement cascades from one level to the next to irrigate the groves of fruit trees; apricot, peach, pomegranate, almond, mulberry, grapes, walnut, figs and nectarines, as noted in 1836 by the intrepid and indefatigable French naturalist P. Aucher Eloy,[1] who zealously explored this region on foot, gathering some 250 different botanical species. He eventually returned to Muscat by the Wadi Samail, weary, fever-stricken and footsore.

A year earlier the pioneer English explorers, J. R. Wellsted and H. H. Whitelock, had plunged recklessly into Oman's heart and had remarked in astonishment and admiration: 'Is this Arabia, this the country we have looked on heretofore as a desert? Verdant fields of grain and sugar cane stretching along for miles, are before us;

streams of water, flowing in all directions, intersect our path; and the happy and contented appearance of the peasants agreeably helps to fill up the smiling picture.[2]

Society on the Jabal is feudal; the majority of the inhabitants are tied to the land. Here allegiance is to faction and family. There are twelve splinter factions of the Bani Riyam tribe dwelling on the mountain, each with its petty sheikh or headman. The four main villages and their populations are Shuraijah (245), Wadi Bani Habib (177), Siq (163) and Manakhar (106). There are two nomad factions who wander over the Jabal and its fierce steep faces on mountain donkeys, proud and splendid beasts the size of mules and able to carry an equal load. They negotiate the steep and difficult tracks up and down the mountain with ease and sure-footedness from a few days after birth. It is believed the strain was introduced onto the mountain fron an East African jackass several hundred years ago; unfortunately it is dying out. These people are the Awlad Awamir and the Shiraqiyin (together numbering about 450). The total population of the Jabal is about 1,600, and the villages are built into the sides of the vast scoops of canyons. Houses are well and solidly built of mud and stone. Roofs are strong and timbered, plastered with a red clay to withstand the winter elements. Ornately carved doors of walnut and sandalwood, sweet-smelling, decorate the doorways.

As we flew on, the canyons widened with tiny patches of green laid out in varied patterns in each curve of the long winding riverbed below, with minute dwellings clustered here and there.

At a nod from Bill Terry, I asked our Captain to do an about face and cover the whole Jabal Akhdhar once more so that Bill could complete his film. Terry, long my partner in African and Arabian exploration, was the photographer who filmed the Japanese attack on Hickham Field and Pearl Harbour.[3] Although it was bitterly cold at this height, Bill was wringing wet from the strain of holding the 16-mm. Bolex out of the cockpit window in an effort to capture every angle.

The pilot made a wide circle and came down again into the very heart of the mountain, weaving in and out of one narrow passage to the next, peeping into caverns and chasms that few had seen so intimately before. It was an experience to watch the tiny shadow that was our plane fall on the face of mighty rocks far below or climb dizzily up some sharp peak right ahead of us. The play of light and shadow, the changing pattern of green, grey and golden yellow, the deep dark canyons and the dazzling sunlight on the highest ridges made a kaleidoscope of sensation and colour hard to forget. Flying into Akhdhar of Oman was truly a mountain-top experience.

After sloping up from the west, the majestic Jabal Akhdhar drops off abruptly on the east and, as observed by Colonel S. B. Miles in 1876, 'The abruptness of the north and south sides render this grand rocky mass inaccessible from the plains, except by means of the torrent beds that ages of surface drainage and the waters of living springs have scored on its rugged flanks.'⁴ Yet back in the tenth century the Persians under Abd al-Qasim had invaded these almost inaccessible, precipitous slopes while the Omanis fought desperately, hurling down huge stones as they retreated upward step by step in defence of their last citadel. According to Ibn al-Athir the despairing valour of 10,000 Omanis could not stem the relentless Persian tide and after total defeat and bitter humiliation at the summit their women and children became the property of Abd al-Qasim's conquering troops.

Several aspects of Jabal Akhdhar, which is visible for over a hundred miles at sea, reminded me of Gibraltar. As we flew on farther east below us appeared houses, miniature cultivated areas and finally, in the distance, the extensive date groves of the Batinah Coast. Our Captain took us low over the twin Omani cities of Muscat (Arabic, *Masqat*, 'falling-place') and Matrah (perhaps meaning 'anchorage') with their blue-green bays, black masses of rocky coast, ancient Portuguese forts and gleaming white buildings.

We were all a little airsick upon landing at Azaiba (Arabic, *Adhibah*), an hour's drive from Matrah. The next thing I knew I was being hugged by beaming Jama, my chief Somali, and veteran of all our Arabian expeditions, who exclaimed in Arabic *ash-shukr l-illah*, 'thanks to God', and welcomed more sedately by Professor Alexander M. ('Sandy') Honeyman. The Sultan had graciously sent Mohammed Amin to give us an official welcome, and next to him stood the Sultan's Military Secretary, Brigadier Pat Waterfield.

The Sultan's Land Rover drove us as rapidly as possible over dry river-beds, past quaint little villages, camels, goats and friendly people. The road from the airport runs along the edge of the sea for a short distance, then heads into the interior past a customs post over a low serpentine pass and through the city of Matrah; three miles farther on one gets a breathtaking, strikingly grand view of Muscat[5] lying at the base of a rocky amphitheatre in a narrow, sheltered cove (the easternmost of five large contiguous indentations) facing a 900- by 400-fathom, horseshoe-shaped rock-girt harbour. This harbour, believed by Lord Curzon to be the most picturesque in the East, is certainly the best and deepest in all of Arabia. Wellsted once stated, 'No part of the world presents a wilder or more romantic aspect than Muscat Cove.' On both sides the bold, grim 350-foot cliffs are inscribed at every elevation with the time-honoured white-washed names of many ships – such as the H.M.S. *Arethusa*, H.M.S. *Surprise* and H.M.S. *Teal*, some dating back over ninety years. Many of the great names of the British Navy are recorded here. The Sultan refers to this as 'my marine autograph book'. Here a unique spectacular panorama unfolds with the whitewashed city bracketed in between the grey-walled Portuguese forts erect as sentinels on the right and left, with dark rocky crags towering behind on three sides. Perched on the highest point of these fantastic serrated ridges are various lookout towers left by the cruel and adventurous empire builders from Portugal. The surrounding dark brown craggy scenery is of a weird, arid and unproductive land.

One finds little or no level coastal plain in the vicinity of Muscat as there is farther north, for the towering eastern Hajar Mountains meet the sea directly in an apparently unbroken line of precipitous cliffs, rising diaphanous and opalescent out of the pale blue waters of the Indian Ocean. There is an austere silent grandeur about these uniformly naked mountains whose bare rocks, devoid of vegetation, exclude Muscat from every cooling breeze during the hot season, sucking up the pitiless heat during the day to release it after sunset with recorded temperatures of over 120° at midnight. 'Those vast and torrid mountains no shade but heaven does hide.' Occasionally on a Muscat summer night a west wind, *gharbi*, sweeps down from the surrounding sun-baked mountains and the already impossible temperature rides to new heights in this geographical furnace. However, as our party entered the city in mid-winter, the weather was cool and could be rivalled but not bettered. We were lucky; the city's climate has had a bad press. 'On the 1st of May, 1810, Mr H. Smith informed the Government of Bombay that "the pernicious effect of the climate of Maskat obliged him to resign all further charge of duties of that station. . . ." The horror in which Maskat was held at this time by the East India Company's servants is not difficult to understand if it is remembered that the climate had already proved fatal to all the four Residents who held office there since the foundation of the Residency in 1800.'[6]

A Persian poet has expressed it aptly. 'Muscat gives to the panting sinner a living anticipation of his future destiny', or in other words, 'Hell with the fires put out.'

But the weather was by no means the only aspect of Muscat which made an impression on travellers in the past. In 1347, Ibn Battuta 'embarked and reached Masquat [Muscat], a small town in which there are many fish,' and in 1507, Affonso de Albuquerque found that 'Mascate is a large and very populous city . . . it is the principal entrepot of the kingdom of Ormuz [Hormuz]', while the noted Italian traveller Pietro della Valle found in 1625 that Muscat contained two churches and a motley population of Portuguese, Arabs, Indians and Jews. In 1672, John Struys noted: 'This City [Muscat] according to its greatness is populous enough, but not so populous as it was soon after Ormus [Hormuz] was taken in by the King of Persia [1622], then serving as an Asylum for the Portugueezes, Indians and Arabians.'[7] In the eighteenth century the harbour was a forest of tall masts and spars and then, as now, filled with intriguing merchantmen and dhows from the Red Sea, Karachi and beyond, with trade to a large measure with Turkish Iraq, the annual visit of the Omani 'coffee fleet' being an important event at Basrah. In 1721 Captain Alexander Hamilton sailed into Muscat harbour on the 250-ton, 12-gun *Morning Star* and noted that 'The City of Muskat is very strong both by nature and art; but the buildings very very mean, as most Bafricks are under the Oeconomy of a People who abominate Luxury and Pride as the Muskat Arabs do. The Cathedral built by the Portuguese, still retains some marks of its ancient

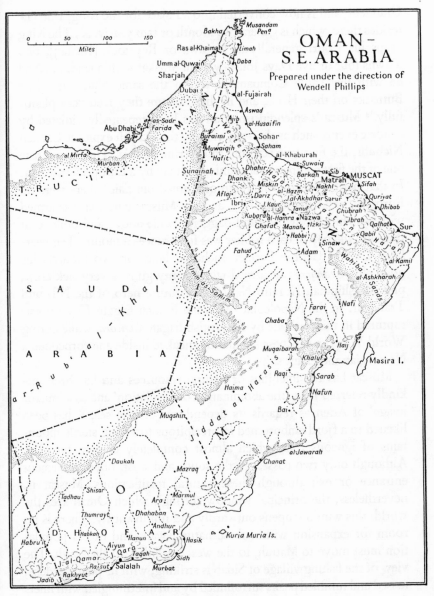

MAP 2. Oman – S.E. Arabia.

Grandeur, and is now converted into a Palace for the King, when he resides there, which is generally a Month or two yearly. . . . The King keeps his Court generally at Nazawa or Reystock [Rustaq], two Towns four or five Days Journey from Muskat within land. . . . And he with his Table Companions sit on the same Mat, with their Buttocks on their Heels, and in that Posture they feed very plentifully.'[8] Muscat's splendid isolation has been repeatedly violated by historic events such as the 1765 visit by the Danish explorer Carsten Niebuhr, the first true scientist to describe Arabia. This man wrote one of the first competent accounts of Oman by a European traveller. In that period (during the reign of Ahmed bin Said) there were no European residents in the city, and the Muscat garrison was armed with matchlocks, swords and daggers, 'wide above and pointed at the end'; the pay of each soldier was four rupees a month. Ten years later Captain George Farmer anchored here for two months; his good ship *Seahorse* was armed with twenty guns, a very sick crew, plus Midshipman Horatio Nelson, the future hero of the Nile and Trafalgar. In the Napoleonic Wars the French frigate *Vigilant* was captured in this harbour by the British frigate *Concord*, while during World War II a Japanese submarine sneaked inside and torpedoed a Norwegian merchant ship.

Muscat has no amenities or natural resources and has been unkindly referred to as 'the abomination of desolation' and as a 'mirror image' of Aden as regards its dependence on the sea. It has been likened to a fjord embosomed in precipitous towering sterile mountains of igneous rock which almost completely enclose the city. Although only two passes, to the south and west, offer convenient entrance or exit through these natural fortifications, Muscat is, nevertheless, the principal window through which Oman sees the world; this window opens outwardly and not inwardly. There is no room for expansion within these natural walls and excess population must move to Matrah, to the west, or Sidab, to the south. The view of the fishing village of Sidab is striking, with its palm gardens, tossed and tumbled peaks surrounded by and intermingled with inlets from the sea. Two small reservoirs in Wadi al-Kabir held by concrete dams supply water to Muscat. There is no main street, just a maze of narrow winding alleys which lead into a sort of central compound.

On the south and west sides of this part of the city is a rather substantial wall with a real moat. The only gate into the walled city large enough for motor vehicles is through the west wall. It is appropriately known as *bab al-kabir*, 'the Big Gate', and was reconstructed some years ago by the present ruler. In a fashion known for millenia in Arabia and bordering areas, this gateway is supplied with built-in benches (in 1950–51 we excavated benches inside the main, south gate of ancient Timna) on the inside for the guards and citizens to sit on as they engage in endless conversation and story-telling. The two heavy-timbered panels of the swinging door are closed every night about three hours after sunset with a roll of drums and three shots from a cannon. The doors will be opened only for vehicles belonging to the Sultan or for others specially authorized. After the closing of the main gate, pedestrians may enter the walled city through a small door in one of the large gates – if provided with the light required by law. Torches just won't do. It must be a lantern; there are no exceptions[9].

On arrival in Muscat one is immediately impressed with the heterogeneous quasi-Arabian character of this city of approximately 6,000 inhabitants (the figure fluctuates seasonally).[10] The gaily-clothed Baluchi women are seen everywhere unveiled, as in 1820, 'having rings of such thickness in their noses, as to make the nostrils, through which they were suspended, hang down, and much disfigure faces which would otherwise have some pretensions to beauty.[11] By contrast the Omani women of today, as those seen in 1847 by Ida Pfeiffer,[12] wear a kind of mask of blue stuff over the face, fastened upon springs or wires, which project some distance beyond the face; a hole is cut in the mask between the forehead and nose, which allows something more than the eyes to be seen.

In 1836 J. R. Wellsted observed with delight that 'In their persons the females are tall and well made, with a roundness and fullness of figure, not however approaching to corpulency. . . . They are, without doubt, in point of personal attraction, superior to any other class which I have seen in Arabia.'[13]

At the time of his visit in December 1816, J. S. Buckingham noted that out of an estimated population of ten thousand there were only three or four Jews and no Christians resident in Muscat. 'From the preference which seems to be given here to hansdome Abyssinian women over all others, there are scarcely any persons to afford this luxury, who are without an Abyssinian beauty as a wife, mistress, or a slave.' He found the people of Muscat 'to be the cleanest, neatest, best dressed, and most gentlemanly of all the Arabs that I have ever yet seen, and inspired by their first approach, a feeling of confidence, good will, and respect.[14]

It has been well said that 'Muscat has one foot in Arabia and the other in India', for the *suq*, 'market', is dominated by shrewd and enterprising Indian merchants (mostly from Bombay) who are called *banyani* by the local Arabs, after the merchant caste of Hinduism. Indian coinage is the usual medium of exchange in Muscat and in the coastal cities of Oman, although the *mahr* (bride-price) is granted the dignity among Muslims of being arranged on the basis of the Maria Theresa (M.T. dollar's value: 4s 6d or 77 cents). The Indian rupee, worth 20 cents, is broken down into sixteen annas, and the anna is subdivided into four pais; the New Indian coinage, with 100 *nia paise* to the rupee is not yet widely accepted in the Kingdom. In addition, the Sultan's own smaller coins are sometimes seen along the coast. They are based on an independent *baizah* (derived, as Indian *pais*, from the old Spanish *bazanta*), of which there are sixty-four to the rupee. Two-*baizah*, five-*baizah* and twenty-*baizah* coins are in circulation. The coolies on the waterfront are exclusively Baluchis, related Zedgalis and Iranians, while the Arabs themselves, who represent about half the population of Muscat and make up the aristocracy of the city, wear beards and turbans reminiscent of the old Persian style. The Hindus living in Muscat, somewhat looked down on by Muslims because of their polytheistic faith, carry on their customs without interference for the most part (although their women lack freedom in public) and even maintain a small temple on the outskirts of the city in the mouth of Wadi al-Kabir, where they take their daily morning bath and wash their white garments.

There is little uniformity in the Arabic spoken in Muscat and neighbouring villages such as Sidab. Long intercourse with Zanzibar and East Africa has had its influence on the local dialect. One individual may speak like a desert nomad, using vocabulary, phrases and sentence structure which are akin to the classical language, while another may use idioms, simplifications and pronunciation resembling the colloquial dialects met around the northern end of the Persian (Arabian) Gulf. In general, however, their language is full of pidgin English and pidgin Hindustani and has a flavour which belongs to Muscat alone.

The poor in Muscat are not happy to be poor and are not content to submit to the mere force of circumstances which in the past they have often accepted with resignation, consoling themselves with the reflection that this must somehow be Allah's will. They have become conscious of their material disadvantages and are more and more determined not to suffer or tolerate them. To them the putative basic mentality of the Islamic East that this earthly life is short and one should concentrate on the eternal promise of future reward has little appeal. It is not indolence nor is it the lack of capacity to which poverty and disease are attributable; few are trained in productive skills, and there is little opportunity for those who are. It is therefore not surprising that the greatest ambition of many young Muscatis is to leave, though not for more than a few years at a time. The influence of this unique cultural island is too penetrating for one native-born to forget it quickly.

The concept of private property is looked upon favourably in Muscat. Both land and houses (usually built of mud and plastered with gypsum-stucco or stone or concrete) may be owned by either native citizens or by foreigners. Land where an individual cannot prove ownership is treated as crown land under the jurisdiction of the government. All building construction comes under the Municipal Law of Muscat and Matrah, which is administered by the Municipal Board.

It will be necessary here to digress for a moment to say something of the origin and purpose of my presence in Muscat. In 1951 I organized an Arabian expedition, my third, to excavate the monumental ovoid Moon Temple of Awwam, in the 'forbidden' kingdom of Yemen, the temple of the god Ilumquh in the ancient capital of the Queen of Sheba.[15] On 12 February 1952, official Yemeni hostility forced us to abandon everything and flee for our lives. I led my party over the soft sand-dunes to safety in Beihan, leaving behind (the greatest disappointment of my life) not only irreplaceable antiquities excavated by the expedition, but a fortune in vehicles, hospital units, photographic supplies and other equipment. It was thus by chance and not design that we first arrived in Oman, but luckily I had already met the studious Sultan in 1949, when I crossed South Arabia and was received by him in Muscat; and he had then invited me to bring my American expedition to his country, to explore and excavate. I explained to him that due to our staggering losses in Yemen we could do only limited work and that if he would have us on these terms we would be honoured to come. He replied that we were welcome on any terms, that he had followed our troubles in Yemen closely and sympathized with us, and that as far as money went he would advance all we might need for a major archaeological programme. It was only months later that we realized fully the kindness of the Sultan, for after we had charged to his account many thousands of dollars worth of expenses, he cancelled the whole amount as his contribution to the expedition. This generosity resulted in the eventual discovery of the extremely important lost city of Sumhuram, the ancient frankincense centre of Arabia.

Hence my fourth visit, with which we are here concerned. Professor Alexander Honeyman of St Andrews University, veteran of our earlier expeditions, had preceded me and had set up our headquarters in a mud-stone-plaster house kindly lent to us by the city's leading Indian merchant, Khimji Ramdas. As professor of Oriental languages at Scotland's most ancient university, Honeyman is a specialist in Hebrew, Arabic, Aramaic, Ugaritic, Phoenician and, what was most to our purpose, Epigraphic South Arabian. All my team on this new venture were veterans with the exception of twenty-eight year old Ray Cleveland. He was studying for his Ph.D. under the great Orientalist Professor William F. Albright of the Johns Hopkins University. Cleveland had been initiated in archaeology under Professor Kathleen Kenyon, during her epic work at Jericho. We were still waiting, before setting off for our objective, Sohar, for our medical specialist, Dr Louis Krause, on his way by air via Bahrain.

The Sultan was an enthusiastic supporter of our expedition and himself contributed not only several vehicles and all the petrol we should need, but, more important, Sheikh Saqr bin Hamad, who had accompanied us on my reconnaissance visit to Sohar three months previously, as our chief guide. Sohar had been chosen as our objective because of the glowing accounts of it given by classical Arab geographers, and the great accumulation of occupational debris.

My mother and sister Merilyn having accompanied me to Muscat, were invited to dine at the gleaming white palace. Before World War I, my mother Sunshine had been a California Sierra gold prospector, swimming instructor, life guard, school teacher and motor cycle rider. Merilyn, a former New York model and sports writer, was recovering from a broken neck recently received in a serious auto accident. I briefly explained to them that his Majesty the Sultan had been born in 1910, three years before his father Taimur bin Faisal assumed the office of Sultan. With the abdication of his father Taimur in 1932 Sultan Said became the King of Oman. The Sultan speaks, reads and writes letter perfect English, is of modest stature, neat in appearance, of a retiring nature and extremely polite and courteous to visitors and guests. He is a devout Muslim, but not fanatical. Though completely Arab, the Sultan has great affection for Great Britain and America and listens to the B.B.C. and subscribes to American magazines. A man of conservative habits, the Sultan owns no Cadillacs, aeroplanes, or yachts but enjoys the simpler life of a man of action. He prefers to drive desert jeeps and trucks himself and is a keen sportsman, excellent shot and avid photographer. The Sultan has one wife, his second, who has borne him three children. The only son, the handsome and extremely intelligent Saiyid Qaboos graduated from the Royal Academy at Sandhurst in September 1962. When Qaboos was a boy his father the Sultan used to impress upon him that he was like all other Omanis; he must work or starve. He was to have no servants of his own.

Now on this present occasion the Sultan greeted us warmly and showed us a beautifully engraved silver bowl sent as a gift by Theodore Roosevelt in 1907 to his grandfather Faisal bin Turki, who was on the throne at that time. It was inscribed, 'From the President of the United States of America to His Majesty the Sultan of Oman'.

The Sultan next led us onto his terrace to view the harbour, which is so nicely framed by the impressive Mirani and Jalali Forts, each perched on a cliff about 150 feet above sea-level. He explained that one of the early Portuguese commanders had been called Mur and as time passed the Western fort, which is slightly higher and more complicated and irregular in design, having been adapted with great skill and judgement to the available space, was called Mirani; whereas, the Persian commander was named Jalal – thus Fort Jalali (it formerly bore the name of San João) to the east, which completely occupied the whole of the top of the isolated, scarped rock on which it proudly sits. Today Jalali, which dates from 1589, although smaller and of simpler construction, still exhibits two tiers of casemated embrasures with a round tower at each end. It serves as the Sultan's only prison, with about eighty-five residents at present, mainly dissidents and agitators from the recently troubled area in the interior. (In Yemen, under the late Iman Ahmed, men of this type would simply have had their heads chopped off by royal decree.) The Sultan's doctor visits the prisoners twice a week and if a man's condition warrants transfer he is sent to the hospital. The only access to Jalali is on the harbour side by a flight of steep steps cut out of the solid rock. Once a prisoner escaped from Jalali by making a rope of blankets; however, once down on the ocean side and finding he had no place to go, he promptly gave himself up.

On 14 February 1963, there occurred the first mass escape known in the history of the Kingdom from Jalali prison. The usual number of prisoners was never more than ten to fifteen to a room, but at this time there were forty-four prisoners ranging from murderers to arms smugglers, kept in one room due to repairs being made. The hands of the prisoners had not been shackled, only their feet; they discovered that a given number of men could pull open the shackles, inspected daily, that had been hammered on around their ankles by the prison warden. The escape was well planned. None of the guards was involved. One of the old cannon embrasures in the main tower wall had not been filled up properly, and this led to the escape attempt. The prisoners had removed the old spikes from the gun cages holding the wheels and had used these to dig at night. During the day they stuffed in old clothes to cover the hole being enlarged. Their extra rations came in gunny bags; these they un-ravelled and rewove the material into ropes which could be used in the escape.

Four of the prisoners were too old to make the escape attempt and were tied up before the others left. They claimed later that they had been beaten before being gagged. The escape rope was found untied on the ground at the bottom of the wall, and it is a mystery how the last man got down the rope and yet untied it at the top at the same time. Brigadier Pat Waterfield feels that possibly one of the four who remained behind untied the rope and then tied himself up along with his three companions. The escapees went down the ropes to the rocks below and then to the beach behind the British Consulate in Cable Bay. They then crossed the rocks to the old cemetery in Sheikh Jabir Cove where they gathered together and left their wet clothes behind. From the beginning, everything went against them; the moon was later than expected and the tide was high instead of low. Thus as they came over the rocks, they were forced to follow a higher track and left a long trail of blood, for the rocks were like razor blades on their bare feet. Before long, some of the escapees ran into a British Corporal accompanied by about eight of his men at Sidab. The Corporal had studied the local language and challenged the prisoners; two were shot as they tried to flee and twenty-six were captured on the spot.

The escape was first reported in Muscat when two of the prisoners broke away from the main party and went into the city where they were stopped for walking around after hours without a light. When questioned, they admitted they were from Jalali prison and that they had escaped along with forty-two others.

By this time, the patrols began reporting in from the surrounding area. Each of the prisoners carried a little package of food. Many were strangers to Muscat and they lacked a plan of action for the outside area. The prisoners received absolutely no help from the local people. Most of the Sultan's troops were away on a training exercise at the time of the escape. However, all the troops were soon alerted and sent out in small parties to block the routes leading out of Muscat.

Within 24 hours, all the prisoners had been captured except one, a Baluch named Bakshut, who had been the ringleader. Two years before, he had murdered his wife for being pregnant without his permission. Now he was on his own – nobody helped him from the outside. He travelled at night, living on the countryside, and was eventually recognized by a former inmate of Jalali prison. At the time, he was about a hundred miles north of Muscat. Bakshut had been free for thirty days when he was arrested by the local Wali.

The following inscription in old Portuguese can still be read over the inner gateway of Mirani Fort.

In the reign of the very high and Mighty Philip, first of this name, our sacred King, in the eighth year of his reign in the crown of Portugal, he ordered through Dom Duarte de Meneses, his viceroy in India, that this fortress should be built, which Belchior Alvares built, the first Captain and Founder 1588.

Professor Robert Serjeant gives us further details about the fort and the inscription:

Kal'at Merani, as this fort is now called, was known to the Portuguese as Fort Capitan. . . . The building of the fortress was commenced by Dom João da Lisboa about 1552, and it was expressly for this purpose that he had been sent out from Portugal. When the town was attacked and taken by Piri Ra'is, the Turks dismantled the fortress and it was left derelict. When Ali Bey, about 1581, raided and pillaged Muscat town, the government at Lisbon realised that measures must be taken to strengthen the defences, but in its dilatory way it let several years slip by before it would sanction the erection of the forts, and it was not until 1586 that the Viceroy was entrusted with the order to build them. Dom Duarte de Meneses seems to have laid down the plans, though it must have been in the final year of his commission when this stone was carved. By this time Portugal had been brought under the domination of Spain by Philip II whose name also figures in the inscription.[16]

This mighty fort was thus erected at a time when the cold and fanatic Philip II of Spain imposed his cruel yoke on Portugal.

There is a single-line Latin inscription over the exterior arched window (now filled up and completely plastered over) on the south-east wall of the circular chapel on the top of Fort Mirani which reads:

AVE MA	GRA.	SA PLA	DOS.	TECV
Ave Maria	gratia	santa plena	Dominus	tecum.

Inscription number three, in Portuguese, is built into the south-east wall of the lower rear court on the harbour side of the Fort. In translation this reads, 'Experience, Zeal and truth built me for the defence of the cross which defends me, on the order of the very high and powerful king Don Philip, third of this name, in the year 1610.[17]

The grey walls of Jalali and Mirani have looked down upon many historical events during four centuries, and to the inhabitants of Muscat they have seemed as eternal as the rock on which they rest. The royal family of Oman has lived in their shadow since Muscat became the capital, and the boding aspect must have made a deep impression on the members of the family. That the family is enor-mously human is a fact which was impressed on me by the father of the present ruler, Taimur, in his late seventies, who resided in Bomb..y as Mr T. F. T. al-Said (he died early in 1965). While I was recently his guest at the Taj Mahal Hotel in that city, he was com-pletely guileless as he explained to me, 'Wendell, I never really wanted to be a Sultan, I wanted to live in Japan. You know I had a Japanese wife and learned to speak the language.' When asked his age he always replied, 'I have ninety-five years in five years going to God – but heart fifteen years old.' Completely devoted to his son, Mr al-Said (former Sultan Taimur), who used to invariably sign his name in private correspondence as 'Abu Said' (the father of Said), spoke in his quaint English, 'I live in Bombay to be near enough to Said if he needs me yet far enough not to be in his way.' He had a charming way of ending a statement with 'God Willing', a pause, and then, 'I think He will.' Of his eight brothers four are still living.

In 1946 Taimur made his only visit to Muscat since his abdication in 1932. After a brief five-month stay he again bade goodbye to his former capital city. His mother, Saiyidah Alia (i.e. Lady Alia), then over eighty, died soon afterwards. Over sixty years ago this coura-geous woman had loaded rifles for her husband when rebels broke into their palace. Her father was Sultan Thuwaini who was assassin-ated in Sohar, her two brothers had been Sultans of Zanzibar, her husband Sultan Faisal of Oman, her son Sultan Taimur, and her grandson Sultan Said. From 1922 to 1927, Sultan Taimur's young Said (the present Sultan) attended Mayo College at Ajmer in Raj-putana, India, (tradition says its first student, the minor Maharaja of

Alwar, arrived at classes on his elephant), where he mastered English and Urdu. Said returned to Muscat in May 1927 and four months later travelled to Baghdad for one year's study of Arabic literature and history at the secondary school. It had been originally suggested he be sent to school in Beirut; however, Sultan Taimur gave a definite no, feeling his son might possibly come under too much Christian influence. At the turn of the last century young Taimur and his brother Nadir had obtained an English primer as they wanted very much to learn the language. One day, somehow, their father Sultan Faisal found out. 'What's this?' he shouted. Taimur replied 'English book.' Faisal said, 'You want to learn "Kafir" language' and immediately ordered their precious books burned, for he did not want his sons' minds contaminated. At this time the Sultan had an Indian clerk named Mohammed Ibrahim. From then on Taimur sent his slave Nubi to Mohammed who taught him English words for transmittal back to his master. Mohammed eventually went to prison for a while and somehow Nubi went along to continue his lessons.

Although he is not one of the famous (or notorious) monarchs of the world, the King of little-known Oman, Sultan Said bin Taimur is a man who has had numerous contacts with the great powers throughout his reign. The first contact was in March 1933, when a special American Mission headed by Paul Knabenshue, U.S. Minister at Baghdad, arrived at Muscat to commemorate officially the centenary of the treaty of friendship between Oman and the United States.[18] Later the Sultan accepted an official invitation from President Franklin Delano Roosevelt to visit America and sailed on the *Tatsuta Maru*, and after a day's visit in Honolulu arrived at San Francisco (accompanied by his father) for a west-to-east tour of the nation, as my friend King Husain of Jordan did at a much more recent time. Leaving the Palace Hotel at the West Coast port of entry, where he was given a sightseeing tour by the Navy, the small entourage visited Hollywood, the Grand Canyon, Chicago and Detroit. After the transcontinental trip the Sultan was formally received by Secretary of State Cordell Hull upon his arrival at Union Station in Washington D.C. on 3 March 1938.

As a White House guest His Majesty was surprised and pleased to hear the United States Army Band play the National Anthem of Oman, a thoughtful courtesy he has never forgotten. President Roosevelt presented him with copies of two books which he had written in his pre-presidential days, receiving in return a gold Omani dagger. The American President arranged for the Sultan to visit the headquarters of the F.B.I., where among other things he fired a Thompson Sub-Machine Gun and inspected the death mask of Dillinger. After laying a wreath on Washington's tomb at Mount Vernon he sailed on the *Queen Mary* for England, where he was received by King George VI and enjoyed an official visit in the United Kingdom.

During World War II, when the fall of Egypt appeared imminent, it was essential to establish a lifeline to India across Central Africa and Southern Arabia. The Sultan did not hesitate to make land near Salalah and Masirah Island available for air bases. Landing strips were levelled by the R.A.F.; the hangars and barracks were constructed by Pan American World Airways on behalf of the U.S. Government, and the bases were staffed by U.S. Army Air Force personnel, the R.A.F. and the South African Air Force. Throughout the course of the war the strategic importance of Oman could not be overestimated and it has been well described as 'the cork in the Persian Gulf bottle'.

It is an interesting thought that Oman, the one country in southwestern Asia and North Africa which has never received a single dollar in American aid, is one of America's oldest and truest friends – this despite the fact that for many years the State Department had its accredited representative to the Kingdom stationed in an adjoining country (Saudi Arabia) which was hostile to the Sultan! In the Sultan's words, 'When a man is healthy no one helps him; sometimes one has to be sick to survive.'

2

RELIGION IN OMAN

*Muslim relics – Christianity respected – Orthodoxy and dissent
Ibadhi Mosques – Christian missions*

> Nothing can be more misleading than a number of general
> statements based on imperfect and incomplete knowledge,
> and no man living has a thorough acquaintance with the
> millions of Muslims in Asia and Africa, to say nothing of
> scattered communities elsewhere, so that he can make
> authoritative pronouncements on Islam as a whole.
>
> Alfred Guillaume, *Islam*

In Oman, where time has little affected values, the world is neatly
divided into believers and non-believers, and the believer still considers it an affront to God ever to commit himself to the future
without adding *inshallah*, 'If God wills'. The Arabian Muslim, like
his homeland, is isolated, aloof, suspicious, proud, independent and
self-satisfied and almost universally impervious (even sometimes
hostile) to foreign religions such as Christianity. Actually, the
thoughts of the vast majority are centred around 'What shall we
eat, what shall we drink and where-withal shall we be clothed?' An
uneducated but far from unlearned *badawi*, 'nomad', was once overheard to remark, 'In the desert we have no water; how then can we
make the prescribed ablutions? We have no money, and how can we
bestow alms? Why should we fast in the month of Ramadhan, since
the whole year with us is one continual abstinence; and if God be
present everywhere, why should we go to Mecca to adore him?'

The Arab, if he thinks about it at all, believes Christianity to be
a form of religion, originally pure in its inspiration, which has become corrupted; while the incomparable Quran is the revealed word
of God. A comparison of Jesus with Mohammed, the human name
most closely associated with God, shows that while the Quran gives

Jesus distinctive appellations, 'Word of God' and 'Spirit from God', and states that Jesus was born of a virgin, Miriam, and sinless, neither of these divine attributes was ever claimed for or by Mohammed, nor did he ever claim to be a worker of miracles (the Quran is adduced as a sufficient miracle). Mohammed distinguished himself in having all the necessary qualifications for chief of a tribal community together with divine inspiration. He became chief of the community of Madinah. In addition to being endowed with the customary qualities, as a prophet he introduced a new element to the tribal community in that he rose above the tribes to become a chief of chiefs. Mohammed not only enforced the customary law, but introduced divine law which essentially was a higher law and of different binding. He created a larger political community, the *ummah* or the Islamic state.

Although Mohammed himself did not make any extravagant assertions about his person, millions of his followers not fully versed in the orthodox teachings of Islam ascribe lofty attributes to him. Drops of blood taken from the Ahl as-Salami tribe of Yemen, whose progenitor, Abbas bin Mirdas as-Salami, once drank some of the Prophet's blood to win *tabarruk*, 'blessing', were sold a few years ago for five riyals a drop. During the battle of Uhud two nails of his helmet entered the face of Mohammed, 'and Abu Ubaida pulled one of the nails out of his face and one tooth dropped out; and he pulled out another nail and another tooth dropped out. And when Abu Ubaidah was taking out the teeth, Sunan Abu Said sucked the blood from Mohammed's face and swallowed it. Upon which the Prophet said, "Whosoever toucheth my blood, him shall the fire of hell never touch!"' [1]

Working against conversion to Christianity, in the rare cases in which it is considered, there is still the very real fear of social stigma, political reprisals and persecutions. 'Religion being a focal concern in the culture of the Middle East, conversion was regarded as apostasy and resulted in an open breach with family, society, and value culture. The convert to Christianity was ostracized by his peers and, what is equally important, since Islam was held with unshakable conviction to be the only true religion, to leave it was regarded as an evidence of utter folly.' [2] However, it is the rare Muslim ruler in this day who would ever think of obeying the old Ottoman code of Islam which was directed at those who deviated from the faith: 'He is to have three distinct offers of life if he will return to the faith and time for reflection, after each offer, is to be given him. If he remains obdurate he is to be executed by strangulation and then his head is to be cut off and placed under his arm. His body is thus to be exposed three days in the most public place.'

Throughout major portions of this present world of Islam, a *nasrani*, or *masihi*, 'Christian', is accepted as a Christian, and the better Christian he is the more respect he commands. Islam, as such, knows little of compromise and does not respect compromise on our part. Recently the Dutch explorer D. van der Meulen observed with regard to Saudi Arabia that, 'If the Americans had, from the start, insisted on entering the country as confessed Christians with open freedom for their belief, such an attitude would have commanded Ibn Saud's respect. . . . These first Americans discarded one essential element in any real contact, for the Arab who believes will only trust the Christian if he shows that he too believes in the One God.'[3]

' "You must be missing your Church today," said Sheikh Shakhbut [the ruler of Abu Dhabi, to the English author Roderick Owen]. "I'm sorry there isn't a church for you in Abu Dhabi."

' "We are," we answered. "But wouldn't you disapprove of a church here?"

' "Disapprove? Of course not. You need your religion as we need ours. Besides, good as you are, you'd no doubt be better if you went to church; and that would be to everyone's advantage."

'This sensible point of view needs to be seen in contrast to the difficulties encountered by churches of all denominations in Saudi Arabia, where ARAMCO's policy of giving way was involving visiting preachers in unheard-of subterfuges to obtain visas. Sheikh Shakhbut was not implying that Abu Dhabi was a suitable field for missionaries, but he was recognizing individual religious rights.'[4]

The happy result of the American Mission in Muscat and Matrah has been the gaining of goodwill and the overcoming of prejudice and misunderstanding, first through medicine, then education. One

of the things, however, which causes the missionary to Arabia most
to despair of his task is that more often than not his kindness, help-
fulness, friendship and acts of mercy are received with gratitude by
the Muslim, and the missionary is loved; but not Christianity.

Nothing of a definite nature is known of early Christianity in
Oman, and it was onto a scene of paganism that Islam first came
there, and it is not to be supposed that every inhabitant of the
country was converted in a day. The process of Islamization undoubtedly spread over a number of centuries and involved a variety
of internal struggles. When the modern period dawned, the religious
situation was much as it is today. The dominant Islamic denomination in the country is not *sunni* orthodoxy, but *ibadhi* sectarianism.
The Islamic world early split into two major religious divisions, the
Sunni and Shi'i. Whereas in Yemen the people were anti-Sunni
practising a type of Shi'ism called Zaidism, in Oman the majority of
the Ghafiri were orthodox, while the Hinawis were in the main
dissenters, followers of the Ibadhi sect of Islam, differing from the
Shi'i and Sunni alike. The sunna 'Traditions' ascribed to the Prophet enjoy a validity second only to Quranic sanctions among the
Sunnis; the Shi'as hold that these traditions are in the main apocryphal. The Sunnis recognize four successors of Mohammed as Caliphs
– Abu Bakr, Omar, Othman and Ali. The Shi'a reject all but Ali
and his family. The Sunni says, 'There is no God but God and
Mohammed is the Prophet of God'; the Shi'i adds, 'And Ali is the
Saint of God', for to them 'Mohammed is a city of learning and Ali
the gate thereof.' The Ibadhis recognize only the first two, Abu
Bakr and Omar, and hold that, when the situation requires, an Imam
should be elected from the faithful. This fact has had a significant
influence on the history and culture of Oman, and the character of
the *ibadhi* profession is a subject which must be discussed in order to
appreciate fully the character of the country.

The Ibadhi mosques in Oman are never decorated in the interior,
for 'any image or visual symbol in religious worship is anathema
to Muslims'; or adorned with the tall slender minaret – which actually
appeared late in the history of Islamic architecture and was never
adopted in Oman; none of the earliest mosques possessed minarets
and the Prophet's *muadhdhin* used to chant the call to prayer from

the entrance of the mosque. In theory Oman mosques are closed to all non-Muslims. They are also forbidden to Muslims who are not religiously clean, but as the Sultan explains it, 'The individual concerned is his own judge in this regard.' The Prophet had once stated, 'Do not prevent your women from coming to the mosque; but their homes are better for them.' A unique feature of Omani life is based on this utterance of the Prophet; there are mosques built exclusively for women.

The cornerstone of Islam is prayer and in Muscat prayers (a preservation against sin) are said in all the mosques on all days except Friday, for the Oman Ibadhis only perform the *juma*, 'Friday', prayer in old capital cities such as Nazwa and Sohar or where the Sultan may specifically direct. The Prophet once said, 'The Lord doth not regard a prayer in which the heart doth not accompany the body, and all the earth is given to me as a place of prayer and is pure except the burial ground and the bath', while the Caliph Omar, the Great, used to say, 'Prayer carries us halfway to God. Come to prayers, come to prayers, it is better to pray than to sleep.'

The Muslim, as ordained in the Quran, prays faithfully and with constant regularity at dawn, noon, afternoon, sunset, and evening.

The Ibadhis, who are a denomination by themselves, differ in the form of prayer from most Muslims. For instance, as a rule they do not fold their hands across their bodies in prayer or raise their hands when pronouncing the words *Allahu akbar* or repeat 'Amen' loudly after the recitation of *al-hamdu-li-llah*.

The Ibadhis regard Islam and *iman*, 'belief', as one and inseparable. He who deviates from *iman* deviates from Islam and becomes an unbeliever. *Iman* therefore is not regarded as the first pillar since it is taken for granted. The Ibadhis regard works as the major criteria of *iman* and reject the Sunni doctrine of justification by faith without works.[5]

The Ibadhis deny that they will see the face of God at the end of the world; they believe that if God sends a man to heaven or to hell he will be in heaven or hell for all eternity with no possibility of escape; the Ibadhis believe that a man will be judged on the deeds he has done on this earth; they deny the existence of a narrow road laid straight through hell on which a meritorious man will safely pass over, and believe that God Himself will select those who have done good or evil; the Ibadhis say that it is a reward of evil and thus wrong to marry a woman with whom you have committed fornication or adultery. 'They hold that the sinner of a great sin may be an attester of the Unity of God, but not a [true] believer, inasmuch as acts enter into faith. They also affirm that power precedes the act; that the act of man is created of God; that all the world will perish as will perish the people under the obligation of obedience [to God]; that he who commits the great sin of denying God's grace is an unbeliever, but that, in denying the denomination of his sect, he is not an unbeliever.'[6] The commission of one of the greater sins by an Ibadhi places him forever beyond the pale of salvation: sins such as murder, fornication, sodomy, beastiality, seducing married women, theft, wine drinking, violence, perjury, usury, slander, forgery, robbing orphans, and repudiation of parents.

In order to comprehend the good and the evil and thus avoid transgression, the individual is required to be acquainted with the source of all knowledge, the Quran: 'Allah is our God, Muhammad our Prophet, Islam our religion, the *ka'ba* our *qibla*, and the Qur'an our *imam*. We exhort what it commands and outlaw what it prevents.'[7] The Ibadhis insist that the Quran should be the only source for judgment or conviction. And there can be no interpretation, *ta'wil*, of the Quran; it must be read literally.

The Ibadhis give man a cosmic significance, believing that if God destroyed man, the world would perish, for He created it for man and without man its continued existence would have no meaning.

The difference between East and West is not only geographical and racial, but between those who have and those who have not come under the influence of the Bible, which was written in the East, by Easterners, and initially for Easterners. It was not until after Mohammed's death that Arabic versions of part of the Bible were written. There is no doubt that Mohammed appreciated the Biblical stories, but the knowledge of them at the time was vague and secondhand, consisting of mutilated, isolated details in part canonical and in part apocryphal, allowing in the view of Christians singular, curious historical errors to appear, such as that 'Mary' (Maryam) the Virgin Mother of Jesus is confused with Miriam, the sister of Aaron, who died in the wilderness before the children of Israel reached the promised land (Numbers XX); (this confusion may be due to the Greek New Testament as well as the septuagint Greek translation of the Old Testament, spelling both alike – 'Miriam'). In the 'Traditions' it is stated 'that the only two persons born into the world who have not been touched of the devil are Mary and her son Jesus', thus hinting of the Immaculate Conception of Mary. Initially Mohammed seems to have regarded Christ as a former prophet (one of the greatest), and he was sincerely and genuinely surprised that the Christians and Jews refused to acknowledge and recognize his claim to present the same message from God as they did. 'He who oppresses a Christian shall have him for an accuser at the day of judgment', the Prophet once stated to Omar, and 'He who injures a Christian injures me.' Nor was this always ignored and one of the most remarkable instances of Muslim tolerance is the extraordinary story of the Christian martyrs of Cordova in Spain, who had to try hard, and then not always successfully, to get themselves martyred.

Christian attempts to make converts during the first thousand years of Islam in Oman were few. The Catalan Raymond Lull was the greatest of the mediaeval missionaries to the Arabs. Not for 500 years after his martyrdom was a new effort made, when Henry Martyn whose zealous motto was 'Now let me burn out for God' landed in Muscat in 1811. But the first Arabic translation of the Bible, Eli Smith's and Cornelius Van Dyck's, was not even brought to completion until 1864. After the saintly Martyn came another dedicated Englishman, Major General F. T. Haig, of the British Army, who in 1886 travelled completely around the coast of Arabia, and into the interior of Yemen. Regarding south-east Arabia he wrote, 'Oman is separated from the rest of Arabia by a sandy desert. It is, in fact, as far as communications with the rest of the world is concerned, an island with the sea on one side and the desert on the other.'[8] General Haig's written reports published in *The Christian* reached the brilliant Cambridge student Ian Keith-Falconer who founded the first mission at Sheikh Othman before he succumbed to malaria after only ten months in Arabia. The fierce climate of Muscat was responsible for the death of yet another missionary leader who had come there from India, T. V. French, Bishop of Lahore; he died of sunstroke in 1891 after only ninety-five days in Oman, but his example inspired two young Americans, Samuel Zwemer and James Cantine, to found The Arabian Mission of the Reformed Church in America.

In 1897, Peter, the thirty-year-old brother of Samuel Zwemer, explored the extremely difficult Jabal Akhdhar in the interior of Oman.[9] He died the next year the first heroic American martyr of the young mission.

In 1909 Dr Sharon Thoms, father of the present Wells Thoms, arrived in Matrah, the first medical missionary to Oman, only to be killed in 1913 at the age of forty-two in a fall at sundown while setting up a telephone line between Muscat and Matrah. Sultan Taimur sent his steam launch to Matrah to bear the casket to the Christian cemetery in a lonely cove east of Muscat. It was twenty years before the mission could send a doctor to Oman again. The former Sultan Taimur recalled that once when he was a young man he had asked Sharon Thoms to remove his Bible so that they could sit comfortably together in the same room. In 1948 land for the contagious disease hospital was donated by the present Sultan in memory of Sharon Thoms (The Sharon Thoms Memorial Hospital). A second building was later added in the same compound for the care and treatment of 'the least of these my brethren', the victims of leprosy. This generous act of the Sultan contrasts interestingly with the attitude of his grandfather, Sultan Faisal, who once said, 'I take refuge in God from a country that has missionaries in it.' Since 1948 over 400 tuberculosis patients and 140 leprosy patients have been treated.

Wells Thoms once said to the writer, 'You probably wonder what drew me back to Oman. Many forces drew me back – my father's love of the people and enthusiasm for the country – the Master's command of "go ye" – but more than any other single thing it was a pitiful group of lepers who used to huddle together outside the city wall of Matrah asking for alms. We lived in a two-storey native-built house on the sea shore near the private walled Khoja quarters. Father used the first floor as his clinic – here he examined and treated scores of patients in the mornings and did operations in the afternoons. Mother did her best to make the second floor comfortable and attractive. This was pretty difficult in those days when it was hot and the flies and mosquitoes and other insects buzzed around in swarms for we had no electric fans, refrigerators, modern plumbing, nor was it possible to screen more than two rooms against the insects. We used to walk out to the date garden, which lay in the middle of the narrow valley beyond the city gate, sometimes in the evening to get away from the smells of the city and to rest our eyes on something green. A stone's throw from the gate, where the city fathers sat (as they did in Bethlehem in the time of Boaz) at sunset drinking *finjans* of coffee and fingering their amber prayer beads, huddled the most miserable, deformed collection of human beings that could horrify a young boy anywhere. They wore rags and gunny sacks for clothes. Some had no noses and most had some fingers and toes missing. I asked my father the first time I saw them, "Who are these people?" He said, "I think that these are the type of people Jesus referred to when He said, 'If you do it to one of the least of these my brethren you do it unto Me.' They have leprosy – and no one wants them – not even their relatives!" I said, "Why don't you take care of them?" He looked sad when he replied, "I would like to, but it is impossible. They are not allowed to come inside the city gate, so cannot come to our clinic, but even if they did manage to get past the guard, they would cause a panic when they showed up in my office for treatment. Besides that – there is no effective treatment at present for this disease. Perhaps some day you will be a doctor here, and then if there is a mission hospital out here and there has been found an effective cure for leprosy you will be able to give them a home and treat them".'

Until 1955 Dr Wells Thoms (and his wife) were the only Westerners with personal knowledge of the interior of Oman. He had on more than one occasion attended sheikhs in the interior and early in 1954 visited the upper room of the great round tower at Nazwa and treated old Imam Mohammed bin Abdullah for cataracts (the first and only time the Imam experienced modern medicine). Today, in addition to Dr Thoms and his charming missionary wife, Beth, the hospital is served by Dr Maurice Heuskinveld, a specialist in physiological problems with years of experience in Kuwait,

Bahrain and Amara on the Tigris River. The missionaries I have known in Oman are eminently qualified for their task, having a great love of the people coupled with the finest of professional training. They are men and women of spiritual power and masters of Arab mentality, language, manners and customs. For example, the De Jongs have been missionaries in Arabia for thirty-two years, having first gone to Kuwait in 1926; there they built the first Christian Church in 1931. Every Sunday during 1957–8, the Reverend Garret de Jong conducted services in his church at Muscat both in Arabic and English. Mrs Everdene de Jong is the author of the finest book of its kind entitled *Spoken Arabic of the Arabian Gulf* (Beirut, 1958). Her knowledge of the subject is extensive.

To sum up: the average Muslim's religion means more to him in his everyday living than does the average Christian's religion. Many a pushing irascible, determined 'Christian' of the West can learn from a quiet, courteous, contented Muslim of the East. Thus the weak-hearted Christian would do well to pause in humility and respect before much that is found in Islam; the sense of simple dignity of human nature and the absolute equality of man before God; the fearless testimony before men of their belief in God, of His providence, and of their complete submission to His will. 'If they are so zealous in their false worship, it must needs be a reprimand to Christians, who are so remiss in the truth',[10] wrote Joseph Pitts, an early eighteenth-century student of Arabic. Would that Christians the world over were as ready proudly to confess Jesus in unmistakable language, as Muslims the world over are to be earnest devoted followers of Mohammed and the fatiguing path of Islam. For 'the highest truth the wise man sees he will fearlessly utter; knowing that, let what may come of it, he is thus playing his right part in the world – knowing that if he can effect the change he aims at – well: if not – well also, though not so well.'

3

TO SOHAR

*Camels – Desert trackers – The motor-road – Date gardens
of al-Batinah – Sohar, Sinbad's birthplace? – Sohar then
and now*

Our team was completed when the aircraft bringing Dr Louis
Krause, our medical member, touched down as expected. An expedition leader cannot help once in a while having a special favourite
and for me such a one was Dr Krause. A valued member of my
pioneer expedition to Beihan in 1950, Dr Krause holds professor-
ships both at the Johns Hopkins and University of Maryland
Medical Schools. While he was a front-line surgeon in World War I,
General Pershing once told him, 'Young man, don't let army regulations make a fool of you.' He never did; during World War II when
Dr Krause was Chief of the Department of Internal Medicine at
Walter Reed Hospital in Washington, the hospital's Commanding
General issued an order for all patients to be out of bed and at atten-
tion when he came through. Lieutenant-Colonel Krause replied,
'Sir, I believe 8.00 a.m. tomorrow is the earliest you can convene
my court martial – if that time is convenient with you, it's convenient with me.'

In the afternoon the Sultan entertained Bill and me at tea, and
approved my request to take Professor Honeyman overland to
Dubai and Sharjah upon the completion of his archaeological programme at Sohar. I was not feeling very well, which was amply
demonstrated to His Majesty when on leaving the palace I absent-
mindedly took his camera with me.

Our scheduled departure the next morning was delayed for twenty-
four hours to enable me to get back on my feet. The Sultan sent over

a kind get-well note enclosed with a letter to his customs post at Aswad en route to Dubai and letters for our return journey to the Sheikh of the Bani Ka'ab and to the Wali of Buraimi. We were also informed that Sheikh Saqr, accompanied by thirty-year-old Talib bin Sulaiman, had already preceded us to Sohar to make advance arrangements.

On Wednesday morning, 8 January 1958, Bill took pictures of our convoy's departure through the main city gate. In biblical times (cf. Genesis 34: 'All those who went out by the gate of his city') as now, the gate of the city is symbolic of the city itself and identified with the life of the community. The two-mile road through the frowning mountains from Muscat to Matrah, our first stop, was opened in December 1929 by Sultan Taimur. The lurching, languid, living ships of the desert and the ships of the sea meet at Matrah[1] where, on the east, a ruined Portuguese fort sits on a rocky eminence and the landside approaches to the town are covered by a series of antique block houses or towers. Matrah, like its slightly smaller sister city of Muscat, is enclosed on the landward side by rugged volcanic mountains; it faces onto a fairly capacious, well protected, less remarkable bay without exposure to the north-west wind which on rare occasions is a problem in Muscat harbour. Matrah, Oman's largest city, contains the Kingdom's principal bazaar. The only really significant Shiite population in Oman consists of the Khoja, followers of the Aga Khan, who have their own walled town within Matrah. The Khojas, like the Zaidis of Yemen, are historically a branch of the Shiite schism, though they are now non-conforming and distinct, belonging to the Ismaili sect. Outside the city wall a stony open area serves as the terminus for the chief caravan routes of south-eastern Arabia. Hundreds of camels are loaded and unloaded daily, carrying the bulk of the trade with upcountry Oman. Here we stopped to photograph a very long dignified camel caravan loaded with Omani dates from the interior.

All camels in Arabia, as in most of Persia and Pakistan, are of the one-humped variety; no shaggy two-humped or Bactrian camels, at home on the high plateaus of Central Asia, are ever seen here. In Oman the rider sits behind the hump, on a very small saddle covered with a sheepskin; this riding style is distinct from that encountered in al-Hijaz and Syria, where he sits in a heavy saddle high up on top of the hump.[2]

In Oman the camel's nose (the slit-like nostrils can be closed during a sandstorm) is left unpierced and the bridle is formed of a thick, camel-hair rope which is attached to a headstall by a chain noseband. The Austrian scholar Von Hammer-Purgstall is said to have discovered 5,744 different names and epithets for the camel in Arabic literature (Philby says this number is far too high), an indication of the great importance of this animal, without which life in much of Arabia would cease to exist. Each camel is branded with its own tribal *wasm*, mark or design – this degenerate conventionalized picture is as significant in the desert as the coat of arms of old, for here a man's wealth is based on the number of camels he owns. 'A man of property is he who sitting on the ground, sees his horizon limited in every direction by the bellies of his camels.' (Horses are not an economic asset, they are luxury household pets, referred to poetically as 'Drinkers of the Wind',[3] which are almost as rare as the oryx in Oman.)

In the Northern Desert areas of the former Aden Protectorates (now the Federation of South Arabia – Protectorate of South Arabia) and Oman, camels are very often let loose to graze for years at a time, and the owner, when he has need of his camels, will go to the place where he turned them loose and track them until he finds them. This obviously takes quite a lot of time and leaves the door open to thieves and raiders. During this time if the camel requires water it will take itself to the nearest water point and wait for some passing Bedouin to water it with his own camels. This is always done as desert custom.

The Arabs say that when the lonely first camel learned that God was going to create for him a spouse he smiled so broadly his nose split down the middle and it has remained so ever since. According to legend, when Allah decided to create the horse, he called the South Wind and said, 'I desire to draw from thee a new being.' The creator then blew upon it the breath of life, and the noble quadruped appeared. But the horse complained against his Maker. His neck was too short to reach the distant grass glades on the march; his back had no hump to steady a saddle and his small hooves were sharp and sank deep in the sand. Whereupon Allah created the camel to prove the foolishness of this complaint. When the horse saw the camel he shuddered and almost collapsed at the sight of what he had wanted to become.[4]

The impenetrable, tranquil camel, however, due to chronic indigestion (a kind of vile belching which appears to erupt from some monstrous gullet suffocating with fury), always wears an expression of perpetual supercilious, cynical conceit, for according to Arab belief of all the world's beasts the camel alone knows the hundredth name of God, the one great name which possesses all the divine attributes. Closer to the truth was the 1867 observation by the English explorer, W. G. Palgrave, in his *Central and Eastern Arabia*, p. 25. 'I have, while in England heard and read more than once of the "docile camel". If "docile" means stupid, well and good; in such a case the camel is the very model of docility.' They asked the camel which he preferred, going up-hill or down-hill. He replied, 'When I am carrying a load, the devil take them both.'

W. B. Seabrook (*Adventures in Arabia*, p. 54) tells the story of the dying camel that painfully dragged himself for miles to a spring, 'not to drink there – so the Arabs take oath – but so that his carcass might pollute the water and poison those who came to drink afterward.' While S. B. Miles, in his *Countries and Tribes of the Persian Gulf*, noted 'that there is a curious resemblance of character between the Arab and his camel. Among the salient points on which they resemble each other are their resentment of injustice, their revengeful disposition, and the ease with which it is appeased.'

One writer tells a story, possibly apocryphal, of a camel killing a man: 'The man ran for his life towards some large rocks and began to climb, hoping to get out of reach, but the camel overtook him. Raising its long neck the infuriated animal got hold of its victim's leg and pulled him down. Then began a sickening scene. The camel bit and mauled the man and then rolled on him until there was only a flattened mangled mass. All day the camel kept watch over the body, from time to time leaving its grazing to return to crush and roll what was left of his victim.'[5]

The camel nomads (*badu*) of Arabia sometimes refer to Oman as *umm al-ibl*, 'the mother of camels', for the Oman dromedary, the *umaniyah*[6] is the Queen of Camels. This term *umaniyah* refers to the female riding camel whose breeding is carefully controlled. With head and neck stretched full horizontal to the ground, an *umaniyah* can travel at fifteen miles an hour. As its great sponge-like feet are tender, pebbly country is avoided when possible. The best Oman breed is the *batiniyah* from the Batinah Coast. It is the highest bred and most renowned of all thoroughbred camels and is particularly famed for its staying power. These camels have been known to average a hundred miles a day for over a week at a time, and one of them once covered the ninety-five miles between Buraimi and Abu Dhabi in under twelve hours. But the history of Arabian exploration is replete with such phenomenal records of the camel's endurance. We have Burckhardt's account of the camel which covered 115 miles in eleven hours; Guarmani crossed 100 miles of the Nafud sand dunes in sixteen hours; Noldre rode a camel sixty-two and a half miles between ten at night and five in the morning; Leachman mentions the story of a rider who travelled the 600 miles from Najar to Riyadh in six days; Lawrence once rode ninety miles in twenty-two hours and Thesiger 115 miles in twenty-three hours.

When the Hadhrami Bedouin Legion first established the Northern Desert Post, camels were stationed at Zamakh. Major T. E. 'Jock' Snell tells this writer that on one occasion one of these camels ridden by the officer in charge of the area and accompanied by some twenty guards on their own camels, chased a raider well over ninety miles, the H.B.L. camel catching up with him after five hours. The desert guards had to change camels twice during the trip. The camel's eyesight is quite outstanding, but his hearing is very poor. Hence, shooting a rifle off the back of even a very young camel rarely disturbs it.

The desert Arabs have a saying, 'The best of women is like a frolicsome she-camel', and all are in agreement that *al-ibl akbar atayat min al-khaliq lil-bashar*, 'the camel is the greatest of all gifts from the Creator to mankind.'

> Dear unto me as the sight of mine eyes
> Art thou, O my Camel!
> Precious to me as the health of my life
> Art thou, O my Camel!

> Sweet to my ears is the sound
> Of thy tinkling bells, O my Camel!
> And sweet to thy listening ears
> Is the sound of my evening song.

Its every part, living or dead, is utilized – hair for tents and ropes, milk and flesh for food, bones and skin for fuel and leather.

'As an aphrodisiac, Indian erotology suggests camel bone, dipped in the juice of the *eclipta prostata* plant; then burnt. The black pigment produced from the ashes is placed in a box also made of camel bone and then applied with antimony to the eyelashes with the pencil of a camel bone. The effect, it is hinted, will be erotic subjugation. . . . Camel's milk when mixed with honey and taken for successive days produces marked potency, according to Arab tradition.'[7]

Even the footprints are of value, for they portray science, history and gossip to the passing caravan. 'The desert and the track cannot lie.' In Arabia there exist trackers who can purportedly determine sex, virginity and skin colour from what is read underfoot. This perfect medium of the sand represents the library of bookless Arabia, there, except on sandless lava flows, all living creatures leave their record or history until the imprints are obliterated by wind and time. We are told that the more expert of the track-masters can recognize the prints of a young camel that he has never seen by the similarity of its tracks to those known tracks of its mother.

A passage from one of Philby's information-packed books gives a tale that illustrates this point:

'Some Arabs,' said Mubarak, 'were riding across a plain, when one of them, a Shaikh of the tribe, called the attention of his fellows to the tracks of his own daughter crossing their path in the direction of a strip of *Nafud* in the distance, "There goes my daughter", he said, "to gather *Nussi* for the camels against our return." They rode on and in the evening they returned crossing the girl's tracks. "Ah! woe is me," cried the Shaikh, "see ye not that when she went forth this morning she was a virgin and now she is such no longer? By God! she shall die for her unchastity, and with her I will slay the man that has dishonoured her; come, help me search him out, for his tracks are not with hers." And so the party, greatly perturbed by the shame that had come upon the tribe, rode off towards the *Nafud* along the girl's tracks searching for those of her paramour, but nowhere finding them; on they rode some distance into the sands until they came to where the tracks ended near by a desert plant, the curious *Tarthuth* vulgarly known as the Desert Penis – *Zubb al Hamad*; and the old Shaikh wept for joy to know that, though his reading of the tracks was right, he had wronged his daughter by his too ready suspicions and had wronged her more by keeping her so long unwed.[8]

Wilfred Thesiger, in *Arabian Sands*, pp. 51–2, tells of an equally pertinent first-person experience:

A few days later we passed some tracks. I was not even certain that they were made by camels, for they were much blurred by the wind. Sultan turned to a grey-bearded man who was noted as a tracker and asked him whose tracks these were, and the man turned aside and followed them for a short distance. He then jumped off his camel, looked at the tracks where they crossed some hard ground, broke some camel-droppings between his fingers and rode back to join us. Sultan asked, 'Who are they?' and the man answered, 'They were Awamir. There are six of them. They raided the Junuba on the southern coast and took three of their camels. They have come here from Sahma and watered at Mughshin. They passed here ten days ago.'

An Omani will tell you, 'Take a Murra Tribesman on a three day journey blindfolded, have him bury a dollar in the trackless sand at night; ten years later he can return to reclaim his dollar with no difficulty.'

The watering of camels varies considerably. The Army camels which have been used to daily watering cannot go easily without it; desert camels will be more used to going for longer and can very often go for a great many days. For instance on one occasion Jock Snell rode a Bedouin camel for seventeen days between water points and during that time he hardly wet his lips. In the remote desert, if a camel lives its master lives, for to quote the phrase of Sprenger, the Bedouin is 'the parasite of the camel'. If only a camel can stomach the water it serves as a portable distillery with its master drinking the resulting milk which has no cream. A large, fat camel can drink and hold up to seventy quarts of water. Contrary to popular belief, however, there is no natural means of conservation of water in a camel's hump (which is largely filled with fat) or stomach. They must be trained to endure obediently the lack of water for long periods.

Its hump is, however, the barometer of a camel's condition. A large fat hump indicates proper food and regular salting and that all is well on the inside.

To thirsty *badu*, a pierced camel bladder with its yellow trickle is definitely more desirable than brackish water. As witnessed in 1948 by my University of California expedition in the Sudan and graphically described by the sixteenth-century traveller Leo Africanus on the road from Fez to Timbuktu, 'When they are so grieveously oppressed with thirst, they kill forthwith some one of their camels, out of whose bowels they wring and express some quantity of water, which water they drink and carry about with them, till they either find some pit of water, or till they pine away for thirst.'[9]

In times of need the *badu* force their camels to throw up the contents of their stomachs. This vomit is drinkable if the camel has had water within four days, otherwise a foul green liquid is forthcoming. For stomach disorders the *badu* will partake of small amounts of young female camel vomit plus urine as a tonic; the urine is also used to warm his hands on a cold morning and is a shampoo much prized by *badu* maidens.

It is generally believed in the Nile Valley that the eating of camel meat by a woman near her time retards delivery. Sun-dried, raw camel meat consisting of leathery muscles and wiry sinews will sustain life for an unlimited period and some find camel's meat pleasant, like coarse beef.[10] I am not included among this number and if offered a choice would select young African lion, crocodile or even rhino in preference. Only *badu* women will eat camel brains, for they are believed to make men faint-hearted. A favourite saying is: 'What we cannot eat ourselves we give to the women – women can eat anything.'

It has only fairly recently been recognized that the domestication of the camel did not take place as early as was long assumed. It was in 1940 that Professor William F. Albright pointed out that there was no clear evidence to indicate the existence of the domesticated camel in south-western Arabia before the eleventh century B.C. It is true that a figurine of a camel, taken from the Iraq Department of Antiquities excavations at Aqarif, has been dated about 1300 B.C.[11] But the earliest mention of the Arabian camel in any cuneiform text, and the earliest relief representation, both occur in the ninth century B.C. from Mesopotamia. Among scores of thousands of cuneiform letters and economic texts from all over south-western Asia between 1800 and 1200 B.C. not one mentions the camel. In short, the effective domestication of the camel for use in caravans and raiding expeditions (like the Midianite raid into Palestine at the time of Gideon, about 1100 B.C.) cannot be dated before the third quarter of the second millennium B.C. Naturally this does not mean that there were no earlier successful experiments in taming camels, or that the camel may not have been partly tamed several centuries earlier. However, we can say positively that the camel was not commonly employed by the Semitic nomads of North Arabia during the first half of the second milleninum, since it nowhere appears in the monumental representations of Egypt and Sinai or in the accompanying inscriptions. All caravans, small and large, represented or described in this period show donkeys, not camels. From the dawn of history to the second millennium B.C. the ass ruled the field undisputedly. It must be emphasized, however, that the wild camel was well known in prehistoric and early historic Egypt and neolithic representations from North Arabia prove that the wild camel was known there also before the early third millennium.

Where was the Arabian camel domesticated? Professor Albright first thought of South Arabia, but the surprising lack of camel bones in the oldest levels of our excavations at Hajar bin Humeid in Wadi Beihan does not favour this view. The young German scholar Reinhard Walz proposed central Arabia, but Philby has pointed out that the Najd is much too stony for the feet of camels, which are ideally suited for sandy deserts but not for plateaus strewn with stones.[12] Since the best camels still come from the hinterland of Oman we must probably look to this direction for the effective taming of the camel. From south-eastern Arabia the domesticated camel spreads rapidly into Najd and south-westward into Arabia Felix, where its value as a caravan beast was quickly understood. By 1100 B.C. the Midianites in north-western Arabia were staging the first great camel raids known to history, and in the tenth century the Queen of Sheba led the first recorded camel caravan when she (or her representatives) journeyed north to visit King Solomon in

Jerusalem. Thanks to the domestication of the camel, Arabia was rapidly transformed from a very sparsely populated region of food gatherers to a flourishing land of camel nomads and intensive commerce. This development took place during the centuries immediately preceding and following the beginning of Qatabanian irrigation in Wadi Beihan, which dates from about the third quarter of the second millennium B.C. We are probably safe in dating the whole process of effective domestication of the camel between 1600 and 1200 B.C.

But we, travelling toward Sohar some 3,000 years after this event, were no longer dependent on the camel. We have a motor road. The simplest description of the 'broad road' (as the *Encyclopaedia of Islam* describes it), is that after leaving the commercial centre of Matrah through Kharashif Pass there is a track which has its only explanation in the drivers' habit of following the traces left by those who went before. The passability of the road is conditioned by numerous ravines and irrigation channels cut across it and even more by the steep dykes, often three feet high, which are part of the palm groves scattered along the coast.

Travel along this curved alluvial low-lying coastal plain bearing the name *al-Batinah*, signifying 'the Lowland' (in Omani Arabic, but 'Inner' or 'Interior' in classical Arabic) is made still more difficult by dozens of large and small ill-defined wadis intersecting and dispersing across the plain to meet the coast at right angles. These valley systems have their origin some fifteen to twenty-five miles behind the plain in the high Western Hajar mountain range. Behind the Western Hajar range lie the two inland districts of adh-Dhahirah and Oman Proper. Adh-Dhahirah, on the west, slopes inwards to the great desert of high dunes, ar-Rub' al-Khali; Oman Proper, the physical centre of Oman, is situated from 1,500 to 2,000 feet above sea-level and discharges towards the Indian Ocean. Behind the Eastern Hajar are the districts of Sharqiyah and Jaalan; Sharqiyah adjoins Oman Proper and Jaalan lies between the Indian Ocean and the south-east corner of Sharqiyah. The outstanding physical feature in Oman is this Western Hajar range which extends south-east in a great crescent roughly paralleling the coast to terminate in the vicinity of Ras al-Hadd, the point of land dividing the Gulf of Oman from the Indian Ocean. From Dhibah to Ras Musandam this rugged

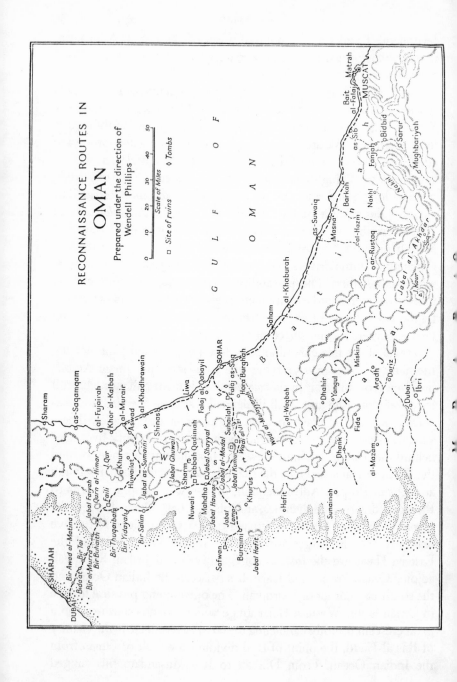

mountainous and precipitous tract is called Ruus al-Jibal.[13] However, only the eight main gorges which drain the seaward slope of
these mountains (Western Hajar) are sufficiently passable to permit
communication and trade between al-Batinah and the interior. The
largest, containing over one hundred villages and 600,000 date palms
is the Wadi Samail, which splits the Hajar into two halves (the
Western and Eastern) and perennially drains the slope of Jabal
Akhdhar into the sea at Sib and represents the chief artery of trade
between Muscat and the interior.

The maritime plains that surround much of the Arabian peninsula
are in many instances barren of vegetation. This harbourless Batinah
Coast (which is destitute of prominent capes), beginning at Sib and
running north for 150 miles, is one of the notable exceptions, and a
third of the people of Oman (practically all inhabitants of al-Batinah
are Hinawi) live and die within the confines of this vast, productive
date garden of Arabia. Indeed the majority of the more than two
hundred recognizable Omani tribes dwell on this Batinah Plain and
in the Hajar valleys, particularly on and around Jabal Akhdhar. The
largest and most important tribes of the plain are the Hawasinah and
the Yal-Saad. Al-Batinah stretches in a repetitious pattern of mile
upon mile of seemingly endless, uninterrupted green acres of fertility, mantled with a covering of drying dust.

The three-fold nature of this plan is immediately apparent. A
gently shelving, unbroken white sandy beach runs parallel to a broad
belt of palm groves which in its turn gives way to an interior of a
shingly plain of brown scrub and acacia extending to the dark,
irregular mountains in the background. The stony, sandy soil
eroded from the slopes is reasonably good. The lack of flowing
springs and perennial streams is made up for by countless copious
wells (called *toyan* in colloquial speech). A remarkable feature is that
though in many places these wells are situated within a stone's
throw of the high-watermark of the sea the water remains entirely
sweet, and it is raised by primitive contrivances, which although
simple, are effective. A rope, one end of which is attached to a large
leathern bucket (*dalu*) and the other to either a bullock or other

animal passes over a wooden pulley wheel held high above the well by a derrick of three or four straight tree limbs. As the beast walks away from the well, usually down a steeply inclined plane to make his job easier, the bucket comes up; as the beast returns, the bucket goes down, while all the time the wooden pulley wheel, called a *manjur*, sends an eerie creaking wail through the quiet groves. This labouring groan is a sound one can never forget, and conjures up al-Batinah in the mind's eye more readily than any other sound or scent. In a typical shallow well, the water raised twenty to thirty feet by two men plus an ox (these are often blind; camels are never used on al-Batinah to raise water), can nourish up to two hundred date palms – with more human life supported per acre by date culture than by any other crop raised in Arabia. There is evidence today of new date groves being planted everywhere along this coast, for storms each year take their toll of palms which are easily toppled over by gale-force winds. There are other hazards: a disease which affects the fruit when forming; water and land becoming salt; but there is always a new tree planted to replace a victim or uprooted tree.

However, the life of the Batinah date-farmer is one of unrelieved drudgery and discouragement; in the main he is a margin-of-subsistence tenant working for an absentee landlord, on land where the price of dates sets the level of life. As the years pass by and extensive slave labour is a mere memory, the dates become poorer and the trees deteriorate, finally turning into wooden skeletons along the beach.

To describe one village or collection of groves is to describe them all. It is, in fact, often difficult to determine where one habitation ends and the next begins. Each of the larger villages or towns has a dilapidated old fort (an occasional one may be quite picturesque) and a few stone or mud houses of some size, but most families live in three-room or four-room thatched huts. The construction of these huts commands some interest. The frame consists of poles lashed together, composed of split palm trees, or *gidwar*. The process of splitting is a skilled trade and hard work, entailing the driving of iron wedges into the palm until it splits cleanly. It is customary for the labourer to demand a measure of ghee and eggs in addition to his pay to keep up his strength for the task. The outside of the hut is covered with the stems of palm fronds (from which the leaflets have been removed) bound on vertically, and the interior is usually covered with mats woven from the palm-frond leaflets. One of these huts is known as *beit-ẓur*, *ẓur* meaning the material from the palm tree. Vegetable gardens are seen at intervals, and clover is grown to be bundled and sold in the market for the villager's family cow. The vine is very ancient in Oman. There are bananas, melons, pomegranates, figs, olives, mangoes and citrus trees, but date palms, the most important and widely cultivated trees in Oman, are by far in the majority and every palm tree is registered; in numerous instances marriage dowries consist of these alone. The date palm, *Pheonix dactylifera*, is either male or female. The female must be artificially pollinated from the male pod by the Arab gardener. A good male palm is utilized and valued like a good stallion. Half a dozen male trees will service three hundred females.

Artificial pollination of the female date palm has been practised in communities since the dawn of history: pollination is clearly shown on Assyrian bas-reliefs, and Herodotus described the operation at Babylon. 'One spring [at Madinah] the Prophet announced that the artificial impregnation of the palm was an unnatural practice, and in the future would be unlawful for his followers. They loyally abstained with many misgivings, no doubt; and in the fall there was no date crop. An indignation meeting was immediately held and a citizens' committee called on the prophet for a heart-to-heart talk, as a result of which Mohammed made a statement to this effect: "You are weak in spiritual knowledge, but are worldly-wise; therefore in the future I will confine myself to the government of your spiritual welfare, and let you manage the affairs of this world to suit yourselves." Next year the palms were artificially pollinated and the crop was as good as usual.[14]

The palm tree has been well compared to the human body: if the head is cut off the tree dies and if a frond is severed another does not grow in its place, and it is covered with a fibre analogous to human hair. A date palm, which grows only below elevations of 4,500 feet and which is notably free from disease, truly needs 'its feet in Heaven and its head in Hell'. In time of war it is considered a major achievement to cut down the date trees of your enemy; to plant them is the first sign of prosperity. The Prophet is said to have addressed his followers in these words: 'Honour the date tree, for she is your mother.'

The missionary Arabist, the late Reverend John Van Ess, tells us his favourite date story: 'Not so many years ago a letter was brought to a camp but no lantern was at hand. So the women promptly proceeded to make a lantern. A handful of dates was kneaded into the form of a cup, a bit of melted fat was poured into it, a few threads from a garment were twisted into a wick which was ignited from the coals. When the letter had been read, the only man who had been able to read the letter threw out the wick, drank the fat, and ate the cup and thus consumed his own lantern.'

Depending on one's state of mind, the state of the weather and the time of day, a graceful date garden can be a scene of exceeding beauty. Oasis life is more refined than life on the open desert, with certain oasis tribes proudly referring to themselves as *ahl an-nakhl*, 'people of the palm'. As a general rule the Omanis eat their dates raw. They claim to possess over one hundred varieties of dates, which are both the 'staff of life' and 'bread of the land', and they assert that a good wife can place before her husband a dish of dates differently prepared every day of the month. As first noted by Carsten Niebuhr in the late eighteenth century, Arabs classify dates into hot or cold depending on the taste. Oman produces a dozen first-class types of soft dates, with those from al-Batinah noted for their flavour and maturing earlier than those from Basrah. The main variety on al-Batinah (not found in the interior) is the *umm silah* which, packed in the palm-frond basket, is well known in the markets of South Arabia. The *mabsali* is not restricted to al-Batinah (found in the interior and on the coast); it is boiled when it reaches the red stage and it is this type which brings the highest price. The most celebrated Omani varieties are the Fardh, Khalas and Khanaizi. Pliny stated in his *Natural History* that if he could remember their barbarous names he could list forty-nine varieties of dates. In all, over 500 different names and epithets are used in Arabia, for the date reigns supreme as the queen of trees. Truly the one-humped camel and the date palm are the symbol of Arabia.

It was out in the open on this Batinah plain that our expedition, about half-way to our destination, Sohar, spent the first night. As though to remind us of our security problem one of the drivers, Khamis, showed us where he had been wounded in the neck by an exploding land mine when rebels mined the Bahla road. Before going to sleep, Bill Terry broke out rifles for all, and our Arab guides and drivers took turns standing guard through the long cold night, as is customary in this part of the world.

After an uneventful night we were off by 7.00 a.m. The day was cloudy, not at all good for taking pictures. It had rained in places and our vehicles had slippery going. From Suwaiq (home of the Sultan's thirty-eight-year-old brother Fahr bin Taimur), which possesses the third ranking fort on the Batinah Coast, to the large unwalled village of Khaburah (at the mouth of the Wadi Hawasinah) the track was narrow, passing in and out of cultivated land and through palm gardens. Even at low-tide travel along the beach was a constant series of interruptions due to rocky outcrops and soft sand accompanied by a continuous onslaught of neglected, noisy pi-dogs.

Mohammed greatly disliked dogs and according to tradition said that 'when a dog drinks in a vessel, it must be washed seven times and that the first cleansing should be with earth.' Generally in the Muslim world, although dogs are despised, it is considered a good act for a man to feed a dog, for it is said that 'a grateful dog is better than a thankless man'.

North of Khaburah several difficult *wadi* mouths were bypassed by turning inland through the date groves. After leaving the coastal village of Sahm our convoy crossed three *wadis* in the final seventeen miles. At three in the afternoon we finally arrived at our destination and new home, Sohar, the principal town on the Batinah Coast.

Oman was ruled by the tribe of Azd at the time Sohar made its first historical appearance in the year 8 of the Hijrah (A.D. 629), when the envoys of Mohammed presented the Prophet's way of life to the two ruling Princes Abd and Jaifar, the sons of the enterprising Julanda, who had ruled for forty years before dying in the first year of the Prophet's mission. After a convocation of Omani sheikhs at Nazwa it was resolved to submit and pay the *zakat*-tax demanded by

Mohammed, and in the main Sohar adopted Islam; it is doubtful if religious conviction played an important role at this occasion, for pride and enthusiasm about Islam was acquired by degrees. The city is next mentioned in the accounts of the funeral of the Prophet as his corpse was wrapped in three robes described as being of Sohari origin.

Soon one of the Azd tribes apostatized under their bold and rebellious leader, Dzutaj Laqit, for Oman was particularly affected by the general shock and unrest which seized the whole of Arabia after the death of Mohammed, which nearly caused the collapse of the new faith. The united Princes Abd and Jaifar, of equal authority, steadfastly true to their recently adopted religion of Islam, fled for refuge in the mountains, but much of the population were dis-affected. In 633 the first Caliph, Abu Bakr, dispatched three generals via Bahrain and Buraimi. After apprising the two princes of the situation, they took up their combined positions outside the walls of the fortress of Sohar. In the subsequent day-long action involving the Omani Muslims and Jaifar plus the opportune arrival of Najdi reinforcements from Madinah, ten thousand Omani pagan followers of Dzutaj Laqit were slaughtered and their stronghold of Daba, just north of Sohar, its inhabitants and wealth fell to the Muslim con-querors; to this day the town has never arisen from its ashes. Hence-forth the 'Day of Daba' marked the nominal death of paganism and establishment of Islam in the land of Oman.

A tradition gives Sohar as the birthplace of Sinbad the Sailor of Arabian Nights fame, while al-Batinah may have been that distant land 'inhabited by monsters and terrible serpents'. There is no evi-dence, however, that a sailor named Sinbad actually existed, although he was and is a very real person to seamen of the Orient. The name Sinbad is of Iranian origin and may originally have been Sindbam, a Persian adventurer. The theme of 'The Shipwrecked Sailor', with its island inhabited by an enormous serpent is known from ancient Egyptian literature; the Cyclops story in the *Odyssey* is similar in most aspects with Sinbad's negro cannibal adventure and Sinbad's valley of diamonds has close parallels in the writings of Epiphanius, a fourth-century Bishop of Cyprus. The appearance of this collec-tion of ancient tales in the *Thousand and One Nights* in the ninth century vividly reflects the great expansion of Arab sea trade under the Abbasid Dynasty 'in a setting of romance, danger, resource, escape, and good fortune'. The tradition that Sohar is the home of Sinbad probably indicates nothing other than the city's former importance as a seaport from which many fearless seamen set out in days of yore.

By the middle of the tenth century Sohar was considered the most important city in Oman and the most beautiful in the Persian Gulf. During this time Istakhri, the author of *kitab al-masalik wa-l-mamalik*, 'the Book of Roads and Provinces', the first Arabic book supplied with cartographs, wrote, 'It [Sohar] is the most populous and wealthy town in Oman and it is not possible to find on the shores of the Persian Sea in all the land of Islam a city more rich in fine buildings and foreign wares than Sohar.' It was the centre for trade with China, Iraq and Yemen and had attained great wealth and prosperity, but its decline soon set in. Masudi, who died in 956 and who had been described as the Arabian Herodotus, wrote *muruj adh-dhahab*, 'The Meadows of Gold', where he says he travelled several times from Sinja (Sohar) the chief town in Oman to Qanbalu (Madagascar). And al-Muqaddasi, who composed his famous geographical work in 985, wrote, 'The two chief ports of the world are Aden and Sohar. . . . Sohar is the Capital of Oman . . . a city of great wealth and excellent markets.'

Sohar has had a stormy history: in 1041–2 it was seized and occupied by a Persian seaborne force as a base for the conquest of Oman; in the mid-twelfth century a governor of Yemen seized control of the Persian Gulf and diverted Sohar's trade with the Far East to Aden. In 1276 it was sacked by an army of Moghuls from Shiraz, yet it was still relatively prosperous and a considerable market for horses when Marco Polo[15] was there in 1293. But by the beginning of the next century it was described by Abu-l-Fida, a Syrian, in one of his compilations, as 'a city in ruins'.

On 16 September 1507, after sacking Muscat, the Portuguese fleet arrived for the first time off Sohar, where under the not so gentle persuasion of Albuquerque the Omani governor revolted from allegiance to the King of Hormuz – until then supreme in the Persian Gulf – and placed himself under obedience to the monopolizing King of Portugal. This represented the first time since the days of Alexander, eighteen centuries before, that European warships appeared in the region.

In the words of Albuquerque's son:

The population of Soar [Sohar] is very large, the town being very beautiful and containing very good houses. There is a fortress of square shape, with six towers around it, having also over the gate two very large towers. The wall is of good height, and proportionately broad, placed close upon the coast in a large bay, which the coast there makes. . . . The fortress is so large that it requires more than a thousand men for its defence. . . . There would be about six thousand and upwards of inhabitants in the place, and five hundred cavaliers, the greater part of these armed with steel armour, covered with plates of iron, arranged after the manner of a roof tiled with slates, and they are strong enough to resist a shot from a cross-bow. . . .

This place Soar [Sohar] contains more nobles than any other place along the coast. . . . The people of the interior are called Badens [Bedouin] and the greater portion of the horsemen are archers, but some carry lances and Turkish maces, while all the footmen go naked from the waist up; they wear hooded caps of felt, lances and bucklers.[16]

The Sohar of today is a rambling town lying between the sandy seashore and the wider expanse of palm groves with no prominent topographical features. The majority of the population live in huts of the *beit-zur* type separated from one another by mud walls and palms. Small square kiln-baked bricks are a unique feature of the local architecture and they were not noticed elsewhere in Oman. These bricks have been used over and over again since ancient times and have been reduced by constant use to about a third of their original size. Saiyid Shihab bin Faisal, the Sultan's uncle, refers to them as the palm of a leper, in allusion to the leper who had lost his fingers. A lofty, squarish fort or citadel in a state of partial disrepair dominates the Sohar area and is still occupied and in constant use. It was originally constructed in Persian times with subsequent Portuguese and Arab alterations and additions, including this Quranic inscription carved in the wood over the outer gate, which was translated on the spot by Professor Honeyman: 'Lo! We have gained for you a manifest decision. Help comes from Allah and a speedy conquest. Made by the teacher Latfallah 1198 on the 12th day of Safar [A.D. 1784, the 5th January]. Buried within the main tower lie the remains of murdered Sultan Thuwaini, whose son Salim could not wait to allow his father the privilege of a natural death.'

The description of the excellent harbour at Sohar in *The Encyclopaedia of Islam* is certainly puzzling, since not only is there now absolutely no harbour of any kind but there is scarcely the slightest shred of physical evidence that there ever was one. The small *khor*, or inlet, at the north end of the city might at one time have been connected with the sea, but it is much too small and unprotected to account for the Encyclopaedia's misleading statement on page 504 that 'The harbour has a good roadstead and excellent anchorage and is well protected', etc. One wonders if there was not some confusion in the author's mind with the harbour of Muscat itself. This is a fair example of the type of misinformation based entirely on written sources, including the romantic and glorified accounts of the early Islamic geographers and historians, on which the western reader has had to rely.

4

DISEASE AND MEDICINE IN OMAN

The tombs of Mulayyanah – Mohammed and Medicine – Cautery as a cure-all – The Evil Eye – Bedouin vaccination – Arab eye-surgery – Mercury vapour baths – Childbirth as a killer

Having settled into the Sohar Customs House which the Sultan had appointed as our residence, and made our household arrangements, we set out to visit all the sites which I had reconnoitred during my brief visit in November 1957, so that everyone should know what we were about. We noted that the hundreds of curious horseshoe-shaped structures, which we took to be tombs, in the Wadi al-Mulayyanah extended on both sides and up the centre for no less than four and a half miles. One of these tombs was circular and built up towards the centre like a giant inverted cup with a hole in the apex. Next we moved on another five miles to Falaj as-Suq, ('Canal of the Market Place'), a ruined city on a hill, which the Arabs believe to have been built by Solomon who, like Alexander the Great, is a folk-hero throughout Dar-al-Islam. We looked at a badly damaged, poorly built wall which circled the top of the high ground with partially ruined watch towers at both ends and noted large quantities of pottery fragments in some of the rooms. Nearby, a plastered water-sluice ran down the terraced slopes and we followed this waterway for nearly five miles in the Land Rover, until we came to two interesting structures, one on each side of the wadi: a pair of beautifully constructed circular water-towers each with a well in the centre. These intact towers (not rare features in Oman) were probably constructed by Persian engineers sometime between the ninth and eleventh centuries and served to illustrate the principle that water seeks its own level. Here the water flowed from the high bank above, through the conduit, into the large circular masonry pillar passing down under the *wadi* floor in a giant U-tube or syphon, to rise and meet its level in the second tower and then on out through the sluice to the distant city at Falaj as-Suq.

Further along the river we located an ingenious, gently sloping aqueduct tunnel cut from the solid rock to avoid loss by absorption and evaporation. This underground channel was connected to the surface by well-spaced vertical ventilation shafts (gaping manholes for the cleaning of the channel) which followed the line of flow like a series of bomb craters and molehills. Whoever engineered this masterful gravity water system, whether Persian (definitely Persian *kariẓ* or *qanat* according to Philby) or Arab, must have had unlimited (slave) labour or an enormous capacity for co-operative community enterprise to carve out these miles of sub-surface canals in this land of desiccation. In Persia it is estimated there were once over 100,000 miles of *qanats* with some of the deepest going down 1,000 feet, as at Gunabad.[1] At present the longest known *qanat* in Persia is fifty miles in length. To excavate these artificial underground water channels and connecting wells in Persia no great labour force is required. There is a special class of Persians who carry out this hazardous occupation on a hereditary basis known as the *muqanni*, or worker of the *qanats*; the *qanats* themselves are known as 'the murderers'. *Aflaj* (plural of *falaj*, 'canal') of this type appear to be characteristic of Oman of the past (al-Batinah excepted with its main dependence on wells) and, as observed by Wellsted in 1835, 'Nearly all the towns in the interior of Oman owe their fertility to the happy manner in which the inhabitants have availed themselves of a mode of conducting water to them, a mode, as far as I know, peculiar to this country, and at an expense of labour and skill more Chinese than Arabian.'[2] Similar underground canals are found all the way from north-western China to the western Sahara.

Sargon of Assyria of 714 B.C. described the underground canals of Armenia, and Herodotus, in describing the various wars in Persia, noted the simple procedure of filling up the wells of a town or city in order to destroy it, while in the second century B.C. the Greek historian Polybius described the 'tunnel well' or underground water system as common in the Parthian Empire in his day and says that they were already old. This Omani water system may have been developed in pre-Achaemenid Persia and been introduced to Arabia in Achaemenian times.

We left Sohar at 8.00 a.m. the next morning for the final day of orientation before beginning actual excavations. Our objective, a difficult two-hour drive from headquarters, was known as Haura Binyan, a high mountain crowned with a double-walled city. This ancient ruin, also recorded under the name Haura Burgha, had first been called to my attention by the Sultan's father in Bombay.

Halfway up the *wadi* we stopped to photograph a small encampment of *badu*. As soon as it was known that we had a *hakim*, 'doctor', with us, they led Dr Krause to where a very sick man lay on the ground. I remarked to Bill what an unbelievable situation this was. Here in one of the wildest, least known areas of the world, a primitive *badawi* lies in the sand extremely ill. Then, without warning, one of America's leading medical specialists drops down as from heaven to serve his most grateful patient.

At one place we came onto an extensive series of regularly spaced, large circular mounds of earth with protected holes in the centre. This was another example of the famous Oman underground waterways, for each shallow surface shaft (some twenty feet deep) was connected to the other by a gently sloping tunnel which ran below the surface for miles. After a quick lunch at the base of our mountain objective we began the steep climb on foot. From the summit a magnificent panorama spread out on all sides with the blue sea (Gulf of Oman) to the east and the dark forbidding Oman mountains to the west.

Three months before, on my first attempt to locate this ruin, my guide had been a badly crippled sheikh who not only had never seen the site himself but knew no one who had. Of course I only learned all of this after we had driven and walked for several hours, stimulated by an intriguing flow of delightful lies as to why the old city lay just over the next mountain. How indefinite guides in Arabia can often be in matters of distance is reflected in the reply so commonly given to the much asked question 'How far?' – the answer – *ramat al-asa*, 'the throw of a stick'. It was eagle-eyed Jama who finally located the distant, almost unrecognizable ruins, which I immediately confirmed through the telephoto lens of my Bolex camera.

The impressive, well-preserved walls, with a uniform thickness of approximately three feet, were constructed of rough fragments of white limestone interspersed with small circular towers. No ornamental or dressed stones were seen and little mortar was employed. Not far from the steep, irregular summit an erect, low-pointed arch still stands. Here the architect must have placed the stones in cement against a wooden scaffold which was subsequently removed, leaving the vaulted arch. Further down the slope on the face of the surface rock I located again the curious man-made cuphole I had seen on my earlier visit; only a few inches across at the surface and shaped downward like an inverted tarboush. Similar holes date back to the Middle Bronze I civilization of the Age of Abraham in Palestine (first half of the second millennium B.C.), where they were used as mortars or querns for the grinding of grain into flour with stone pestles.

Drainage systems, dams, sluices, plastered baths, and a square tank were examined and photographed, and from certain rooms Ray collected potsherds. However, Ray concluded that there would be little to be gained by excavating here, for even though these ruins were well preserved there appeared to be no stratified remains, just walls on top of the mountain with no deposits or accumulated debris left.

The following story, told me by Colonel Colin Maxwell and still told to children in Sohar to this day, is probably as old as these ruins themselves.

There was a Prince who ruled Oman and lived in a palace at Haura Burgha who had a tall and beautiful wife. She had an amazing gift of being able to see clearly over great distances. One day she climbed up to the highest part of the palace and cast her eyes towards the town of Sohar and there in a garden she saw an exceedingly handsome man beside a *falaj*. This *falaj* ran straight and true from beneath the palace to the garden where the man was working. The princess plucked the largest and sweetest lime she could find, and taking a piece of jewellery she wore, with a rare gem stone, she embedded it in the lime, which she then placed in the *falaj*. She then returned to the top of the palace and waited and watched the lime being swept along the *falaj* to where the man was working in the garden at Sohar. She saw the man pick out the lime, break it open and extract the piece of jewellery. The next day the man, realizing that such a rare piece of jewellery could only have come from the palace, went to Haura Binyan and returned it to the princess. The prince learned of his wife's unfaithfulness and of her amazing power of sight, and he made her blind.

Tradition ascribes this spectacular wind-swept site to Jemsetjerd, capital of the pre-Islamic Persians (Sassanians)³ although the ruins appeared Arab to me. In those days of slings and bows this fortress must have been considered quite impregnable. It was here, according to Sheikh Sirhan bin Said, that in A.D. 629 the Prophet's personal envoy, Amr bin al-As, who was from Mohammed's tribe, the Banu Quraish, and had been converted to Islam the year before, first demanded the allegiance of Oman to Islam. At his invitation all accepted Islam save the Persians, who were slaughtered or forced to leave the country. In desperation the Persians remaining took final refuge in Jemsetjerd, where after withstanding a vigorous siege they sued for terms, which included safe withdrawal on condition all gold and silver remained behind. Subsequently this renowned general and wealthy Meccan merchant, 'a man of subtle intellect', swept through Egypt and Syria commanding, 'Give up your heresies and fear Allah and his Prophet'.

On our return to headquarters I received word from Sheikh Saqr that he was bringing the new Acting Wali of Sohar to meet us, and later that evening we received him, Sheikh Ali bin Hamad. He was an agreeable man, responding to our flowery language, coffee and fruit, although obviously somewhat awed by us all. He told me that he was of the Maawil tribe and had served, in various parts of Oman, in the Sultan's service for six or seven years. He agreed to supply me with thirty workmen, and we came to terms about their pay. They turned up the following morning and Sandy Honeyman divided them into two teams of fifteen, each with its foreman. More turned up than we had asked for, and I added three to each group; they were to receive four rupees a day for an eight-hour shift.

It was agreed that Sandy and Ray would take one group of eighteen workers and initiate work at the high *tell* of Sohar, not far from our headquarters. The *tell*, meaning 'hill' or 'mound', in this instance the accumulation of occupation, at Sohar stretches for about a mile along the coast, rising immediately behind the sands of the beach but having at no point a width greater than a quarter of a mile. The principal mound with its scattered sherds is nearly all covered by the present-day city, which consists of large buildings with thick rubbly walls gradually being replaced by huts made of palm fronds. A small *khor* marks the southern limit of the mound and another separates the main mound, surrounded by a moat, from a less extensive one to the north. The northern part is unoccupied, though generously supplied with recent burials, except for a narrow line of huts along the beach. Both of the inlets are separated from the sea by sandbars, but either or both of them might have served as small boat harbours in ancient times if the passage to the sea were open. At the same time Bill, Dr Krause and I would take the second section of coolies (Arab workers in South Arabia refer to themselves as *kuliya*, 'coolies', the term not having the connotation we associate with it) and excavate the mysterious circular structures lining the walls and floor of the Wadi al-Mulayyanah.

I shall not enter into details, tedious to the lay reader, of our digging. The structures yielded bones and beads[4] and we were able to confirm that they are, in fact, tombs. Some eighty-five years ago Colonel S. B. Miles had observed and reported these curious horse-shoe-shaped structures as the remains of an extensive ancient Arabian town. 'Rectangular and oval heaps of black basaltic stones mark the place of habitations . . . and I learnt that the town flourished during the occupation of the Persians in the days of Ignorance, that is before the introduction of Islam, and that it was visited by destruction by God on account of the refusal of the Persians to accept the true faith.'[5] Fifty years later Bertram Thomas disregarded both the house idea *bait al-jahl* 'House of the Days of Ignorance', and a possible military function, in that where there was a long interior axis it had no common orientation and these clusters of mounds faced in various directions commanding no particular field of view. He felt they had some 'religious after-death significance' but did not attribute them to tombs.

We know now that these are pre-Islamic tombs, not city buildings.

We assume they must be pre-Islamic for they are unique cairns numbering many hundreds with nothing like them known elsewhere in Arabia. Admittedly I have not seen every antiquity in Yemen, the former Eastern and Western Aden Protectorates, and Oman; however, I have explored South Arabia as fully and perhaps seen more of it than anyone else; and I have never seen anything similar to the ancient tomb field in Wadi al-Mulayyanah. Thus, here in Oman, sometime in the distant past a people of unknown origin, date and history constructed, at enormous effort, one of the world's largest cemeteries.

The majority of Arabian explorers have observed and reported burial monuments of some sort.[6] In 1950 my first expedition to Beihan passed through the lower part of Wadi Adim in Hadhramaut, two miles south of Sah, and continuing for five or six miles were hundreds of cairns lining the upper portion of the canyon walls. Many were shaped like pillboxes, others were mere mounds of stone. There were never more than three in a group and numerous ones were isolated. Tombs in ancient Arabia usually served only as ossuaries, with which size is not a major criterion. So far no Bronze Age or Stone Age burials have been positively identified. The problem of dating these monuments is further confused because certain present-day *badu* bury their dead under cairns. In 1947, my University of California African Expedition[7] opened a modified pillbox cairn in Sinai; I climbed in to find, much to my embarrassment, a relatively recent group burial with the muscles and hair still attached to the bodies.

Leaving Ray to direct our excavations at the main mound north of Sohar, Sandy Honeyman and I spent an hour investigating the high area within the walls of the old Persian fort which stands at the south end of the city. After we had measured and marked out an area six by thirty feet at the most likely looking spot, I led Sheikh Saqr over by the hand and obtained his permission to dig; this automatically led to the Wali's approval. Sandy immediately set his men to work in this trench near the west wall of the fort compound in a space left vacant by the collapse of a rubble building. The corner of a large building, diagonal to the sides of the trench, was uncovered some six feet below the surface. Its preserved height about the bottom of its foundations was approximately three feet and it was built of small square, kiln-baked bricks of a type characteristic of later Islamic times. This building may have been erected during the Portuguese occupation of the city. For a number of reasons work was terminated after a depth of fourteen feet was reached. The potsherds and small finds even at this depth indicated that the excavation had not gone below the twelfth century. The deposit was not packed and one wall had collapsed into the trench, which had only been vacated a few minutes before when threatening cracks had appeared. The rubble within the walls of the fort had built up very rapidly in recent centuries; this meant that it would be much easier to uncover older materials outside the walls.

One of the advantages which the archaeologist gains from the employment of local labour on a dig is that by contact with his labourers he learns much about the people; and not only the people as they are now but, from the persistence of traditions, about what they were in the past, so that every archaeologist is also something of an anthropologist. The work of Dr Krause with our expedition led us, naturally, to an interest in native Omani medicine. As Ailon Shiloh has pointed out,[8] 'The essential philosophy underlying the system of [folk] medicine in the Middle East is that all illnesses or injuries are subjective affairs arising out of personal actions conducted or not conducted, or caused by someone or something possessed with power. Illnesses or injuries do not just occur – they befall a certain victim, at a given time, and in a definite manner because of specific causal actions.' Such attitudes are rapidly vanishing however. There is only one direct reference to medicine in the revelation of Islam. 'From the bee's belly comes forth a fluid of variant hue which yieldeth medicine to Man.' Tradition affirms (Baidhawi's Commentary) that one of his followers once came to Mohammed and explained that his brother was ill with a violent pain in his belly. The Prophet ordered him to give his brother some honey. Soon the man returned and said that the medicine had done no good. Mohammed replied, 'Go and give him more honey for God speaks truth and thy brother's belly lies.' The Prophet appears to have realized the infectiousness of certain diseases, for he stated, 'if you hear of plague in an area never go near to it.' In addition the Prophet is believed to have said, 'There is a medicine for every pain; then when the medicine reaches the pain it is cured by the order of God.'

Now I am a firm believer in the power of faith and so is that great Oman missionary doctor Paul Harrison, who said, however, that 'the patient with a strangulated hernia who is treated by faith instead of works, just simply dies, and that is all there is to it.'[9]

Actually Arabs have a strong passion for medicine and medical treatment, and the Quran, Sura 35, says, 'He who saveth a soul alive shall be as if he had saved the lives of all mankind.' Yet the study of anatomy with its required human dissection, in no way condemned by Quranic precepts, has been looked upon with horror by Arabs (though ideas on such subjects are now rapidly changing). It was in part based on the popular belief that the soul does not immediately leave the body at death, but remains in it for a period, which caused dissection to be regarded as inhuman and cruel, while belief in bodily resurrection was another factor. Even if the dead man had swallowed the most precious pearl, and that pearl was not his, the opening of the body was forbidden. There is nothing peculiar to the Moslems in this. For more than ten centuries the Christian church opposed surgery and put every possible obstruction in the way of medical science. The Fourth Lateran Council prohibited surgical operations by priests, whereas at the time of the 'golden period' of the Baghdad Caliphs, when the European world was sunk in profound ignorance, with the practice of medicine still forbidden by the Church, the Arabs regarded medicine as 'the most precious of all forms of instruction', and they alone held high the torch of medical science, 'the best index to a nation's genius'. This Arab medicine was composed of elements transmitted from the Greeks, with Indian, Persian and Syrian accretions, along with additions and developments from within Arab civilization, notably the work of Ibn Sina (Avicenna).[10]

But that was long, long ago. Since then over the subsequent centuries few people, until this century, remained more unprogressive than the Arabs of Arabia with their hesitant appreciation of new truths. In the main they have forgotten the Prophet's admonition that, 'Who so pursueth the road of knowledge, God will direct him to the road of Paradise.'

Native medicine in Arabia is 'a weary and unrelieved desert of quackery and ignorance.' In the former Aden Protectorates the tying of a thin black goat hair cord around the upper part of the calf of the leg is considered an infallible insurance against snakebite, while in Yemen a string tied around the big toe prevents rheumatism, and a raven's intestines, if administered in an agreeable form, are considered vital to improving a child's memorizing powers. There is scarcely one Arab in a hundred in all the Arabian Peninsula who has not some cautery scars on his body, for the hot iron[11] is accounted the universal panacea for man and beast in Arabia, the underlying idea perhaps being to create an extreme counter-irritation which becomes a festering sore. Even infants are burned cruelly. A hot iron over the spleen is prescribed for malaria and one at the base of the skull for boils. In bad cases of consumption the bottom of the tongue is branded, causing it to swell, filling the mouth with unbelievable agony so that the patient cannot speak or eat. A popular Hadhrami cure for acute abdominal pain is the deep burning of the patient's heel with a red-hot iron stake. The shock effect alone usually succeeds and the sufferer exchanges his stomach ache for a ten-day limp. If the hot iron fails, the Arab resorts to written words from the Quran, which the patient takes by swallowing paper and all or by drinking water in which the ink of the writing has been dissolved. In most of these instances the patient is armed with one or several popular amulets[12] or shields consisting of a chapter or verse from the Quran folded in a small leather case and hung on the person. Babies are adorned with charms which not only serve to keep off the evil-eye, but are amusing playthings. In addition, old teeth, coins, holy earth and beads are used, as well as the spittle of a holy man applied to the ailing organ of the body. This sure protection and guardian from the excessively dreaded influence of the evil-eye (blue eyes are particularly nefarious) is applied as well to camels, horses, donkeys, houses and fishing boats. For here sickness is due to the hand of God or the evil-eye which is ever going to and fro to discover its prey. 'It empties the houses and fills the tombs.' More than half of all deaths are attributed to the evil-eye, which must somehow be misled, deceived and deluded and its effects dissipated.[13]

Among the Shiites of Iraq (or for that matter anywhere) the name Omar is not used, being that of a Caliph whom they regard as one of the great villains of Islamic history. However, if a Shiite family loses a succession of boys by early death, they will sometimes call the next child Omar so that the devil will be deceived into thinking it is his own and will not molest it. Unattractive or repulsive names are likewise sometimes given for the same reason.

The beautiful, healthy and happy children are especially attracted by the evil-eye. The evil-eye is in reality a covetous and envious eye; thus young children are kept purposely encrusted in filth, ragged and unkempt, particularly when out in public as a disguise to distract, delude and confuse the dreaded eye 'of the enviously malignant gaze of some evilly disposed neighbour'. To arouse disgust in the eye of the beholder is far more desirable than to arouse compliments. Children, esteemed the greatest of blessings, are never praised and male children are often dressed as females under false names to negate any possibility of correctly directed admiration. Women appear as frequent possessors of the evil-eye. The writer is unaware of any truly satisfactory explanation for this 'singular sex speciality'.

Enlarged tonsils are brought about by taking a bath in the full of the moon, and cholera is believed to be caused by the yellow wind when the moon and stars are unfavourable. In Sinai it is widely held that malaria originates from the eating of unripened dates and in the former Aden Protectorates it is believed malaria is caused by drinking dirty water in different places, whereas hernias are thought by Omani Arabs to originate in excessive indulgence in sexual intercourse, bad smells and the wind.

Smallpox (the first definite account of the disease was written by Rhazes who appears to have prescribed a form of vaccination for treatment)[14] is one of the most dreaded diseases of the settled areas of Arabia, where frequent epidemics cause havoc. The Arabs have a saying, 'There is no face left after smallpox, just as intelligence dies after madness.' Pockmarked faces are seen more among the immigrants, as opposed to the indigenous population. However, when the disease strikes it is a dreadfully devastating scourge. The poor sufferer is isolated far from his tribesmen to live or die alone subsisting on food and water deposited several hundred yards away.

'In Muscat the father of Abdullah, one of the Sunday school boys, locked his son inside the walled yard and defied anyone to come for him [refusing to let him be vaccinated]. He declared that Allah alone would decree whether or not his child took the disease. Ten-year-old Abdullah not only contracted smallpox but lost his sight as well.'[15]

In Yemen many of the Saiyids are medicine-men with a large following. On occasion they will put their spit in a glass of water and the patient after paying a fee drinks the water in the belief that the spit of the Saiyid has healing powers. One Saiyid once explained to the writer the genesis of smallpox. 'It is purely a disease of the blood. When the navel cord is cut the blood should be fully drained off, for otherwise what the embryo has derived from the mother remains in the child, and this is likely to erupt in the form of small-pox.'

As soon as *hasbah*, 'measles', is confirmed in what was the former Aden Protectorates, the whole body of the patient is covered with *kuhl*, a black compound made of antimony. The *kuhl* is even put in the eyes, sometimes to such an amount that the conjunctiva is burned with consequent ulceration of both the conjunctiva and the cornea. The child is kept in a room with all doors and windows shut for over two weeks. At the door of the room and at the main entrance of the house raw eggs are broken and left on the floor with the idea that the *jinn*, 'evil spirits', will get busy with the raw eggs and not enter the house. The *badu* are particularly concerned over various smells and their effect on progress toward recovery. It is a common sight to see nostrils plugged with dirty pieces of cloth, it never occurring to them that the air must therefore be inhaled through the mouth, with possibly worse results. The 'smell of a woman' rates high on the list of scents dangerous to an open wound. In spite of the Prophet's admonition, 'Cleanliness is piety', the Arab sometimes has his own idea of hygiene. She-camel urine is used as an antiseptic for wounds; as a purgative, eyewash, hair-oil and general tonic. A widely used cure for *haʒaʒ*, 'ringworm', is the extensive application of human urine. E. A. Powell, in his *By Camel and Car to the Peacock Throne*, says that he saw two Bedouins who joined his caravan near al-Garah loosen their hair, which they wore in long braids, schoolgirl fashion, and shampoo it with rotten eggs whipped up in camel's urine.

Personally I have always regarded health as being more important than education. It has been said that within limits 'health is a purchasable commodity' and therefore unobtainable to the majority of Omanis, who are extremely poor, victims of the Oriental species of poverty which is unknown in the western world. One never loses the memory of beautiful young Miriam already condemned to an early death by tuberculosis; of little Hasanah lying in the sand doomed to a lifetime of blindness by advanced trachoma; of the lovely slave girl's uncontrolled tears as she held up her emaciated baby suffering from diarrhoea; of the countless thin outstretched arms burning up with fever; of miserable pot-bellied tiny Fatimah covered from head to foot with open dirt-filled sores and clothed in unheeded and unmolested flies as she crawled about the village dunghill; of her father, a blind beggar; of the week-old girl, a mere bundle of skin and bones, her father unknown, abandoned by her mother, and nursed by a slave woman who had lost her own baby; of the little shrivelled-up girl married at eleven whose first two children went blind due to poverty, malnutrition and obnoxious quack treatments and whose husband died before the birth of her third, when she was expelled from her miserable date-frond hut by the pious (prayed five times a day), rent-conscious landlord to find eventual shelter in the Mission.

What a privilege it has been for me to observe Dr Wells Thoms at the Mission Hospital in Matrah, being used by God to restore sight to scores of the blind who number thousands in Oman. The main cause is trachoma, followed by smallpox and gonorrhoea. There can be few experiences more thrilling than that of watching a patient's face light up with joy when the bandages are removed and he finds he can see once more. An Arab is sure to exclaim *al-hamdu lillah* 'Praise be to God.'

On one occasion Dr Thoms was operating on an Arab woman for trichiasis and allowed us to photograph the proceedings. With this disease the lids turn inward, causing the eyelashes to rub against the eyeball and injure the cornea and conjunctional covering. It is usually caused by trachoma. The operation consisted of replacing the scar tissue on the inner side of the lids with a graft of mucous membrane taken from the inside of the lower lip. If left to their own resources the Omanis sometimes brand the eyelids with a red-hot iron. The scar tissue formed from the resulting ulcer may cause total blindness or, in rare instances, with extremely mild cases, uncurl the lid and effect a cure.

The operation for a cataract among the untrained Arabs of the former Aden Protectorates is a very ancient one, practised all over the Near East and also in India and Pakistan. No doubt this operation requires a considerable amount of skill on the part of the operator. The instrument used is a sharp needle about four inches long with a handle. The operator sits in front of the patient and inserts the needle at the corneoscleral junction and breaks the suspensory ligament of the lens, with the result that the opaque lens falls in the vitreous chamber and the patient immediately sees. After the operation the eye is closed and sealed with kneaded flour. The patient is not allowed out of the room for forty days.

In about 95 per cent of these cases, the couched eye is spoiled and the patient loses his sight in a few weeks. In the majority of cases the point of the needle, in an attempt to break the suspensory ligaments punctures the capsule of the lens, and a foreign body reaction is set up in the eye. In a few cases both the operator and the patient are lucky, the capsule is not damaged and the whole lens drops in the vitreum in capsules. Dr Mohamed Mazhar of the Queen Elizabeth Hospital, Aden, has seen a few cases where the patients have after couching retained good sight for fifteen to twenty years. Dr Mazhar has also seen cases where the opaque lens is hanging in the vitreum, still attached to a few fibres of the suspensory ligaments. In such cases a very interesting phenomenon takes place; the patient sees very well as long as he is in an erect posture, but as soon as he stoops the opaque lens falls back in position again and the patient cannot see.

To Arabs in the more backward parts of the Peninsula a hospital is the last resort of the diseased and dying after all brandings, purges, chants, incantations and holy potions have been in vain. They enter in hopeless despondency, in the firm belief that this is the end, that they will be forever swallowed by this hungry hospital that feeds on the sick. Those Omani adults who survive soon come to appreciate among other things that bigger and better babies are produced in the Mission hospital than under a thorn bush, thanks to pre-natal care, a well rounded diet and anti-malarial treatment; the good news soon spreads across the desert. Dr Thoms recalled one instance where Sheikh Yasir bin Hamud of the Janibah was so comfortable where he was he refused to go to the hospital. Sheikh Yasir had fallen from his camel and broken his right femur in 1958 near Firq. He was not moved from the place where he fell but remained right there until the bones knit crooked and shortened. A barusti was built over him, and his sisters, wives and tribesmen camped about to care for him.

From the day of our arrival in Sohar Jama worked with Dr Krause in the running of our field clinic. Dr Krause saw a great many cases, and he has kindly allowed me to draw here upon his brief, general report on disease in Oman.

He noted that outside Muscat and Matrah there was no sign of modern medicine, treatment being based upon folklore medicine. He noted the existence of all the diseases with which Europeans and Americans are familiar at home, and in addition a number peculiar to the region. The usual diseases of childhood and those of the respiratory organs are common. Certain diseases he found chronic throughout Oman, noting in particular those secondary to trachoma and the other infectious diseases which occur about the eye. Nothing was done for these during his journeyings, for at that time no effective remedy was known, though one has since been found. Trichiasis is common: it is successfully treated by surgery at the Muscat clinic, where Dr Thoms operates on a number of such cases every week. Dr Krause found tuberculosis to be common: 'I saw acute forms and the sub-acute chronic forms repeatedly, with the rather rapidly devastating form of galloping consumption.' Yaws cases were noted, though perhaps less commonly than on the other coasts of Arabia; the yaws most commonly seen in Oman is the facial form, with destruction of the facial cartilages and tissues. Remarkable cures of this were obtained with penicillin, excepting in the chronic stage of the disease where contractures about the joints or about the face and eyes had occurred. Intestinal diseases were very common, usually acute and subsiding rapidly, but occasionally severe and needing treatment, for the most part successful.

We were interested in the observation of blood pressure during the time in which I was in the former Western Aden Protectorate and also in Oman. I did not see any elevated blood pressures in the natives at all except an occasional one on the coast; all had normal pressure. Where I was able to get a history of a stone or confirm the presence of bladder stone which is still fairly frequently present, then only did we find elevated blood pressure. Needless to say the use of salt was very restricted in the interior of Oman, as in the former Western Aden Protectorate. It is difficult to get salt. We did make a visit to the great salt domes at Aiyadin which is an unusual geologic phenomenon in that area. The natives must travel a great distance to chop away some salt at these great salt domes. Salt is relatively rare, and therefore it becomes more expensive, and for that reason it is used less frequently than we do in the western world. The rarity of the use of salt is probably one of the contributing factors to the normal pressure that we see in these natives in the desert areas. An interesting thing was the frequency in which blood vessel disease still occurred. We did see in the older age group the obvious changes that you find in blood vessels when you palpate them at the wrist or in the peripheral arteries of the leg. We saw a number of recent injuries and some old fractures. We noted the result of improper care and faulty reduction of the fracture with its consequent deformity in the healed stage. This was particularly distressing to see in the individuals with broken bones in their lower extremities, because in a land where one usually depends on one's own legs for locomotion it is quite a handicap for these folks to have a deformity as a result of a simple fracture that could have been otherwise prevented. Malaria is still very rampant and in some of the oases it was apparent that it was very extensive in its distribution. If one depends on the presence of a large spleen (which is probably as good a guide in this area as any) as an indication, the incidence would be remarkably high, forty to sixty per cent in the youngsters. I saw no spleens associated with Kala Azar such as one sees in Egypt, and here the splenic enlargement is a better index for malaria than in Egypt. Of course this area has not been open to anyone except a very few people from the western world, and no attempt has been made to control the mosquito population in this particular area of the world, so malaria is just about as frequent as it always has been. One of the frequent places in which the mosquito larvae were found was in the drinking jars. The water in these rather large jars was rarely emptied completely so that there was always a residue of water to which fresh water was repeatedly added, so there was always a certain number of larvae present that would come to maturity, and in many of these huts it was easy to see the source of the mosquito population. All in all there is still a great deal of education and enterprise necessary. The people are very willing; they were extremely cooperative and were very eager to get some help for their illnesses, and we had no difficulty persuading them to accept the therapy that was offered to them.

One of our hopeless patients was an eighteen-year-old Arab with a bilateral pulmonary tuberculosis (galloping consumption). He had long been treated with a hot cautery iron and bore seven scars on his left chest and five on his right. He was too sick to sit up, although we did get him moved a little into the sunlight. The boy was grossly emaciated, a sickly brown parcel of bones, weighing about eighty pounds. (A normal human skeleton by itself weighs fifty to sixty pounds before moisture leaves the bones). Dr Krause dissolved acromycin in a coffee cup so that he could swallow it – he was too weak to take the whole pill. This would help take care of secondary infection in the chest but nothing could save his life, for he had huge multiple cavities in both lungs. Dr Krause told Jama to tell the boy's father that he would die within a week. Jama spoke briefly to the father apart, but Jama, with whom strict honesty was an unvarying principle, betrayed that he was hedging. Dr Krause, puzzled, asked, 'Did you tell him?' Jama, himself an intelligently devout Muslim, replied, 'No, sir, I could not tell him that, because these people believe that only God takes life and only He knows the time a man will die.' Three days later the boy was dead. The body was immediately washed (it is forbidden to look deliberately on the nakedness of a dead man) by his male relatives (women wash the bodies of women). The one performing this operation washes (if water is unavailable then sand is used) first the right hand and then the left of the dead, having first washed his own hands. The washer must not catch hold of the genitals of the dead except his hands be covered with a cloth and the washer must not hold onto the hands of the dead. In the case of an infectious disease having caused the death the body is only washed from the foot to the navel. Buried (the body of a good and pious man never rots in the grave) the same day, the body is clothed in new white cotton cloth; this custom is prevalent all over the Near East and dates from classical antiquity.

This is followed by a period of mourning and prayers lasting three days. Complete self-control is the rule of the male mourners, whereas abandoned hysterical wailing, outbursts and piercing shrieks are expected of their united female counterparts, to attest in a non-melodious dirge to the violent bitterness of their mingled grief at the loss they have sustained.

Living in the same house as this boy was a young woman with a terrible eye. There was a marked protrusion of the eyeball, to such an extent that she was unable to close her lid. The eyeball had lost some of its roundness and was now discoloured with white patches. She explained that her sight in this eye had gone several months before and that it was now no longer painful. On her chest she had been treated so often with the hot cautery for bronchitis that an over-production of scar tissue or keloid formation had developed. The whole family, including the children, had their palms, nails and toes painted red with henna as a form of beauty culture. Tattooing on individual fingers is believed by these people to relieve pain in the joints.

We had a case of night blindness show up one morning. Jama politely inquired of the man if he could see during the daytime. The patient nodded yes, whereupon Jama said, 'That's enough.' In the afternoon a *shayib*, 'old man', came to us with a horrible knee – it went out sideways. This was an example of Charcot Joint – a loss of the articulating surface caused by yaws or syphilis.

Yaws, particularly of the facial variety, appears to be less frequent here on the east coast of Arabia than on the west. 'Another visitor to our [expedition] hospital [Beihan, 1950] will never be forgotten by any of us who saw him. He was an Arab boy with no face – or at least with nothing that could be called a face. There were jaws and some teeth, two holes where a nose had once been, and a mass of diseased flesh. Only the two eyes remained, and the forehead above them. The eyes now stared fixedly at Dr. [James] McNinch, who explained to me that the boy's face had been eaten away by yaws'.[16] Penicillin is extremely effective in stopping the disease.

The incidence of syphilis is high. The Omanis treat syphilis with mercury vapour baths by digging a pit in which they make a fire. When the fire has burned down to glowing coals they put in green leaves which they have smeared with a home-made ointment of lard or butter and quicksilver stirred up together. When the heavy vapour rises, the victim (i.e. the patient) sits above the fire and vapour on a couple of branches laid across the pit and becomes enveloped in the vapour. Dr Thoms has seen several Omanis badly poisoned by this treatment. Extreme salivation, gingivitis with a loosening of the teeth and swelling of the gums often results. One man who had eczema and not syphilis was given this treatment, and he never recovered from its effects. He died of heavy metal poisoning manifested chiefly by nephritis, oedema of the ankles and stoppage of urine secretion.

In Arabic *jamb* means 'side', and when a child is suffering from broncho-pneumonia the intercostal muscles have to do extra work and that is why the disease is known as *jamb*. In the former Aden Protectorates as soon as the diagnosis is settled the child is put in a room where a fire is burning and giving off smoke. Then all the doors and windows are shut and all the odd crevices are blocked to make absolutely certain that no air enters the room. This idiotic prescription in itself often kills the child in question. The treatment for pneumonia in Oman is about the same as in Aden, only in Oman they often burn the patient with three or four long searing swipes of the cautery between the ribs on the affected side and sometimes apply a poultice of wheat gluten. Dr Krause explained how some 50 per cent of all appendicitis cases including the mild forms will recover of their own accord. Among the septic ones the death rate is much higher than elsewhere.

The Iranians have a saying, 'In the spring the peasant swears by the life of his child and in winter by its tomb.' Here at Sohar numerous babies were treated for swollen abdomens due to intestinal worms. Diarrhoea and dysentery were found to be prevalent during the child's second and third years. Enlarged spleens were common in both young and old due to malaria. Typhoid was present in every village, but so far no heart disease, cholera or cancer has been found at Sohar.

In one day alone, Dr Krause saw over fifty patients in his improvised clinic, not to mention those treated during his village visits. Keeping an orderly clinic was anything but a simple task, because Arab women are incapable of any type of regimentation. They arrive in groups, and confusion reigns supreme as each one wants to be treated first. In several instances women closely veiled with narrow slitted indigo-dyed masks brought children to the doctor, leaving the mother at home; here a whole group will look after the child – it is sometimes difficult to know who the mother is. The Arabs glory in the quantity of their children, for a man's status, prestige and stature are to a great measure based on the number of his male progeny. A wife, asked if she has children, will reply, 'I have nothing'; and 'nothing' means a girl. An Omani grandmother once refused to kiss her grandchild for many months because she was born a girl. Motherhood counts more than wifehood – be fruitful and multiply is the golden rule. A tree that does not bear, cut it down, for it is outside the stream of creation. An Arab once referred to his wife as a woman of rare excellence: 'She brought forth sixteen children and she suckled them all, generally two at a time, and when she ceased from bearing she died.'

In classic times a wife who produced ten male children was considered ennobled, and the chief motivating desire of these women is to bring forth a constant stream of male children and thus, in spite of the pangs of childbirth, they attempt to keep continuously pregnant – mere human cows, bearing and giving milk. At the same time, as in biblical days, a woman will breast-feed and pamper a male child until it has reached the age of three or four years; breast-feeding usually stops when a girl is twelve to eighteen months old. According to the Quran, 'Mothers shall suckle their children for two whole years, for those who wish to complete the suckling'. Among the *badu* in Oman a legitimate pregnancy of three or four years is considered not at all impossible, in fact not at all abnormal (the child sleeps in his mother's womb for up to four years);[17] this view, whatever its medical merits may be, actively demonstrates the wisdom of our desert sisters whose husbands may be away from home for extensive periods; the supreme calamity is barrenness, all the more so as it is believed by many that adultery causes sterility.

One day an Arab approached the writer at our field hospital. 'Sir, there is something outside – God forgive me for mentioning such a thing in your presence – and I want some medicine for it.' The 'something' turned out to be the man's wife. Thank Heaven that all the Arabs of the Near East do not take such an extreme view of women's inferiority as we find in isolated areas of the Arabian Peninsula.

In Eastern Arabia, half-blind, feeble women, often old and dull of senses, always vermin-infested and filthy, untrained, ignorant, armed with their rusty scissors or knives, are preferred as midwives. Usually the dirtiest rugs and mats are assigned for the confinement, where if possible, every particle of fresh air is eliminated from the area. If there is a slight delay the midwife rubs her ring-encrusted, long-clawed hand on the dusty, germ-laden floor, to give it a better purchase as she thrusts it brutally inside the agony-filled mother to begin a pulling and twisting tug-of-war with the reluctant child, who may eventually emerge in detached pieces with an arm or leg torn off at a time. Broken glass or a rusty tin can is used to cut the umbilical cord. The newborn child is peculiarly susceptible at this stage to the 'evil-eye'. Omani midwives have been known to butt the mother's stomach with their heads, and even jump up and down with both feet on top of their extended stomachs to hasten delivery, which may be long delayed, even for five or six days. In the northern parts of the former Eastern Aden Protectorate, Arabs adopt a somewhat novel means of dealing with protracted or difficult childbirth due to mal-presentation. A large flat stone is placed on a fire and heated thoroughly; it is then laid over the patient's abdomen, and in most cases the unborn child alters its position, thus facilitating its delivery. After birth, if the placenta does not make its appearance within minutes it is ripped loose and dragged away by hand.

Once again comes the agonizing cry, 'Come quickly, doctor, my wife is in labour and can't deliver!' 'Is this her first baby?' 'No, it is her second. She had no trouble the first time.' Atresia – that was what the doctor suspected and what he found to be the trouble. Atresia, a condition which causes the death of many a mother and her unborn child in Muslim lands, where polygamy is practised and divorce obtained, is caused by fear – fear of divorce. Atresia is a condition where the normal tissue of the vagina has become inelastic scar tissue. When this condition exists the child cannot be born. The woman in labour suffers agony, for in her body the irresistible force of birth contractions propels the foetus against an immovable barrier of rigid scar tissue, which has closed the birth canal like a purse string. Suddenly everything rips open.

How was scar tissue formed? The answer is that it results from the packing of rock salt into the vagina after childbirth – after the birth of the first baby. Why salt? The answer – to contract the vagina lest the husband, not deriving the satisfaction from his wife which he experienced before delivery, should divorce her. They do it in ignorance, not having learned to associate cause and effect because the next pregnancy and delivery seems a long way off. By then, if a woman dies in childbirth it is God's will, *maktub*, 'Written down', final and irrevocable. The salt treatment of two years back is out of mind! Surgery alone, done in time, can save the mother and child. Every year a score or more such operations are performed in the American Mission Women's hospital in Muscat.[18]

According to the rules, the husband must abstain from sexual intercourse for at least forty days, although there are numerous cases where this rule is broken the next day. After childbirth drugs are applied to induce the vagina to return to less than normal size to please the husband. A newborn baby is immediately dipped in female camel urine and its eyes are rubbed with antimony to make them strong. Then its body is powdered with dry camel dung. Soon the majority of the babies have their little neglected bodies ingrained with dirt, their single unwashed garments untouchable, their eyes uncleansed, inflamed, pus-ridden and full of hungry flies, and their heads encrusted with filth and open running sores.

In the words of the Muscat missionary nurse Allene Schmaltz-reidt Lee:

When patients with hemoglobins of 10–15 per cent depend on us to cure them and we have no blood bank;

When a child is gored by a bull and is bounced in a truck over unspeakable roads for five hours, only to expire shortly after arrival;

When the searing hot winds of May and June seem to visibly draw off body fluid and the children especially become dehydrated and feverish;

When a lad whose feet were nearly blown off when his donkey stepped on an American-made land mine finally walked again and wanted his first pair of shoes like the doctor's;

When sick, tired bodies, young and old, are brought in only after all the local remedies have been tried and the skin seared by the branding irons;

When patients don't understand about taking their medicines and either take many doses at once or else store them all under the mattress while we wonder why they don't improve – that's nursing in Oman!

5

THE WILL OF ALLAH? FATALISM
AND SLAVERY

*Fish-traps – Sardines by the billion – Religion is the law and
law religion – The death penalty – Schools – 'Calvinistic' fatalism
Jews of Sohar – Mohammed and Slavery – Slave-trading by air
Slaves in Oman today*

One afternoon Bill and I took our party and explored up the coast
a distance in the direction of the most northern province or extremity
of Oman, a lofty, precipitous, highly indented inhospitable peninsula
known as Ras Musandam, which means 'Anvil Headland'. It is this
unscalable, projecting horn of black rocks,[1] the *Mons Asabo* of
Pliny, which separates the deeper, cooler water of the Gulf of Oman
from the Persian or Arabian Gulf. At the present time this mountainous country of Ruus al-Jibal is the home of the curious composite
Shihuh tribe of non-Arab, Persian or Central Asian origin, with a
language (Kumzara) of their own. This primitive and inoffensive
tribe numbering three to four thousand live in caves and stone
dwellings existing in the main on fish and shellfish. No ancient cities
were discovered so we settled for innumerable sand-castles inhabited
by large quantities of crabs, one variety of which is called *abu-
maqass*, 'father of scissors', by the Arabs. While holding one up for
the camera's benefit I almost lost part of a finger. Later when I was
relating this to the Sultan he smilingly remarked, 'You have received
your just punishment for having murdered so many poor crabs with
your six-shooter.' *En route* back to Sohar with hundreds of vermilion
flamingos overhead, Bill photographed an elaborate fishing sequence
with the entire labour force of racially mixed Arabs, Negroes and
Baluchis operating a huge *ghal*, 'net', for a great haul under the
direction of a man totally blind. These communal Batinah shore

seine nets may be over 400 yards in length with the central section
twelve feet deep. The netting itself is usually made by the fishermen
from Indian yarn. Fish-traps are made of split date fronds about four
feet in diameter or less. Here the seas abound with dolphin, barracuda, horse mackerel, turtles, sharks and sardines. Quantities of
valuable sharks' fins are sent as far east as China; however, the pre-
ponderance of the catch (utilizing twenty-five-foot throw nets) is
always tiny sardine (*sardinella longiceps*). You can imagine our surprise at finding that the word 'sardine' was used in Arabic in Southern
Arabia today; *sardin* was also used in Dhofar in earlier Islamic
times. To pass by an area where billions of these little fish are drying
in the sun for camel fodder, oil and fertilizer is an unforgettable
experience, for they are allowed to rot into a dark flaky material with
the inefficient and wasteful runoff of blood, oil and miscellaneous
juices collected in an adjacent trench to be used as fertilizer.

Where sandy areas predominate along the Batinah and central
Dhofar coasts, these small sardines are the major netted catch. From
Muscat to Sur in the rocky districts sharks and tunnies are the most
abundant. The 'rock fisherman' uses the *huri*, 'dugout canoe', which
is made from a single tree and imported from the Malabar Coast of
India. The ingenious *shasha*, used by the 'sand fisherman', is made
of sewn, bound palm fronds, usually about ten feet long with a
pointed upcurved bow and stern and flat bottom. This is a singular
illustration of the successful adaptation of materials at hand to the
necessities of life. It takes two men two days to make a *shasha*. It
floats half immersed by reason of its substance (not by reason of the
water displaced) and *shashas* are paddled and sailed for journeys of
fifty miles or more along the Batinah coast by the thousands. In
most instances a man will own three so that when utilized in succession two are always drying in the sun before being put in the water
again, for the fragile *shasha* becomes progressively heavier each
hour it remains in the water, as do the *tankwa* of Lake Tana in
Ethiopia.

Here the abundant harvest of the sea is the coastal Omani's
livelihood, and the life of the poor illiterate fisherman who lives in
his own community is rated far above that of the Batinah date
grower. Whereas Doughty scornfully dismisses the Arab fishermen

as being mere ignoble 'fish eaters' and therefore beyond the pale of noble tribal scions, few would deny that 'it is no mean feat to hook and play and stow away in the bottom of a ten-foot dugout canoe, alone and far out at sea, an eight-foot long sailfish.'[2] Oman fisheries export 40,000 tons a year out of a total annual catch estimated at 100,000 tons. This works out to a probable figure of four tons per man of an estimated 25,000 fishermen, a truly prodigious amount. The Indian Ocean dhow traffic which exports this fish is of great size and immense importance to the economy of Oman.

That evening white-bearded Sheikh Saqr sent us a parting gift of oranges, for he was leaving the next morning to report to the Sultan. Remembering always that the personal factor is the prime one in dealing with Arabs, I replied with an appropriate monetary consideration for the fifty-six-year-old Sheikh whose home was in Sib, one of the few Batinah centres of population not exclusively a date garden, for there limes, mangoes, sweet potatoes, eggplants and guavas flourish.

Two days later I received the following message from the Sultan, sent through his army wireless, 'Greetings thank you for your message I am very glad to hear of your progress and hope your expedition will be most successful inshallah best wishes Said.'

The next evening I sent Jama to inform the Wali that I would like to call on him to discuss our taking pictures of his morning court and of the children's school. As the Wali had a houseful of guests he came to see me. He was most agreeable to both my suggestions. When I tried to close the meeting on a happy note over refreshments (*rahim allah man zar wa-khaffaf,* 'God bless him who cuts short his visit'), the Wali said that there was something important still to discuss. I tried to avoid this for I had a fair idea of what was coming, keeping in mind the Omani proverb: 'If the speaker is mad, the hearer should be wise.' I listened carefully. It seemed that various of the local sheikhs had been complaining at great length about my continually employing the same men on our excavations. The sheikhs wanted all new teams each week so that our money would reach more needy hands, including possibly their own. They believed with Bacon that 'money was like muck, useless unless spread'. I could sympathize with the Wali's problem but had anticipated this previously with the Sultan, who had assured me of my absolute control over the hiring and firing of our workers. While both Bill and Sandy gave graphic on-the-spot demonstrations of archaeological technique, I pointed out the importance of continuing the use of our trained labour. For with such knowledge as they had already acquired they were by far the best, most eager and enthusiastic workers we had ever encountered, most nomadic Arabs having an ingrained loathing for manual labour.

In the spirit of Cromwell – 'a soldier fights better when he knows what he is fighting for' – I always attempt to explain in detail the why and wherefore of things to the amenable Arab, although Arabs in general regard as a sign of weakness the willingness to come to terms quickly. They have a strong aversion to that which might offend and always avoid a blunt refusal to any demand if at all possible. On this occasion the Wali pointed out how easily new men could be trained each week, and Sandy countered with the well-known fact that many archaeological expeditions bring in the majority of their labour force. Jama added the example of the excellent Egyptian Guftis we had imported into Beihan and Marib on previous expeditions.

The Wali replied that he would write a full report of all this to the Sultan and was more than slightly taken aback when I eagerly endorsed his suggestion. After a moment's pause he relaxed and said I certainly knew best and the two of us should not bother the Sultan over these small matters, to which I agreed in full with much hand-shaking.

The following morning began with a warmer sun than had been experienced up to that point. Bill had disappeared earlier in a successful effort to shoot dove and quail for our dinner on the alluvial drainage plain behind Sohar. A thin jungle of shrubs and peculiar-looking trees covers areas of this plain; the lower portions of all the trees are trimmed to an approximate height of ten feet from the ground by many industrious trimmers represented by thousands of neck-stretching camels grooming the trees in their search for the choicest leaves. Bill returned before noon in time to photograph the

Wali holding his morning court inside the old fort. Next to him sat a long-bearded *qadhi*,[3] judge (of Islamic law), apparently listening to several cases simultaneously.

Few Muslims in the past have dared question the Quran's standing as the Word of God wherein the basic regulations for life are clearly stated for all to read. Not so with the present generation of Islam's intellectuals, who are demanding a fresh orientation and redemption from the immobility of their faith, for in spite of temporary setbacks and all appearances to the contrary notwithstanding, the traditional world of Islam is spiritually, though reluctantly, moving in the direction of a freer society such as is known in the West, as an amenity of religious liberalism. In the United Arab Republic Islam has even been 'disestablished'.

In the domain of social and personal relations, however, Islam still reigns supreme, with one of the Muslim definitions (Abu Hanifa) for the science of law being 'the knowledge of the rights and duties whereby man is enabled to observe right conduct in this life, and to prepare himself for the world to come'. Under Islam, 'religion is the law and the law is religion', for the two streams flow in a single indistinguishable mass; the real basis of jurisprudence is the Quran and Tradition, with the legal system of Arabia, the *shariah*, considered to be the revealed or canonical law of Islam.[4] The jurisdiction of this *shariah*, or divine law, reaches from the humblest secular details of the faithful's existence to the highest of spiritual issues, for Islam is an all-embracing religion, covering every branch and aspect of human relations. Actually there are not many mandatory verses as such in the Quran. Of about 6,000 verses approximately not more than two hundred deal with legal matters. In accordance with the requirements of Arabian society of that time Mohammed established or confirmed a body of customary law aimed at bringing offenders to justice and protecting the weak and safeguarding their just rights. The present difficulty about *shariah* law which is considered to be based on Mohammed's practice in Madinah, is that it does not always appear to be flexible enough to meet the needs of the present century, yet it is considered, at any rate in some degree, to have divine sanction behind it. Yet, given the circumstances and the age in which *shariah* law evolved, it would seem to have been a system in many respects very well suited to the society whose conduct it was aimed at regulating.[5]

In the Book of Genesis it is written, 'Whoso sheddeth a man's blood, by man shall his blood be shed'; while in Leviticus, 'And if a man cause a blemish in his neighbour, as he hath done, so shall it be done to him; breach for breach, eye for eye, tooth for tooth; as he hath caused a blemish in a man, so shall it be done to him again.' The absolute Biblical law of death for death and blood for blood was to be sternly applied to the guilty on the principle of strict retaliation for the crime committed. In contrast the Quran prescribes the penalty for murder in this fashion: 'Oh, Believers! the law of death for death is ordered for murder, a free man for a free man, a slave for a slave, a woman for a woman'. In *shariah* practice it is an eye for an eye and a nose for a nose, with a fixed scale of *diyah*, though in actual Omani usage *diyah*, 'blood money', payment, pardon or imprisonment varies greatly according to the *qadhi*, locality and status of the individuals involved, for the Islamic code and tribal customary law permit much greater use of monetary compensation to the victim or the aggrieved, as opposed to retribution from the aggressor or the guilty, than does Roman law and the impersonal and objective legal codes based on it.

Under the Ibadhi concept of justice it was the duty of every Muslim to exhort others to do good and refrain from doing evil; the Ibadhis equalized all Muslims (i.e. true believers) regardless of colour or racial origin. To them all upright Muslims belonged to the community, whether rich or poor, Arab or slave. The highest place belonged to the most pious. They maintained that the law applied to every Muslim even if he were not aware of it.

The sources of law were limited and carefully chosen. To deviate from the true source would constitute *kufr* and result in eternal damnation. The Ibadhis confined themselves consciously to the Quran, the Sunna of Mohammed, and to the precepts extracted from these two sources by their pious Imams. Consensus (*ijma'*) and analogy (*qiyas*) for the most part were rejected by Ibadhi jurists. *Ijma'* was understood to be the unanimous confirmation by the Companions of Mohammed of certain rules and procedures and as such was recognized to a limited extent as supplemental to the Quran and the Sunna. The first two caliphs, Abu Bakr and Omar, were highly respected by the Ibadhis and their legal precedents were often followed.

Legal obligations were associated with religious ideals. The Ibadhis resorted to a greater degree of ethical consideration than did the Sunni in their interpretation of law. Transgressors of the law were condemned for unbelief. Abdullah bin Ibadh stated: 'He who fornicates is an unbeliever; he who steals is an unbeliever; and he who drinks wine is an unbeliever.'

The old Islamic legal institutions, which enjoy a range of adaptable flexibility, are today found in Arabia and to a lesser extent in Afghanistan, Nigeria, etc., much of the rest of the Muslim world having succumbed to western models of secular civil, penal and commercial law derived from Roman law as compiled under Justinian, based on commonsense justice strengthened by precedent. As the Sultan said to me on a subsequent occasion, 'What is good in one's eyes, is not necessarily good in another's, but certain things are bad in all eyes.' The Wali in Sohar explained that divorces, marriages, inheritance and local disputes were handled by the Qadhi and himself, and unless the Sultan or the Minister of the Interior forwards a particular Sohar case to a court of appeal the decision of the Sohar judge stands. Murder cases are always referred directly to the Sultan for judgment.

In 1933 while in Sohar the present Sultan was sitting at the usual morning court with his tribal leaders, when suddenly, without warning, two men presented themselves carrying a small sack from which they promptly produced a man's head; they had been sent as messengers from their sheikh, who had cut off the head of a highwayman from the Sohar interior in order to show their Sultan that they had successfully captured him.

On 16 September 1960 an Omani was executed under Fort Mirani at Muscat. He had murdered a man accursed as a witch in the bazaar at Samail. The condemned man stood in front of a cave from which he was shot by his victim's relatives. First the Sultan passes judgment, then if the murdered man has no relatives, the State becomes the guardian and dispatches the murderer.

Wali Ismail bin Khalil of Matrah is the head wali of al-Batinah, although he does not overrule the local *qadhis* in matters of law.

Wali Ismail joined the Sultan's service in 1928 as a schoolmaster from Palestine. He was appointed Wali of Matrah in 1939 and serves as the channel between the other Batinah walis and Saiyid Ahmed bin Ibrahim, Minister for Internal Affairs, who is responsible to the Sultan for all of the internal affairs of Oman with its thirty-three governors (seventeen coastal, sixteen interior). The Wali of Dhofar operates directly under the Sultan. Recently, upon the retirement of Colonel Hugh Boustead, the Sultan appointed William T. Clark – twenty-six years in the Sudan Political Service – as 'Development Secretary' (responsible for health, communications, agriculture, education, buildings and administration), and Martin Wynn as 'Administrator' in the Municipality of Muscat and Matrah.[6]

The Municipal Committee is a body of eight members, including a Chairman appointed by the Sultan, and is representative of the various communities in Muscat and Matrah. The Administrator works as Secretary to the Committee. The Municipality is mainly financed by a small surcharge of customs duty, shop rents, motor vehicle registration and driving licence fees. An annual budget is prepared and the money spent on sanitation, anti-malarial measures, fire-fighting, street lighting and public works, which include the construction of the cement-surfaced Muscat–Matrah road. Meetings of the Committee are held not less than once a month under the Kingdom of Oman Municipal Law.

On ceremonial occasions during the Sultan's absence he is represented by his uncle, Saiyid Shihab bin Faisal, who is six years older than His Majesty. However, present or absent from his country, the Sultan always keeps three matters in his own hands – finances, the army and foreign affairs. In an actual sense the government of Oman can be considered an extension of the person of the Sultan.

Under the guidance of the chief *askari* of the Wali of Sohar, we next visited the little schoolhouse outside the fort. An *ajuz*, 'old woman', wearing a horrible *burqa*, 'mask' (consisting of a black vertical strut covering the nose plus a pair of horizontal face bars leaving two bulls' eyes for light), objected strenuously to our taking pictures until Bill began to feature her. Then all went smoothly. Of the thirty-six pupils half were little boys grouped together and the rest attractive little girls. Each attentive pupil sat on the floor with a huge Quran held up in front by a forked holder so that it never rested below the waistline of the reader, for this would dishonour the Holy Book. Everyone was screaming from the Quran at the top of his or her respective lungs – believing that the one who could drown out the others took first scholastic honours.

Although knowledge (the ultimate aim of knowledge is the knowledge of God), said the Prophet, 'Lighteth the way to Heaven; is our friend in the desert, our society in solitude, our companion when friendless; it guideth us to happiness; it sustaineth us in misery; it is an ornament amongst friends, and an armour against enemies' – in the eyes of many, with the exception of the Quran, Arabia is the great bookless world. Actually it is not, and throughout his country the Sultan is attempting to show his people that more knowledge and modern technology can improve their lives and enrich their living.

Two independent systems of education, spanning the elementary grades, operate in Muscat and Matrah. The largest is represented by the government school, *al-madrasah as-saidiyah* (named after the ruling dynasty) which enjoys a relatively large new building just outside the south wall of Muscat. Instruction is in Arabic through all six grades, with several years of English offered in the final grades. Its primary aim is the preparation of young men for government service. This school (and the one at Matrah), which has teachers coming mostly from Lebanon and Palestine, and the somewhat similar but smaller school at Salalah, are the only Arab schools in the country which depart from a purely Quranic education. The Indian community supports its own elementary schools, which insure some education for all its boys and girls. English is strongly emphasized as the language of culture and commerce in the Indian community, but the elementary instruction is in the appropriate Indian language. Indian youths are sent to India for secondary education. No provision is made in Muscat for the young Baluchi, who may or may not have a usable knowledge of spoken Arabic (his own language, widely spoken in Muscat, is not written). The mission school was the first school giving secular education in modern times in Oman. In 1897 the Reverend Peter Zwemer founded a boarding school for eighteen freed slave boys with the brand of the slaver's iron forever imprinted on their cheeks. The present school had an enrolment of about sixty children in five grades under the direction of the Reverend and Mrs Jay Kepenga. This is the only elementary school for girls in Oman. Several members of the Albu Said family as well as government employees and merchants received a basic education in the mission school.

The increased emphasis on liberal education and the emergence into self-responsibility in several of the Arab states is the most encouraging sign on the Near Eastern scene. Modern Muslims, as represented by the middle classes, the artisans and students, are beginning to awaken from the mere repetitious performance of duties and blind imitation in matters of belief; 'the first condition for knowledge is doubt'. Today these Arabic-speaking peoples are receiving much more than an elementary education in the Quran, especially in the way of science, literature and the social sciences. Thousands of politically conscious, highly vocal students graduate yearly from secondary schools with a knowledge of the wide world and with the desire to live more productive lives. The small number of national colleges and universities are attempting to raise their standards and quality and may eventually be on a par with American and European institutions of higher education. But no educational institution can rise above the level of its teachers. We in the West owe our advance ahead of the East to our teachers. But we were not always in advance – on the contrary; and if free enquiry and general education become established in the Arab world, there would be nothing to prevent the Arabs from drawing level with us. After all, while Christian Europe was still under the Church's ban on learning and free enquiry, the ninth-century schools of Baghdad were marching proudly from effects to causes. We have learnt to use inductive reasoning, but the Arabs were our masters, as the Greeks had been theirs. And the Arabs were listening to their greatest teachers while we were still busy burning ours at the stake or forcing them to recant.

Why did the Arab world lose its intellectual lead? The earlier and tireless search for truth and knowledge in the Islamic world was

H.M. Sultan Said bin Taimur —
King of Oman

Wendell Phillips,
author of *Unknown Oman*

Professor Alexand[er]
Honeyman *on the left* a[nd]
Dr Ray Cleveland *on [the]
right* directing excavatio[n]

Below: The ruins of Has[ik]
which lies on the we[st]
side of Kuria Muria Ba[y]
to the east of Salalah

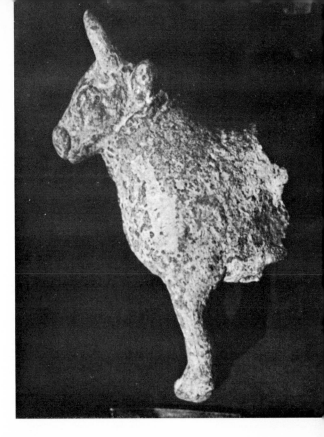

A bronze bull representing the moon god Sin; this was excavated at the Lost City of Sumhuram in Dhofar Dependency

An extremely important inscription discovered at Hanun in Dhofar which has since been lost

Expedition Field Director and photographer, William B. Terry,
with ancient Omani Fortress of Rostaq in background

Wendell Phillips and young Sheikh Hilal bin Sultan from the village of Khabura on the Batina, to the South of Sohar

Below: This ancient ruined fortress is located approximately two miles from Shabwa

The notorious camel raider Sheikh Janazel bin Said, of the Bait Musan section of the Bait Kathir tribe, who was our guide across the deep sands to the Sultan's waterhole

Below: The local Dhofari members of the writer's expedition in search of the lost city of Ubar. On the right is the Bait Imani chief guide

Below: Pre-Islamic tombs, unique cairns numbering many hundreds; nothing like them is known elsewhere in Arabia

Head *askari* in Dhofar

Sheikh Hamud bin Hamid, the Wali of Dhofar, and Wendell
Phillips erected an official monument at the well of Khasfa,
and there the Wali raised the Sultan's flag

Sheikh Abdulla bin Salim
serves the expedition lunch
at his headquarters in
Mahdha

The ingenious *shasha*, 'floatboat' used by the fishermen of Oman, is made of sewn and bound palm frond ribs and is usually about ten feet long with a pointed upcurved bow and stern and flat bottom

The scraggy picturesque frankincense shrub, *Boswellia carterii*, grows wild in Dhofar

Dr and Mrs W. Wells Thoms with the writer's sister Merilyn and a group of lepers
from the Mission Hospital at Matrah

Omani baby adorned with charms designed to keep
off the 'evil eye'; they serve as amusing playthings
as well

Qara aborigine. They
among the most primi-
people of the entire
East.

w) Accompanied by
ting and the beating
drums, the Negro
men of Salala in
far dance on any and
ll possible occasions

Dr Louis Krause examines an Omani woman at Sohar who is suffering
from an enlarged spleen caused by malaria

An Omani mother presents her ailing daughter for examination at the expedition field clinic in Sohar

An extremely rare photograph, showing an Omani bride
in Muscat awaiting the arrival of her husband, whom she
has never seen

checked and finally halted by the 'Scholasticism' of Sunni dogmatism; in the darkness of that creed the spirit of enquiry came to be considered a manifestation of the devil; innovation became synonymous with heresy. It is written in the Quran, 'God sees all things'; thus he must have eyes and the faithful must accept their wretched lot in this world in the belief that it is His intention. Since what is, is necessarily according to the will of Allah, then it cannot be altered, and enquiry and innovation are not only blasphemous; they are pointless. And in so far as this is still accepted, the twentieth-century follower of the Prophet must abandon his judgment to ninth-century orthodox Sunni dogmatists.

It is claimed that Muslim fatalism or divine and absolute predestination, which is a religious dogma, fosters the personal endurance of mental and physical travails and prevents useless regrets, despair and remorse in time of adversity; however to many it is best understood as complete stagnation; benumbed, helpless, defeatist resignation to one's miserable physical state, to ignorance, poverty, and disease. The exercise of reason and industry are renounced, for all is predetermined by divine will 'so that nothing can happen in the world, whether it respects the conditions and operations of things good or evil, or obedience or disobedience, or sickness or health, or riches or poverty, or life or death, which is not contained in the written tablet of the decrees of God.'

The Ibadhis of Oman are charged with holding to the doctrine of predestination in such a sense that God is made the author of things evil as well as things good. There is nothing new in this: 'I form the light and create darkness; I make peace and create evil; I am Jehovah that doeth all these things' (Isaiah 45:7). The Ibadhi belief recalls the sombre doctrine of Calvin: 'We call predestination the eternal decision of God, whereby he has determined what he wishes to do with every man, for he does not create them all in a like condition, but fore-ordains some to eternal life and others to eternal damnation.' The Ibadhi fatalism teaches, 'Why fight the inevitable?' and *al-muqaddar la yatahawwal*, 'Destiny cannot be reversed.' 'A calamity is a mercy in disguise' and 'misfortunes serve as good tidings and as forerunners of heavenly blessings.'

To many progressive Muslims, however, fatalism signifies little more than a realization of God's sovereignty and of man's dependence, and the sum of total attainable wisdom is more extensive than the mere blind repetition of old formulas. 'Trust in God but tether your camel!' They like to replace the words fatalism and predestination by premeasurement; everything created by God is for good in the given use and under the given circumstances and only its abuse is evil. The great problem of predestination is partially comprised in that God knows what man is going to do, but that man is free to do it or not to do it. Man is free to make his own decisions since no compulsion is laid upon him; but even the Christian holds that he cannot reach God by any but the one way.

Is fatalism intrinsic in Islam? Has Islamic belief in determinism produced social stagnation, or have Muslims sought refuge in God's will in the face of political disintegration and economic collapses? The fact is that together, in spite of at times having social and economic stagnation, Muslims never murmur against their creator and constantly voice the greatness of God and the unchangeable course of His plans; but whether one caused the other and if so which caused which is quite something else again. More often than not religious viewpoints merely reflect circumstances. Thus, before we pass too harsh a judgment on Islam, let us recall that the early centuries of Islam did not produce men of lethargy and stagnation who relied on God while they sat immobile in their tents, but vigorous, incorruptible men who depended on armies and generals to gain and hold the lands they wished to possess and rule – men who believed that they had to carry out God's will if it were to be done on earth, men often with an enlightened sense of civic responsibility.

Perhaps it was the sophisticated mystic philosophies of the conquered Persians which started the change toward speculative theology; the collapse of the central government, the scourge of the Mongols, the coming of the Tartars and the Turks, along with the arrival of the Crusaders, who drove helpless men into a state of mind which demanded acceptance of God's will. Going a step further, could it be that a formal statement of 'acceptance' has less to do with the present economic stagnation than formerly believed? Could it not be that poverty in natural resources, backwardness in industrialization and the stultifying hand of absentee ownership has more to do with the standard of living than the mental attitude of the people? In 1817 Sheikh Mansur observed of the Arabs of Arabia, 'If, therefore, the inhabitants of this vast peninsula are considered, and in some respects deserve to be considered, a degraded and slothful race of beings, we must attribute the justice of the charge entirely to the nature of their government and the laws under which they live.'[7] Perhaps the whole interpretation is based on the notion that every people is to blame for its own condition – since 'God is a just God' – meaning respectfully that everybody who works hard enough will have plenty. It must be recognized, however, that there are causes in history which are simply not controlled by the humans who suffer their effects. However, this does not imply that endurance of the effect is in any way commendable.

As the season which Professor Honeyman had allotted for our dig drew towards its end, it was necessary to put in as much work as possible if we were to get through all we had set ourselves to do. In mid-January I decided that we should, if possible, work on Fridays, the Moslem sabbath. This was arranged by raising the day's wage by one rupee, paid to the six of our best workers whom we wished to retain. Our immediate objective at this time was an ancient Jewish cemetery located a mile and a half from Sohar, where approximately two hundred graves covered about two acres. Wellsted, in his *Travels in Arabia*, Vol. 1, p. 231, had recorded the presence of about twenty families of Jews in Sohar in the first decades of the nineteenth century, and also a small synagogue. Some of them had, it seems, taken refuge there from the cruelties of the Governor of Baghdad, Daud Pasha. During the period when Dr A. S. Jayakar was Surgeon at Muscat (1870–1900) there were still a few Bani-Israil living at Sohar, but they had long forgotten the origin of their tribe and could not give the date of their immigration into Oman. In 1958 nothing remained of them but their cemetery.

On reaching the old cemetery, at a place called 'Gumbida' by our workmen from Sohar, we selected a reasonably intact tomb. Next to it was the very eroded outline of an older grave which was to be our second effort. The visible parts of the tombs, about six and a half feet long and four feet wide, were all of brick bonded together with mortar. Three feet down we hit the top of the actual casing composed of mud brick covering one half of the tomb. Soon several holes began to appear and by using a flashlight I could see a complete skeleton on the inside. A curious burial practice was observed, in that the body was placed at a diagonal, not directly under the surface monument as one would expect. Examination of the jaw suggested that the skeleton was that of an adult male. The teeth were full of cavities and the bones exceedingly fragile. Close by, Professor Honeyman was measuring the cemetery's one standing brick structure of curious rectangular shape. On the outside were inscribed numerous Jewish names, such as Moses, Joseph, and Jacob, in Hebrew characters.

Work now started on the eroded tomb next to our first effort. For some reason this grave did not have the partial mud brick roof found over the first tomb. Three feet down he came onto a wide platform of hardened soil. Inset off to one side and lower down lay the burial chamber, again not under the surface monument. Since the pelvic outlet was triangular, it was assumed we had another male skeleton – this one with the face turned to the East. Bill rigged up a white sheet to reflect light down into the tomb, enabling him to take a film of the full-length skeleton thus exposed.

While everyone set to work to fill up the graves almost as good as new, one of our best negro workmen was reciting out loud, 'What is the world coming to, here am I a good Muslim working eight hours on our day of assembly digging up the bones of a long dead Jew.' He explained that his father had been stolen from Zanzibar at the age of fifteen and subsequently married a free woman, so his son, our philosophizing digger, was free. Later this same worker seriously proposed that he would be delighted to be my slave for life if I would give him 300 M.T. dollars and take him to the States with me.

The Prophet Mohammed as the pre-eminent exemplar had a distinction, very remarkable in that age, of not owning a single slave. He actually adopted a slave, Zaid ibn Harithah, as his son and married him to his first cousin. Zaid's son, Usama, became Commander-in-Chief of Abu Bakr's army which comprised many of the noblest leaders of the Quraish.

Although the Prophet, seemingly without question, regarded slavery as part of the natural order of the universe, he constantly recognized in forcible words the self-asserting humanity of the slave, ameliorated his condition, and enjoined mercy. The Prophet also recognized that strong men have always preyed on weaker men. Thus Islam gave divine sanction to the institution (slavery was also sanctioned by Judaism and Christianity) which is recognized although not established in the Quran and is still found in parts of Arabia; for Arabs are among the most conservative of all peoples. They remain patriarchal, and the ancient custom of slavery is congenial to this system, which favours the complete dependence of all members of the household on one family head who is vested with practically unlimited powers. The slave participated in his master's dignity and the master shared in his slaves' humble services. In the time of Mohammed the freeing of a slave was considered an essential act of penance for those who had unintentionally killed a believer, and obviously one cannot free a slave unless one first owns one; it was thus within the reach of each Muslim slave owner to ameliorate his slaves' misfortune. This was not always the case however in nineteenth-century America, where 'With respect to emancipation, it may be stated as a principle, without an exception that, as slaves are considered property upon which creditors have a right to look for payment of their debts due by the owner of slaves, regard must be had to the rights of the creditor; and no act of emancipation is valid when these are violated.'[8]

Although the Prophet is reported to have said, 'The worst of men is the seller of men', in the early days ruthlessly inhuman slave merchants ransacked the whole known world for choice young females; many of these captured, male or female, who rejected Islam or failed to pay the prescribed tribute were liable to enslavement. Tribute was never accepted from idol worshippers, only from the 'people of the book'. Thus originally all the slaves of Islam were non-Muslims. Today in Oman this condition is a thing of the past, for there is little traffic in slavery; in the main only born slaves exist. There is still a minor slave trade with children, particularly girls, and a few adults, stolen mainly during summertime. They are seized or purchased from the Makran Coast of Persia and Pakistan, landed along the Batinah Coast and taken through or around Buraimi for eventual sale in Saudi Arabia, where in time parentage, country and creed are all but obliterated from childhood's misty records. Since the slave follows the religion of his master, all Omani slaves are therefore Muslim.

In most instances slavery under Islam, which was fettered by religious laws, 'never became the frightful engine of cruelty and wickedness that subsequently disgraced certain more civilized and Christian countries.' Present-day slavery in Oman does not entail the shameful and sickening horrors of the old British West Indian or American plantation variety, or the unspeakable cruelty practised often with full approval of the various Christian sects, of old Southern States slavery, the literature of which is vast. A graphic representation of this period portrayed the American Flag of Liberty with a slave chained to the flagpole, and a man standing over him with a lash. Any reader of this book who is inclined to consider Omani, and in general Arab, slavery as entitling him to look down on the Arabs, is referred to that literature; but he will need a strong stomach. Many Omani slaves would never think of leaving their masters, for they are considered part of the family. Here under Islam a master and his slave in the spirit of brotherhood may eat from the same plate[9] and wear the same clothes, a slave can own slaves, as in the late Assyrian period of Sennacherib, with the master owning all. If a slave works during the day his night must be free. An Omani saying goes, 'The slave is the slave of his master, but otherwise as free as you.' In the words of the Prophet, 'A man who behaves ill to his slave will not enter into Paradise.' Mohammed, upon whom unfair deprecatory criticism has been heaped, was far above the hypocrisy of Christendom in its fancied devotion to the principles of the Sermon on the Mount. Can a slave in Oman divorce his own slave wife? The answer is no, this exclusive prerogative rests with the master. 'Slaves may marry with the consent of their masters.' According to most jurisconsults, slaves may have only two wives (slaves or free women), but according to the Malikites they may have four like free Muslims.'[10]

If any Omani slaves however choose to leave their owners they are never made to return against their will by the Sultan. Thirty years ago the notorious Baluchi slaver Birkat,[11] from the Iranian Makran Coast, kidnapped several of his own people and shipped them to the Batinah Coast for eventual sale via Buraimi to Saudi Arabia. One slave escaped and reported to the Sultan, who immediately freed all of the others. If Birkat had been captured at the time, he would have long been a resident of the Sultan's prison. On this occasion the Sultan fulfilled the extraordinary Old Testament slave ordinance: 'You shall not give up to his master a slave who has escaped from his master to you' (Deut. 23: 15).

As late as 1951-2 a number of tragic slave-trains passed from the Oman coast through Buraimi each year *en route* north of Liwa Oasis and south of Qatar. Approximately 25 per cent of these trains were intercepted and captured by patrols of the crack Trucial Oman Scouts. On one occasion a heartless Adeni was in charge and another time the slave-train was commanded by a vicious Saudi who had among his dozen slaves six beautiful African virgins of ages ranging from fourteen to sixteen.

One of the British representatives in the Buraimi Oasis at the time of the frontier dispute, 'began to watch the departure of Saudi aeroplanes. . . . Except for a Pakistani pilot, all the air crews were American. Shortly before the take-off, a lorry would drive on to the airfield and about forty children would be driven out of the lorry and literally pushed into the plane. . . . "When I took this job", the American pilot replied, "I was told to keep my mouth shut and my eyes shut as to some of the things that go on around here. And that's the way it's going to be. Another seven years of flying for King Saud and I'll have made enough money to retire for life." This information about slavery was reported to the Foreign Office, but no mention of it was made during the Buraimi frontier dispute in October 1955 – or indeed since. In fact, no positive action is taken about slavery in Saudi Arabia for political and economic reasons, arising from American influence in that country.'[12]

Why do the Foreign Office want to believe that Slavery does not exist? [said Viscount Maugham in a speech before the House of Lords on 14 July 1960]. Your Lordships have heard from the noble Lord, Lord Shackelton, that Saudi Arabia is the greatest slave-buying area in the world; and there are over half a million slaves there today. The main oil

Unknown Oman

company operating in Saudi Arabia is the Arabian–American Oil Company – 'Aramco' – and if it were known that children are enslaved in Saudi Arabia this might be taken as a criticism of Aramco's general moral influence over the country. Moreover, Aramco wields considerable influence in Washington; and the Foreign Office does not want to embarrass the Government of Britain's largest ally.[13]

Perhaps the worst aspect of slavery is its treatment of children. In June 1960 the slavery investigator Lord Maugham told the British House of Lords how Arab slave boys between twelve and fourteen were regularly castrated (one can question the truth of this allegation); and how a group of children were seen in Buraimi Oasis, heavily shackled by their ankles. More recently an East African publisher, Sean O'Callaghan, has described his visit to a 'slave baby farm' in French Somaliland, where he found in one dormitory a number of little girls, kneeling in a circle, their bare buttocks red with weals of a cane. In the next dormitory he found another pathetic little circle, this time of boys – and was horrified to find that they had been castrated. O'Callaghan and other observers have also reported on terrified boy slaves being pawed and fondled by quite obviously homosexual buyers at the slave auctions.

Whereas the Quran declared in Sura 100, in terms that permit of no ambiguity, that the liberation of slaves is most pleasing to Allah, the Apostle Paul condoned slavery to the extent of admonishing them, 'slaves be obedient to your master as slaves of Christ, doing their work as unto him and not unto men.' About A.D. 62 this same Apostle sent back his dear friend, Onesimus, the fugitive slave, to his master, Philemon, a leading Christian of Colossae in Asia Minor, with the words, 'no longer as a slave but more than a slave, as a beloved brother.'

The Caliph Othman is said to have purchased and then released over 2,400 slaves during his lifetime; an improvement over the pious Mississippi planter, who professing a languid horror of slavery, said, 'I cannot bear it; it goes against my conscience to keep slaves. I mean to sell mine!'

'He who frees a Muslim slave will have for every organ of the emancipated slave an organ of himself redeemed by God from hell fire.' Under Islam when a slave is freed the master gives a paper or repeats in front of witnesses that this slave is free. There are many examples of the owner freeing a slave girl and then the girl in question marrying her former master of her own free will, thus fulfilling an Arab proverb: 'The slave girl from her capture, the wife from her wedding.' The Quran further states, 'Marry not idolatrous women until they believe, for surely a believing slave girl is better than an idolatrous free woman even though she pleases you.' When a slave marries a free woman the children are free; thus when you hear of a slave the mother must have been a slave, for all slaves must come from a slave mother. In this instance Islam, in fulfilling that terrible saying that 'a slave womb could only produce slaves' has retrogressed from the ancient Babylonian Code of Hammurabi where irrespective of whether the slave was the mother or father the resulting children of a mixed marriage were free.

In 1930 Philby visited the Daka, or public slave market, of Mecca. 'It was hidden away in a blind alley of a poor and unsavoury quarter of the city; and even the man in charge seemed to make no effort to pretend that his goods were worth having. They consisted of a single family; a rather wretched looking man with a still more miserable wife with three children of various ages, all to be disposed of collectively or separately, as their owner sought to rid himself of the burden of their upkeep. The quality of mercy is rare in the commercial circles of Arabia.'[14]

Three years later, before the Royal Central Asian Society, Philby stated this Arabian truism which to the uninitiated may seem hard to comprehend in the light of the above paragraph: 'If instead of pointing the finger at Arabia as a hotbed of slavery, the European nations would contribute the cost of a few hours' European war, every slave in the country could be offered the doubtful advantage of legal freedom if he or she wanted it. And many, very many, would refuse.'[15]

A royal [Saudi] decree of 1936 authorized slave trading by traders licensed by the Minister of the Interior. Currently told is the story of the seventy-two year old Saudi who paid $25,000 during a spirited auction for a very beautiful sixteen-year-old girl. In July 1956 *The Observer* said with regard to Saudi Arabia, 'The influx of American oil royalties has increased the demand for slaves, the market prices for which in 1956 were around $420 for a man and $1,260 for a girl.' (In ancient Babylon female slaves were cheaper than male slaves). Prices have since sky-rocketed and fantastic sums are paid for youthful and healthy slaves. The main source of slaves is still Abyssinia, though there is a steady trickle from Southern Iran and Baluchistan, where parents are sometimes eager to sell off surplus daughters.

On 6 November 1962, however, the new Prime Minister of Saudi Arabia, Prince Faisal, issued a decree from Riyadh abolishing slavery in the country.

As one of the few living Americans who has had slaves working under his direction and has been responsible for their welfare to God and the Sultan, although I am opposed to slavery in any form and under any terms, my sympathy goes out to the well-meaning individual who ever attempts to free His Majesty's personal slaves. For to be a slave of the Sultan is a mark of honour and distinction, like being a cabinet minister. All of their requirements are taken care of and they enjoy considerable prestige among the rest of the population. On occasion these slaves, who are rarely apathetic and never under-privileged, have risen to be Omani governors, somewhat paralleling the case of Bilal, the blind Abyssinian slave whose glorious stentorian voice made him the first *muadhdhin* of Islam. (It may be noted that colour prejudice is and always has been almost unknown in Moslem countries and negroes are able to rise to the highest and most honourable offices). Bilal's freedom had been purchased by Abu Bakr, who addressed him as 'our leader' and 'our Lord'. On solemn occasions he preceded the Prophet, carrying a lance in his hand. Subsequently it was Bilal who discharged the mission of suspending the famous general Khalid Ibn Walid from his office, while Usama, the son of Zaid, the Prophet's former adopted slave, led Abu Bakr's expedition against the Greeks (when the army departed Abu Bakr walked some distance in the company of Usama while the latter rode), and Kutb ud-Din, the founder of the Muslim empire in India, was a slave.

'Take away that black man! I can have no discussion with him!' exclaimed the Christian Archbishop Cyprus (who combined the functions of Byzantine prefect and Melkite or imperial patriarch), when the Arab conquerors had sent, to discuss terms of surrender of the capital of Egypt, a deputation of their ablest men headed by the Abyssinian negro Ubadah, as the ablest of them all. To the sacred archbishop's astonishment, he was told that this man had been personally commissioned by the great general 'Amr, conqueror of Egypt. 'Well, if the negro must lead, he must speak gently,' ordered the Greek prelate, 'so as not to frighten his white auditors.'

The prophet once stated, 'If a negro slave is appointed to rule over you, hear him, and obey him though his head should be like a dried grape.' Thus under Islam it is possible for the slave of today to be the Grand Vizier of tomorrow; and it has been said of slavery in Oman that 'Religion endorses it, the social order depends upon it, and the welfare of the slaves themselves demands it.' However,

> A day, an hour, of virtuous liberty
> is worth a whole eternity in bondage.

As the years go by there are fortunately fewer and fewer born slaves and happily the day will come when the humanity of men will triumph over the violation of essential human rights (no man is good enough to have complete control over any other man) and all slavery, which has had a place in every society at some stage of its development, will be dead in Oman as well as the rest of Arabia, for slavery bears the curse of inherent injustice; an outrage on human personality, it is an ugly thing at best.

> Did not He that made me in the womb make him
> (the slave) also?
> And did not One fashion us in the womb? (Job. 31: 15).

6

TRUCIAL OMAN

Workers of Sohar – The tongue of angels – Lawrence's Arabic
British protection or Saudi imperialism? – Dhows and 'Booms'
Unspoilt Dubai – Bahrain – Empires over the Gulf
Pirates and Pearls

During all my expeditions my colleagues and I have made at least
some attempt to find out something about, and to get to know, the
men who worked for us. On an archaeological dig it is easy to joke
about the laziness of the workmen; but how hard would *I* work for
under four shillings a day? And if I were undernourished, and
debilitated by disease? We did our best to avoid that state of mind
in which such words as 'workmen', 'Arab', represent a faceless
crowd.

In most Arab lands a boy will work hard; but by the time he is
twenty-five he is exhausted, by the time he is thirty he has passed
his prime, and by the time he is thirty-five he is probably dead, without ever having 'lived' in our Western sense of the word. A lad of
fifteen perhaps believes that, by working hard, he can better his
condition; he slaves away for ten years and receives in return a
pittance, hardly a bare livelihood at the lowest level; then he
realizes that he was dreaming of pie in the sky, and he settles down,
in weakness and apathy, to wait for death. The severity of his
poverty is a bondage as bad as slavery; his spirit is broken by disease
and shackled by ignorance. His lot is to look upon his wretched
world,

> Famine in his cheeks;
> Need and oppression staring in his eyes:
> Contempt and beggary hanging on his back.

Even the single individual of outstanding ambition is not able to escape the backwardness of his oppressive childhood environment decades after he has left it. The dynamism of our American and West European society is something which had taken generations to develop, starting with the example of early settlers in America, who often represented the most ambitious members of society in their homeland. Good proof of the worth of the Arab individual are those who have been fortunate enough to get an American visa and who, while condemned to poverty in their homeland, have entered American society with the same energy and success as native-born Americans. Perhaps of a similar nature to the alleged lack of ambition supposedly prevalent in Arabia is the problem of 'corruption' in the non-Western world. John Marlowe, speaking of Iran, has a plausible explanation for it which does not involve the 'character' of the people: 'The fact that in U.K. and U.S.A. people usually pay their taxes, and usually obey the law in such matters as building licences, statutory declarations and so on, is not because people in U.K. and U.S.A. are less "corrupt" or more public-spirited than they are in Iran but because the machinery of administration is, by and large, effective enough to ensure that people cannot "get away with" not paying their taxes and disobeying the law generally, however much they might dislike doing so.'[1]

The evening after Sandy had regretfully laid off his Sohar crew he received a note from one of his disappointed workmen:

To My Dear Sar: Will you please Eksept me Because I have not Brither only I and you make me Dercharch frome your job and I am a fastman in your work will you Hilph me and Thank You.

Saud bin Amer.

After a masterpiece like this it was agreed that Saud could join the other work party the next day. In our cumulative experiences, these workmen hired at Sohar were certainly the best to be found anywhere in the Near East. In other areas of Arabia, Sudan, Egypt and Jordan the men tended on occasion to be quarrelsome and only in part interested in doing a good day's work. Here at Sohar all of our labourers were anxious to do the work, never engaged in arguments and did not try to withhold their strength for a future day.

Partly to satisfy our own curiosity and partly because of whatever value it might have, we talked to some of the workmen to find out just what sort they were. There were no bachelors among the typical eight we interviewed as to their private lives.

Jumah bin Abdullah, aged thirty-one, sole possession – hut of palm leaves; married Sarfah, who after one year, died in childbirth at the age of fourteen; married Fatimah, who has given him two sons, seven years ago when she was fourteen.

Mohammed bin Saif, aged twenty owns a house of palm leaves and 150 palms; two months previously he married Ammah, aged fourteen.

Jumah bin Farhan, born a slave thirty years ago, was purchased when he was nine years old, after fourteen years he ran away and was liberated in Muscat. Married Mozah six years previously, when she was eleven, who produced one daughter; has one slave wife, Huwaidmah, of uncertain age, who produced one son, one daughter.

Ahmed bin Salih, aged twenty-five, owns house of palm leaves, small palm grove, one small cow and one small ass; married Halimah four years previously when she was fourteen; she has produced one son and another child is expected at any moment.

Abdullah bin Hashim, aged between thirty-five and forty-three, owns palm leaf house. Married Ammah, age unknown; they have one three-year-old daughter.

Salman bin Bilal, aged thirty-five, owns palm leaf house; married Zaharah, aged twenty, no children; later married Maryam aged twenty, who produced four sons. Both wives live in the same house.

Nasir bin Mohammed, aged forty, owns house of palm leaves; married Salimah ten years before when she was seven,[2] no children. Previously married Fatimah who died after fifteen years of marriage at the age of thirty; she produced seven sons, all of whom died.

Ghumdan bin Mohammed, aged thirty, owns two palms, one goat, one sheep, married Sarifah, eight years previously when she was twelve; they have one son aged three.

Sohar, as with many maritime towns, has been subjected to much alien linguistic influence. Thus, in admonishing the men to do good work, the foreman would shout out the Indian word *shabash*, meaning approximately 'well done' or 'bravo'; and out of a group of twenty of our workmen, only one claimed to be pure Arab and could

name his tribal origin. Most were Baluchi or part Baluchi, with two
or three Persians and several Africans. The common language was
Arabic, although the Baluchis spoke their own language among
themselves, but even this was Arabic with many Persian and Baluchi
words. On being questioned, some of the men were unable to identify
certain words as Arabic or Baluchi, the fusion of the two languages
had advanced so far.

Arabic belongs, of course, to the Semitic group to which ancient
languages like Accadian, Hebrew and Syriac, as well as the Ethiopic
languages, belong, and is as different from European tongues as
East is from West. It has been characterized as 'a pure and original
speech of the greatest flexibility, with an enormous vocabulary with
great grammatical possibility, fitted to convey theological, philo-
sophical and scientific thought in the highest manner.' Arabic has
'remarkable delicacy, its bold and energetic sublimity, adapted
equally to the simple pathos of love and elegy, the piquancy of satire,
or the loftiest efforts of popular oratory.' With the exception of
English, which has borrowed hundreds of Arabic words, Arabic
itself has had more to do with the destiny of mankind and has extended farther over the face of the earth than any other language,
and with the exception of the Bible no book in history has so in-
fluenced the course of civilization or affected the lives of more
hundreds of millions than has the Quran.

The Arab scholar Mohammed ad-Damiri quotes the saying,
'Wisdom hath alighted upon three things – the brain of the Franks,
the hands of the Chinese and the tongue of the Arabs.' To the passionate Arab, flowery expressive language has a special significance
unequalled by any other attribute, for if language is the house of the
soul then Arabic is at once a house and a temple with the most
magnificent thoughts clothed in words of power. The Arab em-
bellishes his powerful prose with arresting and beautiful proverbs
and parables, for eloquence and volubility are the hallmark of the
Arab and exercise an irresistible influence; they are considered *sihr
halal*, 'lawful magic'. In 1903 Lieutenant-Colonel A. S. G. Jayakar
wrote in the introduction to his invaluable and rare list of *Omani*

Proverbs: 'Even a casual observer cannot help noticing the extensive use the Omanees make of proverbial sayings in their conversation and admiring the facility with which they adapt them to the circumstances calling for their use. . . . Upon the whole, however, the moral principles inculcated in the proverbs and aphorisms of the Omanees are sound, and may be considered the heritage of mankind in general from remote ages.' As observed by Wellsted, 'The Arabs never perform the most trifling undertaking or engagement without an enormous expenditure of words.'

To the Arabs, Arabic is the language or chosen vehicle through which God made his ultimate revelation to man – the mother tongue of Paradise. In heaven God speaks Arabic and will judge the world in this 'language of the angels'. The elements of beauty in the language are many, with its boundless vocabulary and wealth of synonyms which are limited in the main to objects relating to the Arabs' daily life, where the narrow sphere of their observations was curtailed by the brief geographical horizon, which tended to multiply their expressions by the relative paucity of objects with which they were conversant.

Throughout the present-day Arab East, the Arabic language shows a vertical differentiation depending on social stratification and a horizontal differentiation based on geographical separation. For the foreigner, progress in attaining any degree of fluency in the language means ceaseless plodding and endless diligence, for Arabic is for the Westerner one of the most difficult languages in the world. In the words of the master missionary linguist Ian Keith-Falconer, 'Arabic grammars should be strongly bound, because learners are so often found to dash them frantically to the ground.'[3]

It has always amused me, and I am sure T. E. Lawrence was equally amused, to read how Lawrence could adopt various Arab dialects at will and travel disguised as an Arab from one tribe to another with no one the wiser. In the words of the English authority, Major C. S. Jarvis, for thirteen years Governor of Sinai, 'No pure-bred Englishman brought up in England has ever accomplished this nor ever will.' 'Talking of disguise in Arabia,' said Douglas Carruthers, 'there can really be no such thing. A European who is a good linguist, and had studied the manners and customs of the Arabs, may pass more freely and without offence if he wears native clothes, but it is not a disguise.'[4]

'One of the myths which grew about Lawrence,' according to Sir Alec Kirkbride (*A Crackle of Thorns*, p. 7), 'was that he could pass himself off as an Arab. This was not so. He spoke Arabic imperfectly. ... Even if his appearance had not been enough to show that he was no Arab, he betrayed his origin the moment he spoke.' Yet to be completely fair to Lawrence I must mention that Sir Hubert Young, who first met his hero at Carchemish, stated from first-hand knowledge that already in 1913 Lawrence was 'capable of wandering about in native dress and passing unobserved among the swarthy and bearded inhabitants, but he had mastered the local dialect and was apparently accepted without question wherever he went as a youth from Jerablus.'[5]

But the fact that Lawrence never, according to the majority of accounts, completely mastered Arabic, does not mean that it cannot be done by a foreigner. Colonel G. E. Leachman, most heroic of the English Political Officers and explorers of Arabia, spoke the language with such perfection that he could and did pass as an Arab when he so wished.

Late one afternoon we had a delightful visit from young Sheikh Hilal bin Sultan from the village of Khaburah on al-Batinah to the south of us. While Dr Krause treated the Sheikh's younger brother, who was already blind in one eye and going blind in the other, Sheikh Hilal and I discussed ruined cities. He mentioned a site some forty miles inland from al-Hijari with lots of broken pottery and extensive ruins both in the mountains and down on the plain. In spite of his kind offer to guide us I regretfully had to postpone this visit until another time. We were all set to leave early in the morning on our carefully arranged journey to Sharjah and Dubai, and one rarely sets out in Arabia on a spur-of-the-moment trip. Everything must be carefully planned and laid out well in advance.

I had decided to leave Ray and Ali at Sohar to continue the excavations during the six or seven days for which the rest of us planned to be away.

Early the following morning we paused briefly at Sohar's Army Headquarters to cable the Sultan before proceeding up the Batinah Coast. In addition to Bill, Dr Krause, Sandy and Jama, we carried two Omanis loaned to us by the Sultan – Abd al-Karim bin Shah Mohammed and Talib bin Sulaiman. Abd al-Karim said he was between thirty-five and forty years old and had been to Dubai several times. Talib was quite certain he was thirty years old and I was just as positive he was much older. The Omani rarely knows his own age but always the age of his camel.

For the first forty-four miles the road, as it paralleled the coast, was a monotonous repetition of the Muscat-Sohar journey. It rained constantly all morning, while off to our right transparent waves broke on the beach. Numerous watercourses, usually dry but now overflowing, including the Wadi Nabur, were crossed with difficulty, and the three fishing hamlets of Liwah, Shinas and Murair, composed of the typical Batinah date-frond huts, were passed but not examined closely. Both Liwah and Shinas are dominated by ruined castles, leftovers from bygone days of splendour; in the month of January 1810 the joint forces of Sultan Said the Great and the British under Sir Lionel Smith battered down one side of the quadrangular fort of Shinas, after a bombardment of several days with over four thousand shots and shells fired. The foreign Wahhabi garrison of Mohammed bin Ahmed, after a most determined, sanguinary and heroic defence, was to a man put to the sword by Sultan Said. This Mohammed used to slaughter ten to twenty Omanis each day and seize their property; he operated under the brave and ferocious Wahhabi invader Mutlaq al-Mutairi who was at this time making bold inroads upon Sohar in 'a swathe of blood and destruction'.

After a cold chicken lunch in the Wadi Aswad we turned into the mountains following the Wadi Qur. This was a land of stunted acacia, tamarisks, oleanders, euphorbias, tall palms, doves and sand grouse. Soon we paid our respects to the Sultan's Customs Post. When Ahmed bin Norok received my letter from the Sultan, he kissed it, then touched it to his forehead. As Bill set up his camera for a picture, Ahmed said *atarakhus*, 'with your permission', and excused himself to reappear wearing a long dignified black coat.

Then before we could stop him, a table was set up by the gate and within a few minutes we were being served generous amounts of coffee, tea, canned cherries, pineapple, mangoes, figs and delicious Muscat *halwah*.

On up the Wadi Qur the scenery reminded me of the Sinai Peninsula – bare mountain traversed by geologic dykes and sills. Between the village of Huwailat and Jabal Qur, we investigated minor ruins at a locality known as Khurus. Very little pottery was visible and excavation would prove of small benefit here.

Toward late afternoon our Land Rover hit deep sand of a reddish colour reminiscent of ar-Rub' al-Khali. Finally the terrain levelled out similar to the Tripolitania Coast of Libya. For the most part the territory was physically uninviting, flat, monotonous, arid and desolate with a coastal maze of treacherous swamps and meandering indented creeks fringed by dangerous reefs which serve as 'a blessing to small craft on evil purpose bent.'

This Trucial Oman (there is no political connection with the totally independent Kingdom of Oman[6] to the south-east) extends from the base of the Qatar Peninsula eastwards along the Persian Gulf to Ras al-Khaimah and across to the Gulf of Oman for a total distance of about 325 miles. Once known as 'the Pirate Coast' it legitimately became the Trucial Coast when the nineteenth-century sheikhs made their truces with the Government of India, the powerful guardian of the Persian Gulf and 'reluctant arbiter of Eastern Arabia's political quarrels.'

These agreements or treaties were known as the Trucial Arrangement or League and contained clauses to exclude foreign powers from the possession of territory, to enforce the maritime peace of the Gulf, to regulate or abolish the slave trade and to put down piracy. Actually the Trucial League was a confused tangle of hatreds and jealousies whose threads were united in the hands of the British Resident in the Persian Gulf. These sheikhs had time and again attacked and absorbed each other's territory. In 1820 eight sheikhdoms, including Bahrain, signed. In 1835 six signed a temporary truce from which the coast derives its present name (Trucial Coast) and by 1914 only five sheikhdoms existed. Subsequently one of the five was split into three and Trucial Oman[7] is now made up of the chain of seven petty sheikhdoms of Abu Dhabi, Dubai, Sharjah, Ajman, Umm al-Qaiwain, Ras al-Khaimah and, since 1952, the small economically unimportant sheikhdom of Fujairah which faces the Gulf of Oman.

Actually no British protectorate has ever been declared over these 'Protected States'. Here English protection under 'exclusive agreements' meant strict neutrality as to internal affairs, and absolute dictation as to affairs with other governments at the diplomatic level. One view was that to protect meant 'to keep matters *in status quo* until the hour was ripe for annexation', giving rise to the amusing chant, 'The English, the English, with hats of height. We hope they die this very night.' The other view was stated at Sharjah by Lord Curzon in 1903 during his stirring address to the Trucial Sheikhs, at the great Durbar to honour the first visit of a Viceroy of India: 'We have not seized or held your territory. We have not destroyed your independence but preserved it.' This preservation without territorial acquisitions is still valid half a century later – preservation from Saudi Arabia whose motives in the past have not always been exclusively inspired by altruism for local Arab freedom.

The people of this coastal region, numbering about 100,000, have a confused mixture of Arab, Persian, Baluchi, Hindu and Negro blood and are seafarers at heart. Prostitution is commoner among the women of this coast than in any other community of eastern Arabia.

It was nearly dark when we raced across the flat-packed sand into Dubai. Here we were told the only real accommodation was at Sharjah, so we back-tracked part of twelve miles and turned off at the Airport Resthouse for the night. Our one-day journey by motor would have taken four days by camel – an ordinary desert caravan travels at three miles an hour.

That evening Bill and I sat down in the comfortable little lounge of the Sharjah Rest House dining room while Sandy went off to wash his feet, having braved the well-urinated mud of the streets of Dubai all day in the briefest of open-toed sandals.

I was surprised to find that a strange Englishman sitting on the opposite side of the room with a Major in the Trucial Oman Scouts had kindly paid for my Kitty Cola. As I thanked him he moved his chair closer and introduced himself as an official of I.P.C. (Iraq Petroleum Company). Bill politely inquired 'if we had passed one of his rigs in operation on the way in.' Our new friend replied 'yes' and I innocently said 'how deep are you?' – which is a question in the oil world very much like what time of day is it. He very haughtily said, 'I am not at liberty to divulge such information.' Before I could even look hurt Bill interrupted with 'it's 6,150 feet' and now it was our friend's turn to look hurt. 'How do you know that?' he stammered. Bill smiled and explained that everyone knows that there are no such things as secrets in the oil business. Actually Bill had simply counted the number of strings of casing as they were pulled from the ground, which accounted for his current brilliance.

Possibly our new friend had been indulging in something stronger than Kitty Cola for when I laughed and said, 'It really doesn't matter,' he almost shouted, 'It certainly does matter', and that we were competitors of theirs. Bill said, 'Oh, are you planning to excavate at Sohar?' and that did it. Our new I.P.C. acquaintance launched into a long dissertation on the Arab world, Americans in general and us in particular.

'Why don't you trouble-making Americans remain at home where you belong? Isn't your United States big enough for you? Why did you have to encroach where you have no right to be? We British have always ruled the Persian Gulf and if it had not been for you meddlesome Americans we would still manage the affairs of the Middle East as in the past.

'You dollar-loving Americans know nothing really about Arabia, you learn two or three words of Arabic which you can't pronounce properly, wear an Arab handkerchief on your heads and think you are all Lawrences of Arabia.

'All of Arabia's oil would be in British hands if your American Companies had not used unfair methods of competition, what real rights do you have taking oil out of Saudi Arabia, Kuwait, Bahrain and forcing your way into Dhofar when we were there first?

'Actually if the truth was told,' and here he lowered his voice, 'England's real enemy in the Arab world is America. So what if you had not been consulted over Suez – (the inglorious adventure that ended ingloriously) – since when did Great Britain have to consult with the U.S. over anything in the Middle East? Right or wrong the U.S. should have backed England to the fullest, for we British know what's best in this part of the world. Then to top if off you Americans price-gouged us during the Suez Canal crisis, charging more per barrel for crude oil.'

While I took a generous swallow he continued in a more friendly tone. 'I know all about you, Doctor Wendell Phillips. Many in your own State Department consider you a major menace. In case you have not heard, our Colonial officials in Aden rate you England's number one enemy in Arabia, for wherever you show up American interests suddenly appear and British interests disappear. I know all about your many Muslim friends in South Arabia, Egypt, Sudan, Libya, and East Africa. If we English had our way you would be as unwelcome in these countries as you are in Saudi Arabia. That's what is the matter with Egypt today, it is full of too many of your Egyptian-loving Americans who treat everyone as equals. It was different when we ruled the world. We all know this archaeology business of yours is just a front to cover up your other activities. What do you and those with you know about archaeology – we British are leaders in this regard, while you Americans should restrict yourselves to digging up Red Indian Mounds where you can't do any harm.'

Somewhere during all of this Sandy and Dr Krause had joined us, but Sandy suddenly remembered he had forgotten something somewhere else.

'My Company will soon convince your beloved Sultan that he had better forget all about you if he knows what's good for him. You have pulled the wool over his eyes for the last time.'

As our dinner was more than ready I again thanked our new friend from I.P.C. for the Kitty Cola and we quietly took our leave. Bill's first words were a direct steal from Kipling, 'For Allah created the English mad – the maddest of all mankind.' Falling back on Byron I replied, 'The world is a bundle of hay, Mankind are the asses who pull; Each pulls in a different way, and the greatest of all is John Bull.'

During the next half-hour Bill remarked from Disraeli 'how much easier it is to be critical than correct', for the disturbing element in all of this is not the mere deliberate distortion of facts by this Englishman, but the hostile attitude of the British in general towards America. The pleasure and satisfaction they seem to realize out of our mistakes and failures, not grasping that America's weaknesses are weaknesses also of the grand Anglo-American alliance which must somehow become permanent and indestructible. It is extremely doubtful if Americans ever received any great pleasure in England's poverty, queues, rationing, and dollar shortages after World War II. It was rather the reverse, with Americans sympathizing deeply and contributing to rectify this situation.

The fallacy so often overlooked is that the mere sharing of traditions, cultural heritage and a common language does not of itself bring into being uniformity of reasoning or reaction to situations. As stated by Sir John Glubb, 'It is the great tragedy of our times that we can be so like one another, and yet so constantly divided by misunderstandings and unfounded prejudices.' The Americans; well, they ought to behave more properly, more properly, that is, according to British standards of behaviour,

> Turn we this globe, and let us see
> How different nations disagree
> In what we wear, or eat, or drink,
> Nay, Dick, perhaps in what we think. (Prior)

Many Englishmen this writer has come up against in Arabia can best be portrayed in the couplet,

> 'You have ten Bedu lances, four Bedu shots to fear';
> But gaily laughed the Englishman, 'I have five bullets here.'

The main city of Sharjah is built along the shores of a filthy landlocked creek and is walled with slums interspersed with numerous crooked streets and narrow alleyways. The important buildings, some with elaborately carved doors, all face the sea to catch any available cooling breeze. Due to the extremely high humidity, July, August and September are appropriately called 'the hundred days hell'. About a mile northwest of the town proper is the somewhat unimpressive white fortress palace of Sheikh Saqr bin Sultan al-Qasimi, Ruler of Sharjah and Dependencies. Some years ago the present ruler's grandfather was murdered while sleeping in his bedroom by having his eyes put out with a red-hot iron and his throat cut. [Sheikh Saqr was deposed on June 25, 1965.]

We awoke the next morning to pouring rain. After purchasing supplies at an Indian shop in Dubai, we were guided into a small boat and across the still unbridged broad winding inlet known as Dubai creek, which separates the two parts of Dubai. This ferry trip was a delightful, leaky experience with one man and two oars doing all the work. The creek itself is too shallow to take anything larger than native sailing dhows and small coastal steamers up to 450 tons. In the Persian Gulf and Indian Ocean the word *dhow* is applied by foreigners to almost every type of native sailing vessel. *Dhow* is unknown to Arabs either as a general word for 'ship' or as a specific word for a certain kind of sailing ship – nor is it found in any other language of the area. Lord Belhaven's suggestion (*The Uneven Road*, p. 176) that it comes from an Arabic word meaning 'gleam' (or perhaps more normally 'light'), common in names of vessels, is the best explanation I have come across. The larger sailing vessels calling at Dubai are the type known as *boom* in Gulf Arabic. The general word for what one would call a *dhow* is *markab*, 'ship', or to be certain that steamship is not meant, *markab shira'i*. The creek is being dredged constantly, and the earth that is dug up is used to reclaim the land along its edge. Here warehouses, offices and even banks overhang the edge and one can look directly down on the busy scene of ships being loaded with every conceivable commodity from camels to sacks of rice.

Dubai existed already in 1799 and it appears to have remained until 1833 as a dependency of Abu Dhabi; after this date it became a separate principality and dangerous rival to its former parent state. In the 1890 edition of the *Persian Gulf Pilot* the population of Dubai is given as 5,000. Today, it is easily the most advanced and populated of the Trucial States and after Bahrain is the largest port in this part of the Gulf and is expanding rapidly. Dubai, whose merchants own about 400 ships, is orientated towards the East rather than the West, for most of its flourishing trade is with south-eastern

Persia, Pakistan and India. The headquarters of the British Political Agent for the Trucial States, having been transferred from Sharjah in 1954, is now in Dubai. The city, which thrives on trade with Persia, has been called with some justification 'an eastern Venice', or 'Venice of the Gulf', although in my opinion the best Venetian comparison should be made from a great distance. Dubai, with an estimated population of a probable 45,000, is over six times the size of Sharjah and far more attractive in every way with its noticeable, at least until recently, lack of Western influence. The trading ports on the coasts of Persia, India or even China in the seventeenth and eighteenth centuries must have looked something like the Dubai of today. On the north side of the dividing water is the district known as Dera, while on the west lies the main city of Dubai. Here the best houses are usually owned by Indian and Persian merchants. Each roof is adorned with a large square Persian ventilator, or wind tower, which effectively catches and sends any moving air to the rooms below.

The picturesque *suq*, or market place, reminded me of the Tihama Coast of Yemen, for both Hudaidah and Dubai have narrow, roofed-over, shop-lined streets with little sky visible through the palm matting. Only now, because of the recent rain, we trudged through a thick layer of oozing mud.

In 1938 Sheikh Said bin Maktum, who was the ruler of Dubai until succeeded by his extremely able son Rashid in 1958, celebrated the successful conclusion of a revolt 'by drawing red-hot needles across the eye of six hapless prisoners, killing one and blinding the rest for life.' In 1940 war broke out between Dubai and Sharjah over disputed territorial boundaries and a complex series of petty intrigues and tribal quarrels. Husah Umm Rashid, one of the wives of Sheikh Said, not only started the trouble but 'tore the veil from her face, donned sword and trousers' and personally led the defence of the main fort at Dubai. The British finally stopped the fighting but not until considerable exchange of cannon fire had taken place aided by clever 'retrievers' who under cover of darkness collected the used cannon balls fired from ancient guns for re-use the next day.

While outside Dubai, in the area of the Bani Yas tribe, Bill photographed a series of unique water wells. Over the top of each was a small wooden box sitting in the sand bearing a huge padlock. It was explained that each well is held by a different family and the water is retailed at considerable profit. Many a deadly fight has taken place over the disputed ownership of these desert water rights in this otherwise waterless region. Certain wells in Arabia are the exclusive property of tribes; however, sometimes an individual Bedouin will own one he has dug himself.

On a cold and rainy Friday morning we bid goodbye to Sandy at Sharjah, from where he was flying the next day to his home in St Andrew's, Scotland, via Bahrain, the classical Tylos of Pliny and the Awal of the Muslim writers of the Middle Ages, which is proclaimed the 'Pearl of the Persian Gulf' or 'pearl set in an emerald sea'. Since 1953 a large and competent Danish Archaeological Bahrain Expedition under Professor P. V. Glob and Geoffrey Bibby has established a continuous occupation for the island's last 5,000 years. Bahrain, long known as the 'Cemetery Island', owing to its more than 100,000 burial mounds, was an important trading centre linking the Pre-Dynastic and Early Dynastic cultures of Mesopotamia with the civilization of the Indus Valley in India. Thanks to these expeditions, it is now possible to date the majority of the island's grave mounds to the second half of the third millennium B.C. It is further believed that Bahrain is the ancient Dilmun (as Peter Cornwell has postulated) of the Sumerian cuneiform documents and that the Melukhkha of these records is in the Indus valley.[8]

Bahrain was ruled by Persia from A.D. 615 to 723, and was occupied by the Portuguese from 1521 until 1602, when Persian forces, supported by the Persian element in Bahrain, drove the Portuguese from the island forever and established a Persian garrison.

The modern history of strategic Bahrain dates from 1783, the year the Persians were expelled from the islands by the sheikhs of the Utubi Arabs, who subsequently paid a trifling tribute to Persia until this was later discontinued. In 1799 Oman (represented by four ships and six dhows), with encouragement from the Persian Beglerbeg of Fars, occupied Bahrain for the third time in the eighteenth century. Remains of the high-walled Omani fort constructed during this last period by Saiyid Sultan bin Ahmed are still visible on the sea-shore of Arad Bay facing Muharraq. After repeated Oman invasions and forced evacuations, in 1811 the Omanis finally expelled the Wahhabis (who had been in occupation since 1803), and the Utubis (who supply the ruling dynasty) were restored to power subordinate to Oman. In 1820 the Utub of Bahrain submitted to Oman and agreed to pay an annual tribute of $30,000 to Sultan Said bin Sultan. Four years later, after losing his younger brother Hamid in a singularly fruitless invasion attempt allied with the Persians (disregarding an offer of British mediation), Sultan Said the Great on 2 December 1829 officially recognized the independence of Bahrain in an informal alliance in spite of his obsessional wish to annex this island. The year before Sultan Said had made one final, desperate attack against Bahrain (in an outstanding display of absence of decision, skill, judgment and energy), in spite of his reassuring letter and presents to the Utubi Sheikhs. His unfaithful and treacherous allies, the Bani Yas, were the first to fly in this heated engagement, occasioning a considerable and unnecessary loss of life, while Said, brought off the field of battle by his trusted Nubian bodyguard, had to swim for his life, receiving while in the water a spear thrust through the sole of his foot. Said's ineffectual fleet was seized by panic and his invading force lost an estimated 500 men.

Filled with depression by his singular defeat, which reflected infinite discredit upon himself, concerned over an outbreak of cholera on board his vessels, weakened by his painful wound and with the fear of further treachery, Said stated that his 'enterprise was disapproved by heaven' and set sail for Muscat with his whole force.

Bahrain's extremely able Crown Prince, Sheikh Essa bin Sulman (Essa = Jesus) and I have spent many delightful hours together in London's Dorchester Hotel, as well as in Bahrain, discussing problems of the Persian or Arabian Gulf. With the death on 2 November 1961 of his sixty-nine year old father, H. H. Sheikh Sulman bin Hamad al-Khalifah, thirty-three year old Sheikh Essa became the Ruler of the independent state of Bahrain (in Arabic the name means 'two seas'). Bahrain is under the protection of Great Britain and all of the pear-shaped island's foreign affairs are guided by Britain; however, Bahrain is not ruled directly by the British and together with Qatar has never been declared a Protectorate. At the present time Persia considers Bahrain incontestably a Persian possession. 'Persia is still resolved as ever to retain her position in regard to Bahrain, considering the island part of her national territory. To Persia, British policy towards Bahrain was one of opportunism and direct intervention; the subsequent actions on the island constituted an encroachment on her territory.'[9]

In the Neolithic age, the level of the arm of the Indian Ocean known as the Persian Gulf (in the Arab world it is now *al-khalij al-arabi*, 'the Arab Gulf') was considerably higher than it is now; however, during historic times the change has not been appreciable (the same applies to the level of the Red Sea). This has been fully established by the excavation of Tell al-Khulaifah by Dr Nelson Glueck and by Professor William F. Albright's remarkable discovery of the ancient Red Sea port of Merkha (while serving as Chief Archaeologist on my University of California African Expedition in 1947).[10] Specifically with regard to the Persian Gulf, as my former expedition Engineer-Archaeologist Dr Richard Le Baron Bowen Jr., wrote, 'The identification of "Hellenistic to Roman Period" pottery at Ain Jawan would seem likewise to preclude the possibility of the level of the Persian Gulf falling over a few feet in the last several thousand years, as the waters of the Persian Gulf even today wash the shores of Ain Jawan when an exceptionally high tide (only several feet above the average) occurs.'[11] It is probable that these waters were the first 'sea' ever to be sailed by ships. By the third millennium B.C. the Gulf, which washes the shore of some of the earliest civilized countries, was certainly utilized by the Summerians and the Accadians and has aptly been described as 'an area of bleak coasts, torrid winds and pitiless sunshine.' This cradle of navigation has, nonetheless, long attracted the world's empires: the Babylonians, Greeks, Persians, Portuguese, Dutch, French, Russians and British.

In 694 B.C. Sennacherib cleared the Persian Gulf of pirates; this implies a sea trade which must have increased with the establishment of security. In the late seventh century B.C. the trade of the Gulf was possibly in the hands of the Phoenicians who had settled in the

Shatt al-Arab marsh lands of the Tigris-Euphrates, but this idea is losing ground.

In 512–510 B.C. Darius, the son of Hystaspes, sent his Greek pilot Skylax, of Karyanda in Karia, the neighbour and probable friend of Herodotus, to explore by ship the possibility and practicability of a short sea route between the Persian Gulf and the mouth of the Indus. Darius subsequently dispatched a fleet into the Indian Ocean by this route and Herodotus tells us, somewhat vaguely, that 'after this circumnavigation Darius subdued the Indians, and made use of this sea.'

The first European to set eyes on Oman and to navigate the Persian Gulf[12] was probably Nearchus[13] the Cretan, one of Alexander's admirals, in 325 B.C. Rome did not control the sea and its littoral until Trajan seized Ctesiphon in A.D. 116. Some of the more famous of the travellers of the Middle Ages visited and described parts of the region: Rabbi Tudela[14] and Marco Polo in the twelfth century, and Ibn Battuta in the fourteenth century. But the Gulf waters and coasts were not charted until Niebuhr did the job in 1764.

During the lifetime of Mohammed the Gulf was under Persian dominion; but by the tenth century Omani seamen had captured most of the trade and power and they kept it until at last the Portuguese took it from them by overwhelming force, under Albuquerque. Next came Spain, followed in due course by the British whose entrance into the commerce and politics of the Gulf states began, under the East India Company, in 1615, with a trade pact between the Company and Shah Abbas I of Persia. Meanwhile the Dutch East India Company was making its way in the same waters and by mid-century was in the ascendant. The Dutch dominated the Gulf spice-trade for a century until, in 1766, the last of their fortified factories was overrun and destroyed by the Omanis and the Dutch were finished in the Gulf.

During 1677, when Dr Fryer visited the Persian Gulf, the inhabitants of Oman had already earned the sad reputation of being 'a Fierce and Treacherous People, gaining as much by Fraud as Merchandize.' By 1695 the Omani pirates had acquired five large ships carrying 1,500 men. It was soon predicted that the Omanis 'would prove as great a plague in India as the Algerians were in Europe.'

In spite of the 'General Treaty of Peace' which was signed with Britain by the Arab princes of the Trucial Coast and Bahrain in 1820, and of vigilant supervision by the Royal Navy, active piracy in the Gulf continued until the arrival of the steamship in the late nineteenth century.

Eventually, through bitter experience, these Arabs by common consent found less and less profit in pitting their lawless wooden dhows against vigilant iron and steel vessels which operated independent of the winds, although as late as 1905 rapacious pirates attacked a British ship and even today one occasionally hears of local dhows having their entire crews murdered.

At the present time these former pirate communities have emerged from the barbarous obscurity that has enshrouded them since the dawn of history, and up until recently they have been engaged in the more respectable occupation of pearl-diving, which has an ancient history (pearls have made history and changed dynasties) along this coast with whole villages taking part in the activities since time immemorial. Arab poets describe the spring rains falling on the pearl banks as finding chance lodgment in the open mouth of the oyster. Each drop distills a gem, a 'tear of the sea', and the size of the raindrop determines the luck of the future diver.

The pearl reefs, which are open to all the maritime dwellers of the Gulf, extend along the western shores of the Persian Gulf from Dubai in the south to Kuwait in the north, with Bahrain the main focal point of the industry. *Qumash*, 'pearls', from the banks near Bahrain are supposedly marked by greater lustre whereas those further north by greater solidity. Deep water pearling, *ghaus al-kabir*, 'great diving', begins in June and lasts until the first week in October. The best pearl beds occur between five and ten fathoms, although it is believed the finest, heaviest, giant white pearls of perfect lustre come from twelve fathoms. Some experts profess a power to distinguish the depth of water and even the neighbourhood from which a pearl shown them was obtained.[15]

The present-day, natural Gulf pearl ('drape your girls in Bahrain pearls') does not peel and is justly celebrated for its firmness. In today's market it has the almost impossible task of competing with the beautiful cultured pearls of Japan which cannot be structurally distinguished from the real thing (on the average only one pearl is found in a thousand oysters), and the Trucial Coast has suffered accordingly with the pearl industry largely belonging to the past. Whereas a quarter of a century ago pearling dhows were numbered in the thousands, today only a few hundred operate.

Along this coast, before a picturesque pearling ship[16] is launched, a sheep or goat is sacrificed over the bow to give a life to the vessel and thus prevent her from taking one. Islam has never uprooted these early Semitic forms of blood sacrifice and survivals of primitive animism and fetishism as exemplified by the widespread belief in magical powers, spirits, and *jinn*. Among the Baharna[17] of Kuwait, the original natives of Bahrain, an old fertility cult existed up to a few years ago in which an agile barren woman would jump over the first length of timber of a new-laid keel, thereby helping her future child but taking virtue out of the future ship, which will now demand a life for a life in repayment from one of the crew.

The pearl-diver's standard of living is very low indeed; hard cruel work, starvation, life-long poverty; it is rated below that of an oasis date gardener. The diver receives scant remuneration for his toil and suffering and is usually in perpetual debt to his employer (everybody is in debt) for an amount greater than what he will earn the next season, so that few can escape from the account book. This amounts to inescapable lifetime slavery (although the worst abuses have disappeared) in an occupation which ruins his health and shortens his life. On occasion formidable monster fifteen-foot sawfish, armed with horrible sharp-toothed snouts six feet long, have cut unfortunate divers, who dread them far more than sharks, completely in two.

DUBAI TO BURAIMI

Arab manners – Law of the Tent – Jabal Shayyal
Joha the Wit – The Falconers – Buraimi

Somehow our Arab guide failed us and we left Dubai on the wrong road. It was Jama who finally stopped a passing camel caravan loaded with charcoal and inquired if this was the way to Buraimi. It was not, and an hour was lost getting on to the right track. In the late afternoon we reached Jabal Sumaini. Here an entire mountain was covered with ruins. Some of the building has obviously been re-used by a later people; I was reminded of the Dhofar coastal remains of Hasik, for here as well it was almost impossible from any distance to distinguish the limestone buildings from the parent limestone rock. From the summit a cold panorama of ruins and walled fields including a small *falaj* stretched out to the west. To the south and east towered high mountains.

As we went on to Wadi Aramiah the weather became even colder. On all sides we were hemmed in by twisted limestone formations in the fantastic outlines of immemorial weathering. It was almost dark when our Land Rovers entered a deep canyon containing running water along its gravel bed which was studded with *samr*, acacia trees. Talib estimated we were probably an hour from the village of Mahdha, our initial destination. As Dr Krause preferred, for health reasons, not to sleep in a village unless absolutely necessary, everyone searched for a spot high enough in the Wadi for protection in case of a flash flood. I finally settled for a rocky elevation formed by a small tributary wadi. In case of a major downpour we could climb up the sides, but the Sultan's vehicles would be lost.

Before turning in, Bill faced one truck up the *wadi* and the second downstream to enable us to catch any possible intruders in the headlights, for it is still true that in the desert the most dangerous enemy is man, until one has made sure that he is a friend. When all the rifles were distributed Talib and Abd al-Karim took turns keeping watch. As there was a rock wall both in front and at the back of us our guards concentrated their efforts in flashing their lights up and down the wadi throughout the night. Once Abd la-Karim tried to waken Jama for his turn but Jama would not respond, although the attempt had the rest of us with our eyes wide open. It was a disappointment that we had not been favoured with a four-legged visitor, for here roam the feral donkey, short-horned ibex and deadly panther. The panther of Arabia is really the Arabian leopard, *Panthera pardus nimr*, regarded when hungry as being capable of attacking and carrying off children. A stuffed specimen once presented to Wing-Commander Alfred Marsack, former Director of Civil Aviation in Aden, was said to have accounted for seventeen camels, five goats and a small child before it was finally killed.

Bill was understandably a little unwell in the morning after a dinner featuring sardines, salami, spam and pickles. Less than half an hour's drive through bare reddish rocks brought us to the delightful green oasis of Sharm, which consisted of a small scattered village and one square white fort tower surrounded by palms. Here Sheikh Abdullah bin Salim al-Ka'abi had been patiently awaiting our arrival for the past four days. In reply to his *salam alaikum*, 'Peace be upon you', I answered *alaikum as-salam*, 'On you be peace.' As the impeccably dressed Sheikh took my hand (signifying no concealed dagger in the palm) he repeated *ahlan wa-sahlan*, 'Welcome', several times in obedience to the command, 'If ye are greeted with a greeting, then greet ye with a better greeting', for here in the desert even a simple greeting becomes an expression of grace and poetry. The aristocratic Arab has truly mastered some aspects of the art of pure democracy, for gracious words and assurances are given by rich and poor alike. My letter of introduction from the Sultan was respectfully kissed but proved entirely unnecessary, for Sheikh Abdullah had already received his orders direct. He was to accompany us to Buraimi and from there give us safe conduct back to Sohar.

In Arabia a friendly sheikh is usually half the battle. It is a rare

I

privilege to be accepted into the desert fraternity. To a very remarkable extent this magic Arabia, the geographical and non-political entity, retains the power of conquering human hearts. Some, like myself, enjoy Arabia as one of the last remaining 'frontiers', and admire the Arabs, having developed a measure of sympathetic understanding for their way of life, which is in harmony with their environment; for, though often unlettered, the Arab is not un-learned, nor is he in any way less intelligent than his Western brothers.

Lady Anne Blunt noted long ago that the *badu* 'look upon hos-pitality not merely as a duty imposed by divine ordinance, but as the primary instinct of a well constituted mind.'[1] Every *badu*, rich or poor, ranks hospitality high, and in the words of the celebrated poet Omar ibn al-Farid:

Welcome to him of whose approach I am all unworthy,
Welcome to the voice announcing joy after lonely melancholy,
Good tiding thine; off with the robes of sadness; for know
Thou art accepted, and I myself will take on me whatsoever grieves thee.

If an Arab's most despised enemy should present himself one day at the entrance of his tent for protecting asylum, *haqq al-bait*, 'law of the tent', with the severed head of the host's most beloved son under his arm, in theory the host would not exclude the killer from an honourable reception, for the ancient and hereditary virtue of the Arab is his unsurpassed *dhiyafah*, 'hospitality'. This boundless hospitality, set in a land itself of so inhospitable an aspect, is a delight to experience. It has been said that hospitality is the virtue of bar-barians; if it be so, we should gain by being a little more 'barbarious' in our own manners. It happens that I have yet to encounter the supreme example of Arabian hospitality, experienced on separate occasions by Burckhardt, Landbert and Lane; in Burckhardt's own words, 'custom requires that the stranger should pass the night with his host's wife, whatever her age or condition'. This extraordinary custom was found among the al-Makhardah tribe of Yemen, but, says Burckhardt, 'to this barbarous system of hospitality young virgins were never sacrificed.... If the stranger ... did not please the lady, his cloak was found next day to want a piece, cut off by her as a signal of contempt.[2] The custom is by no means universal, however, and moreover what the guest can, or should, do, that is how far he can go with the lady, seems to vary from tribe to tribe and place to place. In south-western Arabia I think that where the custom is found it is confined to men of tribal and noble standing.

On some occasions, however, Arabia's proverbial sacred bond of hospitality has left a lot to be desired. For example, explorers Seetzen, Huber and Hermann Burckhardt were murdered; Palgrave, Doughty and Leachman beaten; Wellsted left Ibri in Inner Oman in 1836 accompanied by 'hisses and various other noises, until we got sufficiently clear to push briskly forward; and beyond a few stones being thrown, we reached the outskirts of the town without further molestation';[3] Von Wrede reported in 1844 that 'as soon as I had arrived among the crowd in the Wadi Doan they all at once fell upon me, dragged me from my camel, and disarmed me; using me very roughly, they tied my hands behind my back and carried me, with my face covered with blood and dust, before the reigning Sultan;[4] the Bents, while *en route* to Hadhramaut in 1898, experienced Arab hospitality in the form of shouts: 'Pigs! Infidels! Dogs! Come down from your camels and we will cut your throats.'[5] And finally my own reception in 1951.

As we pulled up at the foot of the present-day village of Marib, we were immediately surrounded by a mob of silent, tough-looking tribesmen and soldiers, covering us with their rifles. They were an ugly-looking lot, dressed in blue robes, their faces painted with indigo. There was no way out. We were surrounded and outnumbered, so there was no use making any strange motions. Their belligerence was somewhat tempered by their curiosity, for they had never seen Europeans or motor vehicles. One man stepped forward for a better look at our trucks, but as he did so the leader of the soldiers viciously swung his rifle butt against the man's skull. The other fell back, and Jama, obviously worried, asked the soldier, 'Weren't you expecting us? Didn't the King send word that we were coming?'

The askari's face remained expressionless. 'No,' he replied. 'When we heard motors we kept looking into the sky for aeroplanes. We had orders to open fire with machine guns. You are our prisoners.'[6]

Two miles beyond Sharm we passed Nuwaiji, where Bill photographed spectacular Jabal Ghuwail off to the right. From here it was only a short drive to Sheikh Abdullah's village of Mahdha, the capital of the Bani Ka'ab, which occupies a central position between the Batinah Coast, Buraimi and the Trucial Coast. The Sultan's flag flew from the top of a large circular tower dominating the fortress of Bait Nad, which was set in a palm grove fronting a bare plain. Attractive, bushy-haired, olive-skinned, large-eyed little girls ran off at our approach only to turn and inspect us shyly from a respectable distance.

As I have long experienced elaborate, time-consuming Arab hospitality (do you not know that when a guest comes into the house 'Fortune' comes with him?), I gently suggested in the spirit of 'something attempted, something done' that we examine first-hand the ruins which adorned Jabal Shayyal just behind the Sheikh's village, before stopping to rest. These ruins were similar in aspect to what we had seen the previous day with numerous rooms with partially remaining watchtowers constructed along the crest of the highest ridge. They differed in that here the people had gone to greater lengths to secure nicely shaped flat pieces of limestone for their buildings.

Back at Mahdha the next hour was expended over tinned fruit followed by the first essential of every visit in Oman – small, handle-less, artistically decorated half-filled cups of strong and rather bitter Yemen-coffee, or *qahwah* (an old Arabic word for wine). The usual polite amount to partake of in the Arab world is three; accept one, never two or more than three (in Oman there is no particular significance in the number of cups taken). After this, you shake the empty cup sideways slightly several times with a motion of the right wrist, signifying you have had enough. The cup then goes to the next in line for a repeat performance of slow reverent assimilation amid a solemn hush, or is returned to the dexterous server who pours out a long, thin jet with his left hand; the cups are stacked in his right hand. If one is being served in doubtful company, the maker of the coffee pours and drinks the first cup himself, to demonstrate the initial absence of poison; however, if your host intends treachery it may be the second cup to fear with its insert of arsenic. This honourable serving of coffee, which is poetically 'sweet as love, black as night, and hot as hell', is a supremely important and solemn rite, one could almost say a sacred ritual, with the *badu*, for coffee is as necessary to the life of an Arab as the air he breathes. It by far transcends the importance of food, especially for the un-invited guest. Honoured is the *badu* referred to as 'a man of many ashes'. His coffee-pot was always ready.

During a polite discussion I again asked Sheikh Abdullah if he would please postpone lunch until we returned later in the after-noon, for I very much wanted to visit a locality some thirteen miles to the north-east. One of the essential qualities needed for Arabian exploration is unlimited patience – only in this instance it was our host who was blessed in abundance with this attribute. I feel certain he viewed me as a living illustration of the Arab proverb *al-'ajlah min ash-shaitan*, 'Hurry is of the Devil.'

At Tabbah Qadimah, ruins covered an area of several acres, but no buildings were intact. Only the stone foundations with wide-spread rock terraces and fences were visible. Not one single pottery fragment was to be found. These remains were similar in certain respects to those at Falaj as-Suq, only here a fast-flowing perennial stream had entrenched itself in the hard rock.

It was a forty-minute return drive to Mahdha; there lunch was again delayed while Bill took pictures of the final preparations in-doors. Our first course was a Mexican-like *zapate* affair overflowing with warm butter accompanied by tins of fruit and *halwah*. Next, serving us with his own hand in the manner of the Patriarch Abra-ham, our Sheikh, with a *bismillah*, poured a thin gravy over every-thing in sight. Here bread (Omani bread, like Bahraini, is baked in large round pancakes almost two feet in diameter), has a symbolic significance as *rizq allah*, 'the provision of God.' We ate using the *abu-khamsah*, 'father of five', method, in other words with our five fingers, while sitting on the floor. Of course the soles of one's feet are never extended in the direction of the host or guests; it would be bad manners.

I remembered well one occasion in Hadhramaut when our host merely blew water through the entrails to clean them out and then squeezed the contents of the gall-bladder over everything as gravy.

In 1833 Wellsted had observed a *badawi* feast in which 'the entrails, with no other cleansing than being drawn through the fingers, and the feet only partially divested of the hair, are placed in a pan over the fire . . . and, after pouring a quantity of rancid butter over them, [they] stir the mess with their fingers over the fire, until well warmed and soaked, and then devour it with much relish.'[7]

A Western traveller finds much to comment upon in the matter of Arabian food. Now while I fastened my fingers in the cavities of the eyes and generously placed before Bill the skull of a sheep complete with eyes, nose and tongue, with part of the neck hanging to it. Dr Krause made the following professional observations: First he noticed a cyst in the omentum, which is an apron of fat surrounding the intestinal tract. On three large fibre plates piled high with rice our doctor pointed out a windpipe, lung, liver, spleen, heart and kidney with a miscellaneous collection of great vessels.

One day some 1,200 years ago a friend of Joha (the unexcelled Arab wit of fiction), arrived from Helwan and presented his host with a fine lamb and stayed on for dinner to help eat it. The next day two men came to Joha's home, saying, 'We are friends of the man who gave you the lamb.' Joha invited them for dinner. Two days later six men came to Joha's door, saying 'We are friends of the friends of the man who gave you the lamb.' So Joha invited them to stay for dinner. After waiting more than two hours, the hungry guests were served from a kettle which contained only hot water with a few grease spots floating on top.

'What kind of hospitality is this?' they asked. Joha replied, 'This water is the friend of the friend of the water in which the lamb was boiled.'

At the completion of the meal the sure way to convey to our host appreciation and gratitude for his bounty and hospitality was a protracted series of expressive belches accompanied by the statement 'Praise be to God, the Lord of all creatures,' for the Devil has power over that food which is eaten without remembering God.

While warm water was poured over our hands ('When anyone eats he must not wash his fingers until he has first licked them') the *askaris* eagerly devoured what remained of our *tell al-lahm*, 'mound of meat'.

In Bedouin eyes the Western custom of men and women eating in company together is very strange; the Prophet is believed to have declared that food eaten by women before men is unblessed. It is also considered a disgrace for children of either sex to eat with men. The *badawi* is always hungry and will eat almost anything as long as he is in private. He makes a rapid business of eating with his perfect finger technique. Quite a ceremony is enacted in pulling open the lower jaw of a sheep's head, and then eating out the tongue with the mucous membrane attached, to be followed by the muscles on the floor of the mouth and the external muscles of the head. The fat of a sheep's tail is also looked upon as a special delicacy. Among these Arabs the meat of the sheep is preferred over that of the goat, and the latter are kept largely for their hair and milk.

One of our fellow guests at this feast had been blind for twelve years and possessed a remarkable foot. He walked on his heel bone in such a manner that from the front view the sole appeared in an upright position. The foot was hyperextended so that it paralleled the leg with a complete loss of the ankle joint, the instep being attached to the lower end of the shin. As there was no shrinkage of his toes or loss of form he must have possessed a good foot at one time. In reply to my question he attributed his condition to snakebite. This did not seem likely to Dr Krause.

Sheikh Abdullah was very proud of his two young sons who marched up to bid us goodbye. While in our presence they never relaxed but always stood at attention. The Sheikh, armed with an appropriate bodyguard, had added his Japanese Land Cruiser to our caravan for the forty-five minute drive to Buraimi Oasis. On the way he pointed off to the left where a really immense limestone mountain, the four thousand foot Jabal Hafit, rose up out of the desert like a huge solitary whale. The year before the body of a man had been found at the base of this barren mountain. Clutched in his hand was a piece of paper on which he had written, 'I am dying of thirst, no one has killed me.' This Jabal Hafit, which is occasionally inhabited by an extremely rare species of wild goat (*Hemitragus jayakari*), is divided between Oman and Abu Dhabi; the latter, extending far into the desert interior, is the largest sheikhdom on the Trucial Coast.

It was just dark when we pulled up outside the commanding fortress of the Wali of Buraimi, the walls of which were loopholed for musketry. After the more than usual confusion with every local personality shouting orders at everyone else, things suddenly quieted down as Sheikh Salim bin Humaid appeared and ushered us inside. Sheikh Salim was a short heavy-set man of about sixty (he subsequently died at Sib in May 1960) and had served here as Wali since July 1957. When I handed him the Sultan's letter he first kissed it, and then touched it to his forehead and breast signifying complete surrender of thought, mind and deed. He explained that he had known the Sultan since he was a small boy. I frantically reminded Sheikh Abdullah to explain that we had just eaten, but this made not the slightest impression on the Wali and so it was another round of food *min allah*, 'from God'.

I offered to set up camp in the sand but the Wali shouted *astaghfir allah*, 'I ask pardon of God', and insisted we sleep in one of his houses just outside the fortress. 'When I suggested that two rooms would suffice – one for us to sleep in, one for Jama to cook in – the Wali almost had a fit. *Allah yusallimak*, 'God save you.' 'You will do no cooking in my village – I will provide all your food.' Now this was what I feared most and countered just as strongly that this was too great an inconvenience for him – that we loved to serve ourselves. We compromised on lunch together for the next day – I insisted on keeping an exact time schedule. Actually, the Wali's attitude and concern for us was a kind of reflection of the beautiful Arabic welcome, *ya dhaifana, law zurtana, law wajjahtana, nahnu adh-dhuyuf wa-anta rabbu 'l-manzil*, 'Oh, Guest of ours, though you have visited us, though you have honoured our dwelling, we verily are the real guests, and you are Lord of this house.' When early the next morning the Wali brought us breakfast, Jama used the excuse, which was not far from the truth, that I was not too well; I settled for tea which Talib obligingly drank for me.

Later in the morning Bill borrowed the battery from Sheikh Abdullah's Japanese Land Cruiser to run his airoflex camera, in spite of the horrified protests of the Sheikh's driver. The Wali was a born actor and once he understood what was wanted he cooperated beautifully with our picture-making.

In front of the Sultan's Buraimi Army Headquarters several Trucial Oman Scouts, who number about 1,000 and have their headquarters at Sharjah, rode up and three of them carried Peregrine falcons on their gloved wrists. Proud and unprotesting were these beautiful hawks each shackled by a chain round one leg and wearing a small leather hood or *burqa* over its huge jet black, unblinking, hard bright eyes. Not all hawks are falcons, but all falcons are hawks. Falcons are usually captured during the winter months while on migration along the Trucial Coast and are easily lost, requiring a tedious training period, during which time the eyelids are sewn together, until they take food. The thread is then removed and a hood is substituted. The winged hunters are released only when an object of prey is in view. A small bird like a swallow is almost impossible for them to catch because of its devious flight. The bird most commonly sought here is the lesser bustard (*hubara*) which is the size of a turkey hen and is good eating. The matchless falcon pursues and strikes it repeatedly on the ground or in mid-air, eventually forcing it to the earth, for the falcon rarely kills in the air.

On the ground it aims at the *hubara*'s neck with its powerful talons and pecks at the eye of the unfortunate victim with its curved beak until the bustard is totally blind. The rule in this part of Arabia is to allow the falcon a few minutes initial feeding time on the brains or liver of the still living bird. Then the hunter must move in fast to cover the unblinking eyes of his falcon and to rescue what remains of its dinner. A good falcon will kill half a dozen bustards, and occasionally more, in a day. Several sheikhs possess as many as a hundred of these birds of prey, who love nothing better than to fight each other; this they are never allowed to do.

Carl Raswan, authority on the Arabian horse and 'blood brother' of the Rwala, was once witness to a bloody falcon attack on a herd of beautiful, defenceless gazelles. 'With desperate plunges and side-springs the terrified gazelles endeavoured to free themselves from their murderous assailants, but without avail. With their talons hooked in the scalp or the eye sockets of the gazelles the falcons struck wildly with their wings and beaks at their eyes to impede their progress.[8] Falconry is considered the main winter pastime of the Trucial Coast; with the exception of the Buraimi area it is not carried on in Oman. This ancient and picturesque sport was practised by the Egyptians, ancient Greeks, Persians (who claim the invention for their King Anushiriwan, contemporary of Mohammed), and Chinese, and was introduced into Spain with the Arab invaders and during the early crusades into Europe, where along with others, Frederick Barbarossa brought falcons to Italy in the twelfth century; there it reached a peak of popularity and fashion in late medieval times.

After lunch Jama purchased four excellent rugs at fifteen *riyals* apiece. While Bill got us ready to depart, I questioned the Wali at length about this famous oasis which only a few years before had made the front page headlines of the world's newspapers when the Saudi Government sent an invading detachment of soldiers to occupy the village of Hamasa.

Buraimi Oasis had been visited by Hamerton in 1840, Chester in 1855, Miles in 1875 and 1885, Zwemer in 1901 and Cox the following year.[9] Its position on the map was first accurately determined in 1905 by Major (Sir) Percy Cox during his second visit to the oasis (accompanied by Lieutenant C. A. Scott of the Royal Indian Marine). Cox found the oasis lies between the foothills of the Hajar Mountains and the sands of Khatam and is situated in the northern part of the Oman district of the *Dhahirah* plateau. Earlier in the day we had viewed the main *falaj* which brings lukewarm water teeming with tiny fish from the distant mountains of al-Hajar to the west.

One looks in vain for an obvious centre to Buraimi. Mud forts, houses and palm groves, some new, others barely standing, show no attempt at orientation to a main point of reference. The oasis actually consists of nine villages. The oldest of these villages, Buraimi, which gives its name to the entire oasis plus two others, Hamasa and Sa'ra, are occupied by the Naim, Bani Jabr and Albu Shamis; they belong to the Sultan of Oman. The remaining six villages, Muwaiqih, Mataradh, al-Ain, Jimi, Qattara and Hilli, are occupied by the Bani Yas and Dhawahir and are owned by an old friend of the Sultan – Shakhbut bin Sultan, the Sheikh of Abu Dhabi since 1928 when his uncle was assassinated.

The earliest known settlers in the Buraimi area were the Azd, who migrated from Yemen before the *hijrah*. In A.D. 1728 Buraimi was recognized as part of Oman in the authoritative writings of Sheikh Sirhan bin Said, but its history had, and ever since has, been stormy: as early as 840 a revolting faction of Bani Julanda captured the place and murdered the Governor, only to be wiped out, together with the rest of their tribe, by a powerful punitive force sent from Sohar. Later in the ninth century the oasis was used as a base for the conquest of Oman by the Abbasid Caliphs. In the seventeenth century it was again under Omani control, with the immigrant Naim tribe settling the whole region, and later becoming one of the most important tribes in the country. Imam Ahmed bin Said, the founder of Oman's Albu-Said dynasty, controlled Buraimi in the mid-eighteenth century. Salil bin Razik, whose grandfather Razik bin Bakhit once saved the life of Imam Ahmed bin Said and served as Clerk of Customs for the Imam wrote as follows in his *History of the Imams and Seyyids of Oman*, p. 166: 'His dominions extended from the end of Jaalan as far as Tawwâm [el Bereimy].'

The first raid on record took place in the beginning of the nineteenth century when a force of Wahhabis under a Nubian slave named Hariq seized Buraimi, built a fort, and used it for operations into Oman. Saiyid Sultan led 12,000 Omanis against Hariq who withdrew into the Najd, but there were other Wahhabi raids to come. One such, led by Battal al-Mutairi in 1819, ended when the raiders went over in a body to Said the Great and thereafter served him loyally. Later in the century Naim tribesmen repeatedly threw back Wahhabi invasions, and on 18 June 1869 they, in alliance with the Imam Azzan bin Qais, finally drove the Wahhabis from Buraimi.

This final expulsion of Wahhabi representatives in 1869, marking the end of their fifth incursion during the nineteenth century, remained effective until 1952, with the exception of a few brief haphazard visits by Saudi tax collectors. The last Saudi incursion in eighty-three years took place in September 1952 when Turki bin Abdullah bin Utaishan arrived at the village of Hamasa with forty armed men after an overland drive from al-Hasa which violated Abu Dhabi territory.

From 1953 to 1954 the Sultan of Oman and the Sheikh of Abu Dhabi blockaded the Saudis in the village of Hamasa. After pro-

tracted and unfruitful diplomatic haggling, the dispute was referred
to an international arbitration tribunal in 1954. At the request of the
Sultan, the United Kingdom acted on his behalf in the arbitration
proceedings.

What followed in this dispute, and its outcome, is dealt with in
full in my forthcoming *Oman: A History*, and I do not propose to go
into details here, but some idea of the subsequent events should be
given. The tribunal, with a Cuban, a Pakistani, a Saudi Arabian and
a British member, presided over by a Belgian, had been at work for
months when the Saudi member, Yusuf Yasin, was accused of in-
fluencing witnesses by bribery. I have met Sheikh Yusuf Yasin and
I found him a brilliant man. As to the accusations, even St John
Philby, always the champion of the Saudis, said (*Sunday Times*,
23 October 1955) that it was clear the Saudi witnesses before the
tribunal had been bribed. As a result the president, the British and
the Cuban member resigned, whereafter the Sultan in alliance with the
Sheikh of Abu Dhabi, supported by Trucial Oman levies, drove the
Saudis from Buraimi by force. Both the Soviet Union and Egypt
went fishing in these troubled waters, supporting Saudi Arabia,
although Soviet atlases show Buraimi outside that country's frontiers.

In all this not a soul ever mentioned oil. But one explanation of
Saudi Arabian persistence in a bad cause may be found in the fact
that the first promising reports of drilling operations in Trucial
Oman had been published just before their occupation of Hamasa.
In January 1956, *Oil Forum* published an official Saudi claim to
Buraimi and a declaration that the Saudi Government would regard
any oil or mineral rights agreement entered into with any other
power claiming sovereignty over Buraimi as null and void and would
act accordingly. Yet even Aramco, the great Arabian American Oil
Company, always eager to back Saudi attempts to extend their
kingdom, place the Buraimi oasis well outside Saudi Arabia's frontiers in their maps and descriptions of the country. In the view of this
writer the fact is that all the evidence, of whatever kind, clearly
shows that Buraimi is not part of Saudi territory and never has been.
And the claim that the Buraimi dispute is a conflict between emer-
gent Arab nationalism represented by Saudi Arabia, and 'corrupt,

blighting feudalism' represented by the Sultan of Oman and the Sheikh of Abu Dhabi in alliance with British imperialism, is mere rubbish; at that time there was no more feudal country left in the world than Saudi Arabia; and, as Philby himself showed, few more corrupt.

One final point should be made: the 'Physical Political Map of the Arabian Peninsula' by Professor Muhammad Abd al-Mun'im, officially prescribed for use in Saudi schools by the Saudi Director of Public Instruction, places Buraimi outside the limits of Saudi Arabia. This map was withdrawn and vanished from circulation in 1949 when, after a lapse of nearly a century, the Saudis revived an imaginary 'ancestral claim' to the territory. And when, today, any man on the Trucial Coast says that he is 'going to Oman', it is understood that he is going to Buraimi, the nearest part of Oman.

8

WOMEN IN OMAN

Child marriage – Unwanted daughters – Infanticide
Arabian beauty – Female circumcision – Divorce
Trial marriage – Unequal status of women
The veil rent

As a babe unwelcome;
As a child untaught;
As a wife unloved;
As a mother unhonoured;
As an old woman uncared for;
As a dead woman unmourned.

In terms of personality, of economics, of politics and of civics, there are no women in Oman; women exist in number always greater than men, but their existence is domestic and servile only. The unequal position of women in Oman is common throughout the Arabian peninsula; the attitude which degrades them is common to the whole Arab world and beyond that to the whole Muslim world; but the worst practices, the excesses of the system, are being abandoned in the more sophisticated Muslim states and are confined now to the poverty-stricken parts of the Arabian peninsula itself. Moreover, and curiously enough, the existence of a desert woman may be less oppressive, freer, than that of her urban sister, if only because of the greater need for her active services in the work of the community, but also because of the greater freedom with which marriage and divorce are contracted; a desert woman may, in her time, have half a dozen husbands.

As soon as a girl in Oman reaches puberty a husband is provided for her; she has, of course, no choice in the matter; and as she may, technically, reach puberty at the age of ten or eleven, the consequences of her marriage, often to an elderly husband, are frequently horrible. The following short account is not that of an exceptional case, but of a commonplace:

A little child! I saw her as she waited in the . . . hospital [brutally pene-trated by an elderly husband who wanted his rights] . . . never can I forget her piteous cries, the horror staring from her fear-glazed eyes, from which all childishness had fled. She crouched, like some wild, tortured animal, trust in everyone, all childish hopes forever gone. A quivering, outraged form; a broken, wounded life; a terror-stricken heart.[1]

There is no future but marriage, which may well begin like that one, for any woman of Oman at the present time. Doubtless economic changes will make a difference there, as elsewhere; but it should be remembered that the Arabs believe that 'a woman without a husband is like a bird with one wing' and that 'a woman's lot is a husband or else the grave'. It was not always so; there is evidence that women in Arabia generally were more free and more respected as full human beings in their own right, in pre-Islamic times. But this may perhaps have been owing to the fact that there were fewer women; for at that time, known to Arabs as the Time of Ignorance (i.e., before the mission of Mohammed), female infanticide was common, and the method particularly cruel, for the infant girls were buried alive. 'The parents look after the son, and God looks after the daughter'; so it was said, and likewise, 'When a daughter is announced to one of them his face becomes dark and full of anger. He hides himself from the people because of the evil of that which is announced to him. Shall he keep it with disgrace or bury it in the dust?'

Various reasons for this practice have been advanced. It was the opinion of Mohammed that the causes were poverty, famine, the natural excess of females over males due to war. The present writer considers that this was sound, but Ilse Lichenstader[2] holds this to be a mistaken opinion. She writes: 'However, neither inability to provide for her, nor dislike of daughters as such, nor even the fear of disgrace were motives for the act, the former notions as far from the Arab's mind then as now. By burying his newborn daughter he wished to impart the life-giving, productive power inherent in the female, to the earth.'

Mohammed set his face firmly against this practice, whatever its

cause, and especially against the burying of the children alive. Referring to the Day of Judgement, Sura 81 of the Quran describes it as,
among many other things, the day 'When the buried child shall be
asked for what sin she was put to death.' The Prophet detested the
rite as much, perhaps, because it was heathen (both Plato and Aristotle, the former in the *Republic* and the latter in his *Politics*, approve
of it and both Lycurgus and Solon embodied it in their laws), as
because it was cruel. He charged the women of Mecca to do away
with this barbarous practice: 'Kill not your children for fear of want;
for them and for you will We provide. Verily, the killing of them is
a great wickedness.'

One inhuman father allowed his daughter to reach the age of six
before ordering her mother to 'Perfume her, and adorn her, that I
may convey her to her mothers.' This done he took his daughter by
the hand and led her to a shallow pit that had been dug by his instructions and having bid his little girl to look down over the edge
he stepped back and pushed her headlong. As she tried to regain her
feet the pit was filled in over her and levelled with the rest of the
ground. We are told that the only occasion on which the Caliph
Omar ever shed a tear was when his beautiful little daughter whom
he was in the process of burying alive, wiped the dust of the grave
earth from his beard.

We have said that not the girl but her parents, in actual fact her
father, chooses her husband. But in present-day Oman (again, this
was probably not the case in pre-Islamic times), even the parents'
choice is narrowly restricted by custom, custom having almost the
force of law. For a girl, whether she likes it or not, always belongs to
the son of her father's brother, her *bin 'amm*; and this is so much the
case that he, her first cousin, must give his permission before the
girl can be married to anyone else. There can be no doubt that this
custom is powerful because it is based on feeling for property: 'He
who marries his father's brother's daughter celebrates his feast with
a sheep from his own flock.' Westermarck quotes a Moroccan proverb which would be equally applicable to Oman: 'Marrying a
strange woman is like drinking water from an earthenware bottle;
marriage with a cousin is like a drink from a dish – you are aware of
what you drink.'³ Until the time of the Prophet there seem to have

been two opposing forces at work in this matter; for whereas the ancient Arabs, like the ancient Israelites, could marry their half-sisters, yet their folk-sayings include much that tends to show they were aware of the dangers of inbreeding. On the one hand we have the old South Arabian proverb, attributed to Noah, 'The ploughman to the ploughwoman, the retainer to the retainer woman, the slave to the slave woman', while on the other we have the equally ancient Arab proverb, 'Marry the distant, marry not the near' because 'the seed of kinsfolk brings forth feeble fruit.' In certain remote parts of the Arabian peninsula, if a girl is bold enough to refuse to marry her paternal first cousin, he is entitled to kill her without payment of blood-money compensation.⁴ A milder version of the same custom; he may refuse to allow her to marry anyone else, and she is doomed to a life of spinsterhood, that is to a life of servility in her father's, instead of her husband's, household, with no hope of the one consolation, the one honour open to an Omani woman, the bearing of sons. And according to Burckhardt if he does give his permission, he is apt to go about saying, 'She is my slipper; I have cast her off.'⁵

Mohammed, although he preached that women should be respected and treated with honour, thought of them only as wives. He said, 'The game of a man with a woman is one of the games the angels like to watch.' He had, however, no need to urge his followers to marry, for the nomadic Arab is very much a marrying man. The Prophet one day fell in with a stranger and asked him if he was married and received answer that he was not.

'Art thou strong and healthy?'

'Verily I am.'

'Then thou art one of the devil's own brothers.'

An Omani Arab employs a relative to propose marriage with a virgin girl, to her father; with divorcees or widows he takes the direct approach. 'A maid weds to please her clan, but a widow pleases herself.' The Prophet taught, 'A widow shall not be married until she be consulted; nor shall a virgin be married until her consent be asked, whose consent is by her silence,' as she is too ashamed, bashful and modest – according to the male ego – to testify to her desire. On one occasion the Italian explorer Carlo Guarmani records how his

Arab companion was prospecting for a new wife of good family and 'the matrons obligingly acceded to his request, and swore to the girl's virginity ... they slapped her on the back without causing her pain or making her cough, which proved that her constitution was sound and robust, and, finally, they showed him her bust. This was intended to overcome all prudence on his part.'[6]

For the contraction of a valid marriage, it is a universal custom to make gifts, collectively known as *mahr*, a sort of reverse dowry, to the girl in question, of money, jewellery, clothes, and on occasion a wedding bed which may only consist of a fancy blanket for use in the sand. The trousseau usually has a special personal significance attached to it by the women and is known in Arabic as the *kiswah*. 'Ask me never so much bride price and gift, and I give according as ye shall say unto me; but give me the damsel to wife' (Gen. 34: 12).

In Zanzibar, among the Wahadimu, certain of their women imitate the sexual act for the eager benefit of the novices, while in nearby Pemba Island the Wapemba tribe dispatch the intended bride to an old married couple for a brief course of instruction. Although Oman long ruled both places, the writer knows of nothing comparable in Oman, and these practices seem contradictory to Arab attitudes. A week before her marriage the girl has all of her body hair removed, usually with each individual hair plucked out by hand; a solution of zinc and arsenic is also employed by the more well-to-do.[7] Excessive fatness is esteemed as an essential to perfect female beauty throughout North Africa, whereas in Oman it is the elegant, slender, light and airy figure with the sinuousness of a serpent which inspires the most impassioned expressions of desire. 'It is not possible to bind her waist even with a hair, lest the hair should cause her slender middle to break.' According to Burton, 'The high bosomed damsel with breasts firm as cubes, is a favourite with Arab tale-tellers,' and a large hollow navel is looked upon as a thing of rare beauty. Whereas to Haji Rikkan, a marsh Arab of Iraq – 'Her cheeks are like young melons, her mouth is a jewelled ring, no bigger; her teeth are sugar. Are not her eyes, Ma Shallah! as big as eggs? And as for her breasts, they are like two Persian apples.'[8]

This minute tabulation of Arabian beauty in a standard of nine 'fours' is by an unknown author quoted by al-Ishaqi followed by

E. W. Lane in *Arabian Society in the Middle Ages*; the model, apparently, was the Khalifah al-Mutawakkil:

Four things in a woman should be black: the hair of the head, the eyebrows, the eyelashes, and the dark part of the eyes; four white: the complexion of the skin, the white of the eyes, the teeth and the legs; four red: the tongue, the lips, the middle of the cheeks, and the gums; four round: the head, the neck, the forearms and the ankles; four long: the back, the fingers, the arms and the legs; four wide: the forehead, the eyes, the bosom and the hips; four fine: the eyebrows, the nose, and lips and the fingers; four thick: the lower part of the back, the thighs, the calves of the legs and the knees; four small: the ear, the breasts, the hand and the feet.[9]

Nearly a century ago Guarmani commented, 'The beauty of the Scerarie women, combined with their strength and grace, is the most positive contradiction to the absurd fable which asserts that the Scerarat, a subdivision of the Beni-Kelb from the southern Arabian desert, have their origin from the monstrous connection of a woman and a dog.'[10] At approximately this same period Palgrave bravely ventured 'on the delicate and somewhat invidious task of constructing a "beauty scale" for Arabia, and for Arabia alone; the Bedouin women would on this scale be represented by zero, or at most 1°; a degree higher would represent the female sex of Nejed; above them rank the women of Shomer, who are in their turn surmounted by those of Djowf. The fifth or sixth degree symbolizes the fair ones of Hasa; the seventh those of Katar; and lastly, by a sudden rise of ten degrees at least, the seventeenth or eighteenth would denote the pre-eminent beauties of Oman.'[11]

The arrangements for a marriage and its consummation usually take place in the following fashion in Oman. After the 'asking', which has been mentioned above, comes the *milhah*, 'commitment', if all goes well; the *milhah* stipulates the amount of the bride money and the contents of the trousseau which the bridegroom and his family are to provide. The *milhah* may also set the date of the wedding, which normally comes after a short waiting period. The actual completion of the marriage takes place with the certification of the marriage contract. This oral certification (or signing in the case of parties who can write) is presided over by a religious judge, a *qadhi*, who merely asks the bridegroom in the presence of witnesses if he will take the girl, and then upon receiving approval from the girl's father or brother or other qualified representative, the ceremony, which is a civil contract, not a sacred bond or *tei* or indissoluble sacrament, is over. The only religious element in the Muslim secular ceremony is that the contract begins with the traditional phrase *bismillah*. The man now legally possesses the full use of the woman for his enjoyment. The bride is not present. When a son has been married his father may take his hand saying, 'I have disciplined thee and taught thee and married thee; I now seek refuge with God from thy mischief in the present world and the next.'

Socially the marriage is not complete until there has been an appropriate wedding celebration, which begins as soon as the marriage has gone into contract. This celebration consists of dancing, singing (where religion permits) and feasting – male and female celebrants do all of this separately, of course. The culmination is the escorting of the newly-weds to their dwelling, be it house or tent, and this is the first moment the bride and groom have been alone together in their lives (at least theoretically).

As Thesiger so aptly puts it in his *Arabian Sands*, p. 152, the *badu* 'consider that women are provided by God for the satisfaction of men. Deliberately to refrain from using them would be not only unnatural but also ridiculous.' Such a view is stated quite frankly in the remarkable erotic manual, *The Perfumed Garden*, written in southern Tunisia by Umar bin Mohammed an-Nafzawi; in this work the Sheikh begins his introduction with 'Praise be given to God, who has placed man's greatest pleasure in the genitalia of women and has destined the *partes genitales* of man to afford the greatest enjoyment to women.' To quench one's sexual thirst in the fountain of love is to the *badu* the ultimate joy of life, a miraculous experience common to rich and poor alike, and many are the tribal eyes and ears focussed on the bridal tent.

In Oman (as among nomads in every part of the Near East, as well as Greece) it is quite good form for the Arab bride to scream and struggle for several hours before giving up her virginity, the essence of all virtues for 'the best and stoutest sons are those born of reluctant wives.' One fears that there is still too much truth in Balzac's saying that in this matter the husband is sometimes like an orang-outang with a violin.

In many parts of Arabia, when an aged but rich husband has paid a goodly sum to a comparatively poor father for his daughter, it is regarded as a solemn duty of the bride to her father to exaggerate her cries during consummation, not only as evidence of her virginity but of her aged partner's virility and prowess. Where through a combination of modesty and embarrassment the bride fails to do so, it is by no means uncommon for the bridegroom, if he tends to be an insensitive person, to dig his fingernails mercilessly into her tender flesh to cause her to cry out. This part of the proceedings is called *midkhal*, 'entering in'.

Lack of nup.ial blood does not, of course, necessarily reflect lack of virginity; however to the Near Easterner blood on the sheet or 'cloth of bliss' from a ruptured hymen in most instances is sufficient proof of the 'tokens of virginity', that the 'domestic calamity' or daughter was sacrified to her husband a *bona fide*, clean maid. 'God whiten your faces, you have indeed kept your daughter pure.' If there is no blood-stained sheet of innocence to pass gaily and triumphantly around the next morning for public surveillance (not true in all of Arabia) the girl may be returned to her parents in shame and disgrace and may in some cases face death at the hands of her honour-conscious male relatives. Some girls devise ingenious methods to fool their husbands as they enter 'the door of life' (sexual penetration does not necessarily mean defloration) and sometimes they succeed.

In Omani, as in most Near Eastern societies, both Arab and non-Arab, if the bridegroom, either because of immaturity or impotence, is unable to attain an erection and perforate the hymen by this natural means, this fact usually becomes community knowledge through the bride's telling her mother (who in any case is standing by to examine her daughter), and thus the bride and her family are protected from the disgrace of an unbloodied sheet for this cause. The bride's family can in such a case allow time for the young husband to demonstrate his virility, even months if they wish, but if he is unable to do so, a disgrace almost as great as unchastity in a girl is weighed upon his family for having produced a son who is not a 'man'. The *mahr* or bride-price is forfeited by the groom as compensation for the wrong done to the girl and her family.

If the truth were told a high percentage of Arab wives are among the world's most embittered and frigid, while the Arab male is among the world's unhappiest husbands. In his supreme effort to ensure marital fidelity the Omani husband in numerous instances has equipped himself with up to four unresponsive ice-cold mates whose genital organs have been deliberately mutilated by having the clitoris cut out along with its foreskin, and in extreme cases the sanguinary ablation of the *labia minora* as well, thus eliminating in most instances all female pleasure and sensation during sexual intercourse and, to the self-centred male, any possible desire in his females to indulge in extra-marital relations. Tradition does not allow total excision in south-west Arabia among the Shafi'i.

It may be necessary to explain, that among the nations of the east, the passion for sexual intercourse is considered in a tenfold degree more ardent in women than in men; and it was in order to abate, or moderate as far as possible the violence of this passion, that Sarah determined to make a slight abscission from the pudenda of the favourite bondmaid (young Hajar).[12]

The survival of slavery and existence of concubinage in parts of the Arabian Peninsula is to a large extent due to the specific need to cohabit with non-circumcised, sexually keen women, who echo the man's desire and derive pleasure from love-making; this demand is filled by the slave women who hold that Caucasians are more virile than Negroes. In Arabia the negro woman is very popular as a concubine in the summer, for her black skin keeps surprisingly cool, while that of an Arab does not.

A slave girl who has been brought up by her master from her childhood in his house is never bought as a virgin, even if she has not had a situation before. Her owner or some relation of her mistress deflowers her as soon as she has reached a suitable age (twelve to fourteen), and the buyer would look upon it as suspicious if that had not been done.

After sexual intercourse, which is described in the East as the 'ecstasy of eternity', the one ennobling 'abiding glory of paradise', both parties, in Oman, have an ablution to the fullest extent available water or sand allows, for all Biblical and subsequent Muslim precepts governing sexual intercourse view all sexual functions as resulting in ritual uncleanliness. During her menstrual period the woman is considered unclean or dangerous or both and must forego intercourse for a full seven days and nights. When questioned the Prophet Mohammed replied, 'It is an illness, so let women alone at such times and go not in unto them till they are cleansed.' As an extreme, women during menstruation must leave the home and live in a menstruation hut or tent for the entire period, returning to their homes only after having been purified. (One might speculate on the emotional, social and physical salutary effects of these monthly absences). Or they are permitted to remain in the home subject to numerous restrictions. Among other things the menstruating woman must sleep on the floor or on a low bed, must have no sex relations with her husband, must not even touch him or his bed, and should not prepare any meals or enter a home wherein there is an ill person or woman in labour.[13]

Throughout the thirty-day annual fast of Ramadhan the Moslem is free to make love between sunset and sunrise only, never during the day, and the act is sinful at night unless followed by water ablutions. If water is unavailable, loose earth or sand is used as a poor substitute.

After the baby arrives, the childbearer and now child-suckler, in her happy interval of glorious triumph if the child be male, is considered temporarily unclean. No man is allowed to taste his wife's milk, as this would be unlawful; for a woman to sample her own milk would disgrace her in the eyes of the husband concerned. Certain Omani communities follow the Levitical prohibition on intercourse for a period of forty days if the child is a boy and eighty days (greater impurity) if a girl is born. According to an early tradition the Prophet once instructed Ali as follows: 'A woman, when she gives birth, goes apart with the child. Her shame is open thus, and then goes together again when the child has come forth and then the angel Gabriel waves his wings over her and it closes.' In going in unto his wife an Arab should say, 'In the name of God, the merciful and compassionate, I go to my wife to put out the fire of my desire; to prevent myself from wanting other women for the glory of God and I pray to God that I will get a male child.' The Prophet, who never once divorced a wife, has said, 'That which is lawful but disliked by God is divorce.' There is a tradition that Abdullah bin Umar divorced his wife when she was having her monthly period. Her father reported the matter to the Prophet, who became very upset and ordered that Abdullah should revoke his divorce and wait until his wife was finished menstruating, after which he was free to do as he liked. According to traditional Muslim practice in socially backward areas, a man may divorce his wife twice and after each occasion take her back again, but not after the strong, extremely inconvenient and irrevocable third time (triple formula) until another has consummated a marriage with her and divorced her.

No exact figures are available for the divorce rate in Omani communities. The formula for divorce in ancient Arab times was, 'Thou are to me as the back of my mother.' To divorce his wife, the Omani must repeat *talaq*, 'divorcement', three times before witnesses (without assigning any cause), signifying that he is through with her and the bonds are severed; that is all there is to it. The post-patriarchal Biblical written 'bill of divorcement' (Deut. 24: 1) establishing for the woman a kind of legal status and freeing her to marry another finds no parallel among the more primitive nomads of Arabia, but written certifications of divorce are otherwise frequently used, though not considered essential.

It should be pointed out that while divorce is easily effected in most parts of Arabia, it frequently involves considerable loss of face to the man as well as to the woman. This is particularly true among the townspeople and villagers of Palestine and Syria, and in these areas the divorce rate would compare very favourably with that of the United States and Europe.

Quranic law makes divorce a financial burden for the man; thus the only chance the Omani wife has is when the husband is too poor to afford losing one half of his wife's bride-price. In theory this half is held back at the time of marriage; in practice, however, the actual divorce payment is a matter of agreement between the parties. The divorced woman must wait three months under Quranic law (in pre-Islamic practice she could marry the next day and if pregnant the child belonged to the new husband) to see if she is with child before remarrying; a widow, four months and ten days. Thus, in Oman, many women by the age of thirty-five have had between six and a dozen husbands. Arab lore tells us of a certain Umm-Kharijah in the days of Mohammed who distinguished herself with forty husbands from twenty different tribes. If a desirable suitor came to her and said, 'Will you marry me?' she would answer, 'It is a marriage', and without any further formality or delay the marriage would be consummated.[14]

Trial marriages are practised to this day in southern Arabia. For example the Saiars once told Harold Ingrams 'that they gave their girls to anyone who wanted them. After about a couple of months' trial the man might marry the girl, otherwise she would be returned with thanks and without ill-feelings.'[15]

Usually no disgrace is attached to the divorced women, and there is little or no unmarried problem among the ladies of Oman. However, hanging over a woman's entire insecure married existence is the black cloud of fear of being thrown back on the open matrimonial market in second, third, or fourth-hand condition encumbered with children and with her charms faded; it is not a pleasant picture, for divorce has become an instrument for destruction not construction. A wife who returns to her parents and refuses her husband gives back his gifts and is divorced. The Prophet taught that 'Every woman who asketh to be divorced without cause, the fragrance of Paradise is forbidden her.' Under Islam, all claims to the contrary, the woman does not have equal rights to the privilege of divorce, an inequality which has had the consequence of gravely lowering the status of women in Islam. Yet in spite of their easy divorce laws, the desert dweller's standard of morality is considered high among the world's societies, with death not barred as punishment for a wife's adultery. Mohammed's son-in-law Ali once imprisoned a confessed adulteress until her child was born; then he dug a pit, into which she was lowered as far as her breasts, and cast the first stone at her.

The startling descriptions of harem[16] life, both in days of yore and in recent times, in some cases have been absolutely true. The less interesting fact is that the institution of the harem as generally pictured in the West is as unknown in Oman, and in most Arab lands, as courtly love in Europe. Plural marriage is the exception among all except the wealthy and is now forbidden by law in some Arab states outside the Arabian Peninsula. The large and carefully guarded harem compound exists only among the wealthy noble class of Yemen, the opulent parvenus of Saudi Arabia, the *nouveaux riches* of Kuwait, and perhaps among oil magnates in one or two other Persian Gulf states. As the number of extremely wealthy is very small indeed, so are the habits of life associated with the class. We may draw a comparison by saying that elaborate harem life in Arabia has been more rare than was luxurious and elegant court life in Europe during its heyday in the eighteenth century. Stories of the harem are as curious and foreign to the modern Lebanese schoolboy as they are to his British or American counterpart – except he knows better where the truth ends.

The Arabs have a saying, 'Dogs will enter paradise before the mother-in-law and daughter-in-law will love one another.' Men cannot live without women and women cannot live without quarrelling; there are exceptions, but they are truly exceptional. An Arab once stated to me a sentiment at one time universal in Arabia: 'What if one of my wives learned to write – she might write to someone who was not her husband.' For 'a woman who is taught to write is like a serpent which is given poison to drink.' *Agila*, 'tethered one', is used in parts of Arabia for a man's wife; the same adjective is used for a shackled camel; here a woman is a docile, almost vegetable-like instrument for pleasure, a factory for procreation always available for the replacement of domestic animals in the field; for the 'female is of all animals the better', say the Arabians, 'save only in mankind.'

Although Mohammed once said, *jannah taht aqdam al-ummahat*, 'Paradise is at the feet of mothers', it is an accepted fact that depending on their social status, with rare exceptions, Arab women are the downtrodden, mindless slaves of their fathers, brothers, and husbands who rule them like tyrants. They bear the babies, carry the loads, cook the food and eat what their men leave behind. The dirty and disagreeable tasks fall to them. This is as true among Bedouin today as ever it was. Whether high born or low, the Bedouin women, even if they have slaves, are all obliged to put up and prepare the tents, to strike and roll them up, and to load and unload them, as is needed; also to attend to all the domestic work, such as collecting wood and dung to cook on; and lastly, to find time as best they can to look after and bring up their children. By twenty-eight the majority I have observed in Oman, Yemen and the former Aden Protectorates are old and worn-out grandmothers, sorrowfully facing an early death from day to day without the slightest security from the ever-present menace of dislodgment through divorce, the indoor sport of Arabia (although the sons usually have great affection for their mothers).

The problem of the status of women (a *badawi* will caress his camel, stroke it and lead it gently, but he would rarely if ever consider offering an arm to his wife), which has steadily declined, places the sincere Muslim reformer in his most embarrassing dilemma; but the feeling against polygamy (wives are an expensive hobby, for a wife means new clothes) is becoming a strong social conviction throughout this 'civilized' twentieth-century world. In all fairness to Mohammed it must be said that he limited polygamy rather than introduced the practice among the Arabs. One is reminded of Solon's words to the Greeks, 'that his laws were not the best that he could devise, but that they were the best that they could receive.'

A regenerated Islam should eventually free itself from patriarchal bondage and eliminate polygamy by authoritative dictum. Orthodox defenders of polygamy (if men and women enjoy equal rights under Islam why not allow polyandry?) argue that Islamic recognition of this state of affairs is superior to the extensive adultery of the West and to corruption by prostitution of the Christian law of monogamy. They forget to mention Islamic sanction and legalization of slave women concubinage (a survival of the militarist days) which maintained the slave trade and that from Islam's birth to the present day prostitution, with its 'circulating beauties' and 'vendors of joy', has been widespread in Muslim society (as in most societies), especially in port cities and coastal towns, though frequently condemned by religious leaders.

Those who defend the Quranic view of women, yet believe that they are not considered chattels (as they were in Britain until 1870), or a mere part of their husband's or father's estate, quote the verse, 'of other women who seem good in your eyes marry but two or three or four and if you still fear that you shall not act equitably then only one.' The Quran's allowance of four wives, based on constant equality, is generally interpreted as a form of enunciation of monogamy and as a virtual prohibition of an excess of one, for the absolute emotional surrender of the heart should be coupled with the surrender of the body; however, this interpretation which illustrates the discrepancy between theory and practice, still leaves the matter open to experiment. Philby's view, expressed to this writer, is simply that the Quran allows four wives and that is that. In his pamphlet *Polygamy and Divorce in Islam*, Mohammed bin Salem Beihani, Imam of the Asqalani mosque in Crater, Aden, suggests that one reason for polygamy was to compensate the man for the seven days of the menstrual period of his wife. Certain Islamic apologists consider 'equity' beyond human power to observe and believe that the Prophet had in view the eventual abolition of plurality of marriage. This is one of the cases in which the first step is everything. The difference between one wife and two is everything; that between four and five thousand is comparatively nothing.

In *Sura 4*, the Quran says, 'Men are the managers of the affairs of women', and further on, 'Those you fear may be rebellious, admonish; banish them to their couches, and beat them.'

Oman and all Arabia will certainly remain among the backward areas of the world just as long as its women are kept ignorant, intellectually starved, secluded and degraded under a permanent seal of subjection. There is still room for affection and love in Arabia, but it is in defiance of the system, and not in consequence of it. There is also room for some drastic improvements relative to the double standard code of morality. The problem of the unmarried pregnant girl in Arabia is much more immediate and drastic, even though forced into this situation by a stronger man against her will. When her condition becomes noticeable it means almost certain death at the hands of her honour-conscious brothers or relatives. Members of my (1951) camel caravan exploring the Wadi al-Ain, a tributary of the Wadi Harib on the Yemen border, were awakened the first night out by a timid feminine voice inquiring for our doctor; upon examination he shook his head sadly for there was nothing to be done, she was too far advanced. It broke our hearts to see this beautiful young girl walk sadly away to a certain and horrible death.

A girl escapes this fate only if there is clear proof that she was forced by a stronger man against her will, in which case he or his family becomes the object of the revenge seekers' vengeance, while the wronged girl looks forward to disgrace and an inferior marriage, if any at all.

Alois Musil observed among the powerful Rwala tribe that 'if the girl cannot rid herself of the Fetus, she presses her lover to marry her at once, but in case he refuses or is absent, she often commits suicide. For should her father or brother find that his daughter or sister is with child, he would coax her on some pretext outside the camp, kill her, cut her body in ten pieces, and then bury them.[17]

One day in 1940 a young Kuwaiti girl's presence in a neighbour's house was reported to her older brother, who without waiting to investigate any present or future misconduct decided to 'wash away the disgrace' and slashed his completely innocent sister's lovely throat from ear to ear and opened her chest, cutting through the trachea, collapsing the lungs and exposing her beating heart. Later, someone shovelled mud and manure through the gaping wound into her chest cavity in a vain attempt to stem the bleeding as she lay on the floor in agony, her dark eyes full of fear, remaining entirely conscious for twenty hours before she died in the Mission Hospital.[18] In the true spirit of intolerance the local immaculate Arab males, overlooking their own varied sexual transgressions, which ranged from adultery to bestiality,[19] and filled to overflowing with self-righteous hypocrisy, were full of wonder and horror at the somewhat heated suggestion of the great missionary, Dr Paul Harrison, who had fought to ease her pain, that the brave brother in question might well have picked on someone his own size and killed the man (in this case there was none) first next time. By far the greatest number of murders in Baghdad – about a hundred weekly, according to a British C.I.D. officer during the Mandate (in the early years of Faisal I) – were murders of sisters by their brothers for an alleged affair with a man, dishonouring her whole family. The offending part of the woman's body was cut out with a knife.

Although as we have seen Mohammed was responsible for putting down the practice of female infanticide, he adopted a method by which all females could be immured for ever in a living grave, by the institution of the *burqa*, the veil. The veil was probably unknown in Oman before Islam, and its adoption in Islamic times was a retrogressive step back into the second millennium B.C. For the institution seems to have been of Assyrian origin, and the Assyrian Code (*c.* 1500 B.C.) makes it clear that the intention of the veil was to show that the woman was a chattel of her husband or her father.[20] For Omanis, the veil, like the harem system, are specifically Islamic institutions.

As described by Burton, 'A man's *sua*, "shame", extends from the navel to his knees; a woman's from the top of the head to the tips of her toes.' The pitiable seclusion of women which wraps them up as a formless bundle and which has not the slightest connection with the basic dogma of Islam, degenerated into the form of black-shrouded enslavement, a walking prison cell or coffin of the living dead which we find today in Oman, where from this sack of humanity only the hands and feet are to be seen, and the eyes which look out from the two slits in the black mask.

Mohammed once said, 'A woman who believes in God and the Day of Judgment may not travel a whole day and night's distance without escort and no woman may be left alone with a man without a chaperon'; thus the Prophet truly understood the morals or lack of them among his companions.

Were I a woman in Oman I personally would infinitely prefer to be a slave girl than a 'free' Arab woman, even though she is usually placid, like a well-fed cow. As opposed to a circumcised, helpless and hopeless, closely-veiled lifetime of rigid physical and moral confinement sinking in the sloth of ignorance and eclipse, the unimprisoned slave girl is relatively free, for she walks unveiled, where she pleases, with whom she pleases. In areas of the Oman interior I have noticed, however, that women merely cover their chin and mouth as a substitute for the veil. Indeed, the British explorer W. G. Palgrave, reporting a visit to Sohar in 1863, claims to have observed what I have rarely seen in coastal Oman. 'But in Oman the mutual footing of the sexes is almost European, and the harem is scarcely less open to visitors than the rest of the house; while in daily life the women of the family come freely forward, show themselves, and talk like reasonable beings, very different from the silent and muffled status of Nejed and Riad.'[21] Palgrave's description more truly applies to Central Oman where one of the most distinctive features is the freedom with which women approach and greet strangers, and the almost complete absence of any face veil or *burqa*.

On Friday afternoon 25 September 1959 history was made after centuries of repression and inertia, when six thoughtful, courageous Adeni Arab girls, faces unveiled, strolled into the editorial office of the *Aden Chronicle* and stated that they had abandoned the senseless system of purdah after a meeting of thirty Arab women who resolved to shun purdah 'as a painful sore', for good. This unheard-of event was followed by selfish and hysterical Adeni male outbursts, expressions of sex-distrust and male domination; their theme was that 'Women commit a sin by abandoning purdah, let their male relatives stop this offence against religion.' Or, in other words, artificial controls are needed to protect female virtue in Aden owing to the lack of male virtue. There had been similar masculine outcries when women in other Moslem lands had endeavoured to emancipate themselves. Thus woman's present degraded status, lack of freedom and education, solely the result of man's selfish tyranny and lack of self control, is attributed to the teachings of religion. The fact is that the practical everyday Omani attitude is that the necessary, degraded, lower-planed evil called woman, inferior and uninformed, is intellectually ill-endowed compared to a man, being weak of reason and open to flattery and deceit and created solely to serve his demands, for sensuality and procreation. Under Islam the value of a woman's testimony is half a man's and the testimony of the woman is inadmissible. On the other hand, it should be remembered that the first convert to Islam was a woman and the first martyr was a woman.

The Omanis, like the men of most Arab lands, have shackled and degraded their own women, and by denying them the chance to live in the world, even the narrow world of an Omani community, they have denied them self-respect as we, in the West, understand it. It has been truly said that the respect in which women are held by the men of a community is in direct proportion to that community's level of culture, and that that level rises with the status of women. But this is a lesson which Oman has yet to learn.

9

THE BADU

*The red sands – The tribal tie – Fratricide as a way to sheikhdom
Badu raiders – Pride in hardship – The Bani Hilal – Amiable lies
Driving down Wadi Jizi*

> 'In that desert dwell many of the Arabians who are called
> Bedouins, ... who are people full of evil conditions ... and
> they are strong and warlike men . . . and they are right
> felonious and foul and of a cursed nature. . . .'
>
> *Sir John Mandeville*

To return, after that excursion into feminism, to our own movements.
Our next object was the ruins of Safwan, north-west of Buraimi on
the edge of the desert, in a region of *mirh* and *ghaf* scrub. Our friend
and guide Sheikh Abdullah was certainly doing his best, but I had to
point out to him that the remnants of buildings to which he led us
were certainly not more than 150 years old. But from here on the
desert scenery was beautiful in the extreme, with high dunes composed of the characteristic red of the great sands. Once you have
seen it you never forget the sight.

Suddenly our lead vehicle stopped dead, for Jama had fallen asleep
and hit his head hard against the wheel. I should have relieved him
earlier. Soon it was my turn to get us stuck, followed by Bill who
slid sideways down a steep dune. While everyone dug and pushed I
finally drove the vehicle out, with Bill on the camera. At the time
Sheikh Abdullah remarked, 'If we were all being killed no one would
be allowed to die until Wendell got his movie.'

At sunset we camped in a deep hollow in the sand. The Sheikh
set up his personal tent for our exclusive use. Next he placed five
guards to stand watch for three hours at a time throughout the night.
Jama soon moved into the Sheikh's tent to cook dinner, as a sharp

wind had arisen. After dinner I invited Sheikh Abdullah and those of
his men not on guard to join us for fruit and coffee. In the meantime
Bill set up his Strobe lights for night colour pictures using an f/3.5
Rolleiflex with a Zeiss Planar lens, while Jama spread out the new
Omani rugs on the sand. Using bedrolls as cushions, we sat in a semi-
circle for a night film, a difficult operation in the best of circumstances
First, all the headlights were trained on one spot, along with al
available lanterns. Then Bill set the Bolex at twelve frames a second
and asked us to move at half speed. Whatever was going through the
Sheikh's mind relative to all of this he was too much a gentleman to
let us know.

Although in desert etiquette it is usually considered a gross
breach of courtesy to ply one's guest with questions about himself
on this occasion Sheikh Abdullah proved most co-operative and
explained that he was born twenty-nine years ago and is today
Paramount Sheikh of the Bani Kaab tribe, whose area stretches from
the Wadi Qur to the Wadi Jizi. The Bani Kaab are both a settled
and nomadic (*shawawi*) tribe. There are two kinds of *badu* (desert
nomads) in Oman: the *shawawi* are those who dwell on or near the
mountains, as the Awlad Awamir; and the true *badu* who live in the
sands or near the sands, as the Al-Wahibah. One never hears the
pronunciation 'Bedouin' in Arabia, and the singular *badawi* has been
mostly supplanted by the plural (or collective) *badu* in Oman. The
Arabs explain that they are so called because they live in the *badiyah*
'desert'. Sheikh Abdullah's tribe, which is Sunni and belongs to the
Ghafiri faction, refers to the Saudi Wahhabis as *ahl al-gharb*, 'people
of the West', and still relate with bitterness how their tribal chief
Ali bin Said was carried off in chains by the Wahhabis to Riyadh
where he was held a prisoner for seven long years, during the second
half of the nineteenth century. Like the majority of well-bred Arabs
the Sheikh had a characteristic quiet noble dignity of manner, with a
ready smile showing good teeth. He possessed fine ascetic features
and was neither robust nor aggressive – just agreeable, extremely
proficient and devoted to his King. As 'father of his tribe' he has
little or no privacy, for always all of his actions and words are seen
and overheard and his time is always on demand. In spite of his regal
dignity and prerogatives of position he remains at all times generously

accessible to all his people and is free from the least taint of arrogance. The original meaning of the word *sheikh* is simply 'old man', but tribal usage has largely eliminated the implication of veneration for old age. I myself was made a sheikh in my thirtieth year when adopted into the Bal-Harith tribe by Sherif Hussein bin Ahmed and Sheikh Ali bin Munasar.

In a personal, one-man tribal administration the sheikh is accepted and regarded as 'the first among equals' and is of necessity extremely sensitive and responsive to the popular will and opinion of his tribal community; otherwise, his tenure of office may be abruptly terminated. As Raphael Patai has put it, 'The authority of the tribal *shaykh* rests not on force, which as a rule does not stand at his disposal, but on the esteem, renown and prestige he enjoys.' A single false step may compromise him; a series might prove fatal.

Here each intensely independent, incorrigible individual forms a link in the tribal chain, and innate and binding loyalty to one's tribe is the number one essential to the maintenance of the collective fighting strength and organic unity of that tribe and forms the ideal behind *badu* law and custom: 'No worse calamity could befall a Bedouin than the loss of his tribal affiliation, for a tribeless man is practically helpless. His status is that of an outlaw beyond the pale of protection and safety.'[1]

As his village of Mahdha does not come under the Wali of Buraimi, Sheikh Abdullah is both Wali and Sheikh, with thirty-two villages under his control, including twenty-four lesser sheikhs and approximately 5,000 Bani Kaab tribesmen.

Twenty-two years before Sheikh Abdullah's father, Salim bin Diyan, had been praying in the mosque on Friday as was his custom. As Sheikh Salim finished he stood up, to be shot down in cold blood by his own brother Maadid who fired through the open window. Maadid had disregarded the Prophet's pronouncement that 'The first judgment that God will pass on man at the Day of Resurrection will be for murder.' Usually murder within the tribe is not an offence against tribal society as such, but only against the murdered man's family. In numerous instances the crime is offset by a payment of blood-money accepted in atonement by the next of kin (kinship among the Arabs, in the larger sense, means a share in the common blood of the tribe). On this occasion the Bani Kaab tribesmen accepted the murderer as Sheikh. There is nothing remarkable about this: among certain tribes assassination by no means excludes the assassin from the sheikhdom, but in Oman it was, in the past (the present Sultan would refuse to recognize a murderer as Sheikh), necessary to get the Sultan's recognition. In the former Aden Protectorates, assassination was quite a normal method of removing a sheikh, the removal being carried out by his would-be successor.

The tradition is an ancient one, of course. Fratricide seems predestined in many tribes as witnessed by the Bani Yas and Bani Ali. Among the sheikhs of Abu Dhabi over half have been murdered, four by their own brothers. 1845 was the choice year of assassination in Abu Dhabi. In July, Khalifah bin Shakhbut and his brother Sultan were treacherously assassinated by a usurper, Isa bin Khalid. Two months later this assassin was assassinated by Dhiyab bin Isa, to be followed by the killing of the assassin's assassin by Khalid bin Isa, the son of his victim. But one need not go beyond the immediate past for ample illustrations of the art of political assassination in the Arab world – within the last few years numerous illustrious figures have fallen, several of whom were the author's friends. Kings – Abdullah of Jordan, Yahya of Yemen and Faisal of Iraq; Presidents – Husni az-Zaim of Syria; Royal Princes – Abdullah and Abbas of Yemen; Prime Ministers – Ahmed Maher Pasha and Nuqrashi Pasha of Egypt, Muhsin al-Barazi of Syria; Riyadh as-Sulh of Lebanon and Hazza al-Majali of Jordan.

To return to the case we were considering, six years after the murder Sheikh Abdullah's cousin, Ubaid bin Juma, personally killed the murderer and became the ruling Sheikh. From 1952 onward he was a traitor to the Sultan and in 1955 was foolishly allowed to escape by the British authorities (to Saudi Arabia) together with Sheikh Saqr bin Sultan of the Naim. On 13 June 1948, Ubaid bin Juma had written to Sultan Said bin Taimur: 'Your esteemed letter reached me, and I understood it and obeyed your order. . . . We are Your Majesty's subjects, and we have no way except the way in which you direct us. The organization of everything is in your hands.

. . I shall let Your Majesty know all the facts which will confirm our obedience and subservience to you. There is nothing here which had been contrary to your wishes.'

In May 1952, approximately three months before the Saudi incursion into Buraimi, this same Ubaid bin Juma wrote to Ibn Saud: 'We are your subjects and our territories are yours, as we have explained to H.H. the Crown Prince, to H.H. Amir Faisal, and to yourself, We rely on God and after him on H.M. the King (Ibn Saud). . . . We are your subject and servants, taking refuge with God and after Him with you, and awaiting your orders. . . .'

Throughout South Arabia the essence of tribal nobility has been the art of war and the destruction of one's enemies. Life is cheap here and the spice of that life is raiding, with everyone for himself and Allah for all. As the *badu* himself said, and in truth still feels, 'Deny me the right to raid and you deny me the breath of life!' The early Umayyad poet al-Qutami summed up the guiding principle of the *badu*, 'Our business is to make raids on the enemy, on our neighbour and on our brother, in case we find none to raid but a brother.'[2] At times great distances are traversed in these raids with success in the main based on the element of surprise. Any spoil which is found in the possession of a defeated raiding party becomes the property of the victors. Camels will only be returned to their original owners if the victors were the earlier victims of the intercepted party. The *badu* like quick results and are not noted for their great tenacity of purpose or perseverance. If the hoped-for booty does not come easily, they rapidly lose their confidence and may well abandon the effort for another day.

A noted and successful raider is received with high honour, for here in the desert murder, robbery and looting as part of the *ghazu*, 'raid', are much esteemed; the national sport of South Arabia is raiding, the father of the blood-feud, and anyone's property is yours if you can get it and keep it.

An unknown pagan Omani poet once recited, 'Hearts are cured of rancour – sickness, whether men against us war, or we carry death among them: dying, slaying, healing come.' Although the Prophet proclaimed from Mount Arafat near the close of his mission that from then on all blood-feuds should cease, and cases of murder be tried by him or his lieutenants, they did not cease. Little blood-shed is usually involved in these raids, the main objective of which is to steal as many camels as possible; however, blood still calls for blood, revenge, attack, counter-attack, plunder and loot, and on occasion casualties are heavy, for quarter is rarely given. The most common disease of the raider is the bullet wound, with more re-covering than one would expect. Mohammed forbade the killing of women and children, and at only one major period under Islam have the lives of women and children been sacrificed on raids, and this was during the early days of the fanatical Saudi Ikhwan. With this exception, the rule of the inviolability of women and children[3] has been strictly adhered to in the Arabian deserts, where the gangster methods of America and Europe are foreign to the sporting killings of the Arab who introduced the art of *muruah*, 'manliness' (i.e. chivalry), into Europe.

In many ways the *badawi*, who remains the Arab *par excellence*, affords an outstanding example of the survival of the fittest, of man's ability to adapt himself to nearly impossible hostile conditions im-mersed in nature and to survive on the margin of subsistence. Born in a cruel, precarious setting of incomparable filth (in spite of the traditional cleanliness of the desert) and disease, in a miserable shelter from the driven sand, blinding glare, scorching heat or biting cold, the squealing, defiant son of the sands arrives despite the 'help' of the most primitive and unnecessarily brutal midwifery. He is 'baptized' in a semi-bath of camel urine into the sacred fellowship of the desert; his tiny form is swathed in a rough plaster of camel dung; he survives to endure his allotted place, on unsteady legs, among the countless fleas, scorpions, ticks and flies, distinguished from the ever-present goats and sheep by the possession of a single dirty rag covering.

Although desperate hunger and thirst stalk as grim shadows be-side him, the poorest and leanest *badawi*, who has in truth conquered poverty by his indomitable spirit in steadfastly meeting nature's harshness face to face, proudly regards himself as the salt of the earth and considers no man his peer. 'Thousands of ladders do not reach his head.' He is content with his starving lot and feels in his heart that his blood alone is the best. To him as heaven's favourite, the outside world with its clashing empires has little or no meaning and therefore little or no real existence. His thoughts 'are bounded by the Present, and over that Present broods God in His encircling might', for without God he can think nothing, say nothing, do nothing. This constant endless struggle in an environment of disease and raiding in the harsh, barren, waterless, desert has made the wandering Arab what he is – an unfettered, unstable, high-strung thoroughbred.

'Oh Lord,' prayed a Bedouin, 'have mercy upon me and upon Mohammed but upon no one else besides.'[4]

This desert dweller, graced with a keen sense of humour and great dignity in repose, faces a life of abstinence and privation without security, unflinchingly; and his misfortunes with resignation and austerity; he is above all things a child of nature ruled by his *sharaf* or 'honour'. With him honour and existence are identical; separate them and he no longer exists as an Arab. Next to his personal honour and exalted self-esteem, he values his family honour above life itself, and the good name of his wife and sister. If one of them strays from the beaten path, death is her reward.

The blackest crime to the *badawi* is to betray a companion. His loyalty, courage and disinterested self-sacrifice for his friends are legion; for his enemies pitiless, relentless ferocity is his code, as his emotions lie always just under the surface. His character is based on virility, a hungry, thirsty existence of extreme liberty, with both tribal war and peace ephemeral. His moral code is cruel, practical and elemental in the extreme. Strength and force are admired and respected; any sign of weakness is despised. Sacred however is the law of sanctuary where the protectors are honour-bound to afford asylum and protection when appealed to, and as observed by Herodotus 'the Arabs keep pledges more religiously than almost any people.' The very finest bit of advice on how to deal with Arabs was given years ago by King Ibn Saud to my one-time opponent but subsequent good friend, the former Governor of Aden, Sir Tom Hickinbotham. 'Be strong, when you are strong then you can be just and when your strength is overwhelming you can afford to be generous, but first and foremost it is strength which is of paramount importance.'[5]

I have found the *badu* to be most courteous, thoughtful, enjoyable, unsubtle, unquenchably cheerful companions. Alert, lean and eternally boyish they are capable of strong personal attachment. The *badawi* is not the casual, careless, haphazard individual that he appears to be at first acquaintance, for in his own way he guards against most eventualities; however, to his conservative nature all change is abhorrent; and he can never be driven. He judges everything only as it affects himself. To him flattery is an everyday art to be applied by verbal caresses and deception, and he will eagerly 'kiss the hand he can't bite and pray that it will be broken'.

He is equipped with an agile mind; his mental processes are simple and direct, supplying him with definite, concrete conclusions, for his make-up has little sentiment, little romance, a world of dignity plus a consuming avarice with the logical outlook of a cynical materialist. In dealing with strangers his first impulse is to lie, for suspicion is his dominant characteristic. His second impulse is to profit by his deception in every way conceivable. He is often a hero, more often a devil, but never a slave. Aristocratic, he is democratic in his social contacts, self-assured and self-satisfied.

Since all human freedom must be viewed relatively, there is nothing absolute about 'being free as the Arab of the desert', for this desert dweller must of necessity follow the rain to adequate pasture or he and his flock will become extinct. The key to his half-starved existence is restlessness, for he is a parasite on his camel and regards physical labour as degrading and not to be indulged in by free men. However, he will never shirk a community task and always noisily volunteers for anything that imposes a hardship on himself. One rarely upsets a *badawi* by refusing his well thought-out and often shameless request; for one's refusal is all again in the will of God. Eternally grasping for a dollar, he is equally eternally generous with his last swallow of water or mouthful of food. 'You are a stranger, he has never seen you before, he will never see you again, yet he unstintingly gives you that of which he has dire need himself.'

No one excels the *badawi* as a host, and his manners are of the very best; however, at the slightest provocation his renowned dignity and restraint dissolve into impulsive, undignified, unrestrained hysteria. It is the easiest thing imaginable for the *badawi* with the clearest of conscience to combine his lethal weapons with an ultra-inflammable temper, fly into a passionate, wild, incoherent, shouting rage, steal and murder, ascribing all to the will of God, forgetting the words of his Prophet, 'When one of you getteth angry, he must sit down, and if his anger goeth away from sitting, so much the better, if not let him lie down.' A remorseful *badawi*, whose 'temper is at the beginning a madness, at the end a regret', can be touchingly overcome with grief at the accidental shedding of innocent blood.

In his desert folklore the Arab loves to ascribe all mysterious or relic objects to the legendary Bani Hilal; an ancient tribe (some sections still remaining in Hadhramaut) whose traditional hero was one Abu Zaid, the Robin Hood of Arabia. In the eleventh century some 200,000 fierce nomadic Bani Hilal streamed westward erupting out of Egypt like hungry wolves. With their wives and families they spread evil and death along coastal North Africa, as they systematically overran, destroyed and pillaged every building and village encountered, an event leading to the total destruction of the old Romano-Punic agriculture of North Africa. To the Bani Hilal, each man of whom was given a camel and a gold piece for the campaign, home was a tent and any more durable structure an abomination.[6]

It is certainly true that as the world's number one exponent of individualism the Arab *badawi* does not always appreciate the Western concept of the blessings of civilization. As the unfettered master of his actions he regards his noble qualities as derived from the tent, his nursery, and the wide desert the only residence worthy of a man. Co-operative social enterprises are usually a total loss from the start. There is an Eastern saying that those who work with the Arabs 'either get to like them or get like them'. In many instances the Bedouin is more the 'Father of the Desert' than the 'Son of the Desert', for he is master and author of destruction and of the art of creating and sustaining a sun-scorched treeless desert waste, through his raiding and tribal strife. The lack of central stable government in

Arabia has been the principal cause of the absence of co-operative development projects, and I have indicated this by suggesting that raiding and tribal strife be blamed, rather than laziness; it has not been so much the total lack of energy, but rather the unproductive expenditure of it.[7]

This, then, was the kind of society we were in the midst of that night as we slept on the sands outside the Buraimi villages. Before dawn, it rained on and off. Bill was out at 5.00 a.m. to photograph the sunrise on the dunes; however, it was a wan and sickly morning, for the sky was cloudy, making it difficult to obtain the best results. Early morning or late afternoon is always the best time for picture-taking in the desert, for then the long shadows are given full play and weird sand effects are obtained.

By noon we had passed Sheikh Abdullah's home of Mahdha and soon entered the Wadi Jizi which was eventually to lead us back to Sohar. The mountains on all sides were composed of fantastic limestone formations – many turned up on end. This was known as the land of Magan to the ancient Sumerians. Sumerian copper contains a certain percentage of nickel, and analysis of copper ores from Oman, Sinai, Western Persia and Asia Minor show that only Oman copper has nickel in the same proportion.

At our mid-afternoon rest stop Bill fired off a few expert rounds with his .300 Weatherby Magnum. Talib wanted to fire our Thompson sub-machine gun so Bill placed it on semi-automatic. After ten spaced shots Talib was not satisfied so he put it on full automatic and went right over backwards with a burst of ten. All of our *badu* eagerly joined in the fun and it was remarkable to see what really poor shots they were. Surprisingly, I could outshoot several of them using my single-action Colts against their rifles. Experience has taught me that the majority of *badu* do not have the patience or self-discipline required to become really good shots. Occasionally you find an exception who is outstanding, but rarely.

At 4.20 in the afternoon we arrived at Jabal Kumur. To our left was this high isolated mountain crowned with a round watchtower flying the Sultan's red flag. On the right the Sultan kept his Army

Post situated within a delectable green oasis of many palm trees. Here maidenhair and wild flowers abound, and millet, corn, lentils, mangoes, sesame and cotton thrive under the shade of the palm. Here the Omani ploughs with a real colter of iron fitted to a heavy frame and securely braced to an upright handle of three bars set at right angles; this is a vast improvement over the crooked, sharp-pronged stick still employed in certain other areas of Arabia. The life-giving mountain springs of this region are kept alive by the rains. These springs flow right out onto the surface, where the water is carefully channelled to the greedy oasis whose liquid requirements seem inexhaustible. This is the happiness of the Arab: 'Green trees, sweet water and a kind face'; these make his garden. An Oman mountain oasis may be several miles in length as it borders a narrow *wadi* but its width is rarely over half a mile. The Arabs truly believe in the *jannat 'adn*, 'the garden of Eden', as a land of paradisical oases which has been likened to a tapestry through which gleams a silver thread.

In the distance near the centre of our view lay an impressive fortress. Extensive ruins, similar in aspect and probable age to Falaj as-Suq, occurred part way up to the mountain. I was far more attracted, however, to the double *falaj* system filled to overflowing which cut across the base of the Jabal Kumur to our left. These mountain *falajs* are different from the tunnelled systems of the plain. They run from their source along the side of the *wadi* bank in a gentle descending surface conduit with gravitational run-offs at spaced intervals, allowing limited irrigation on the slopes.

Bill wanted to camp here for the night, but I had just been assured by Sheikh Abdullah that we could make it down Wadi Jizi all right. This was a sad mistake. The *wadis* in this part of the world are the true arteries of life, the circulatory systems of Oman, and they become watercourses or rivers after a heavy rain and on occasion raging torrents which reach the sea. Only the largest are perennial, the majority afford but intermittent pools of water. In this instance Wadi Jizi was not only full of massive quantities of boulders but of water as well. For the next two hours Sheikh Abdullah ran forward in our headlights attempting to find a passable route through the rock-strewn *wadi*.

My low-range gear kept giving trouble and several times I hung my Land Rover up in the air. By 8.30 p.m. we had covered a mere ten and a half miles after two and a half hours of driving. Poor Sheikh Abdullah felt very bad because of our difficulties. He kept encouraging us onward because he thought that was what we wanted, for many an Arab is so anxious to avoid causing any feeling of disappointment that he will lie optimistically even though he knows that the real truth will soon be apparent; he feels that any delay in the discovery of the actual situation is for the best; in truth 'the tongue has no bones, you can turn it in which way you please'.

Bertram Thomas believed 'one Bedu in ten is a good guide, one in fifty a reliable informant.' The desert Arab usually related time in terms of distances; such-and-such a place is 'a day's journey by camel', equalling approximately twenty miles; the Western minute and hour has no meaning for him. Although always observant and never a daydreamer, his mind is not distinguished for precision or accuracy and the exaggerated information he gives you is rarely twice the same within the hour. Actually the faithful appear to love to deceive the poor mapmaker who must check and re-check every place name over and over. As noted by Sir Percy Cox, 'The question of topographical names among Arabs is always a difficult one; it often happens that different communities know the same features by different names.'[8] I have done my best with regard to the localities encountered, first checking with Sheikh Abdullah and later with the Sultan, but I quite agree with Philby, when he says in his *The Land of Midian*, p. 89: 'The vagaries of Arabian nomenclature in the mouths of different guides are the bane of the Arabian explorer.'

Bill finally asked if he, Sheikh Abdullah, would drive on if we were not with him. His immediate reply was *abadan*, 'not at all', that he would never have driven at night if we had not been there. That settled that, and we camped at Suhailah, a broad area in the wadi next to the river. While the rest of us tried to sleep in the freezing cold with all clothes on, our Arabs were quite content to huddle around their camp-fire, the delight of the *badu*, talking and gossiping throughout the long night, for the dominant recreation of the *badu* has always been conversation. They love to reminisce endlessly. Lack of sleep never seems to worry them. It is difficult for the *badu* to adjust after the deadly summer has passed, for he is little prepared physically to endure cold and he actually prefers hot weather. It was obvious the next morning that had we not stopped of our own accord, the wadi would have done the job for us. On two occasions we had to rescue each other with ropes tied to the trucks. Our average speed was one or two miles an hour, and we had time to note, on the right side of the wadi at Magham al-Kalba, the remains of another city with several *falajs* in use and in ruins. This part of Oman is certainly characterized by elaborate water systems and by ruined cities, none of great antiquity. At noon our fight against boulders, sand and water came to an end; by this time none of us believed in the old Arab saying 'Running water maketh the heart glad.' We gratefully left the floor of the *wadi* passing the pair of remarkable water-towers observed during our first two days of orientation. We had conquered Wadi Jizi.[9] After Falaj as-Suq it was only a matter of an hour or so beyond the horseshoe-shaped tombs to Sohar.

10

SOHAR TO DHOFAR

Archaeology at Sohar – No ancient city – Lush Dhofar
The Qara Range – Lake Darbat – The four tribes of
the Qara – Circumcision – Pagan vestiges – Dietary laws

During our absence Ray had kept a full crew excavating at Sohar.
On the day we bid goodbye to Sandy at Sharjah he had opened a
third area fifteen feet square on the inland slope of the main mound,
somewhat south of the centre of the city. It was directly on the
opposite side of the mound from the Customs House, located next
to the beach, which served as our expedition headquarters. This excavated square was some 150 yards inside the ancient west gate of
the city wall, which has nearly all collapsed except for the brickwork
of the arch. Although excavation went through nearly fifteen feet of
accumulated clay and debris, beach sand was reached without the
discovery of objects earlier than about the tenth century. A series of
hard surfaces, probably the floors of huts, were found in the upper
three feet. The lowest of these surfaces had several large jars buried
up to the brim, like jars (of a type known as a *hubb* both in Oman
and in Iraq) found at several sites in Iraq. No building remains were
found in the lower levels, although a brick-lined well was disclosed
near the north-east corner of the square. The south part of this square
cut into a large rubbish pit full of ash, sherds, and lumps of dark-
coloured glass or glaze. This indicated that a glass or pottery factory
had existed nearby, though it did not extend into the excavated area.

Although our allotted time was about up, Ray and I agreed to
make one more attempt to find the ancient city of Sohar, if such a
city ever existed. We decided to take the unusual step of working
two successive shifts, the first eight hours beginning at dawn and
the second eight hours in the evening and extending into the night.

There was some difficulty initially in getting work started in the first light of dawn, as many of the workmen lived at a half-hour's walk from the site and, without clocks, had no way of knowing when the dawn was coming and when they should wake up and set out for work. This fourth and final area was dug just above the present *suq*, in a space comprising the highest part of the mound. Nearly twenty-four feet of Islamic occupation rested on beach sand. Quantities of sherds of the famous 'Persian' blue-green glazed ware (mostly eleventh to thirteenth centuries) were found in this square as elsewhere at Sohar, but nothing suggesting a pre-Islamic occupation was uncovered.

Potsherds are truly the archaeologist's 'Index Fossil' and being impervious to chemical changes have endured as an important guide to history, whose significant characteristics are assignable in the 'Library of Civilization'.

Our total pottery finds at Sohar, although they included only three or four complete pieces, were diverse and interesting. They ranged in date from the seventh century A.D. to the nineteenth century and in addition to Islamic wares included a piece of Chinese celadon and Siamese imitations of celadon, as well as the later blue and white porcelains which displaced the celadon wares in the fifteenth century. In addition we found two pieces of European faience with tin glaze from levels later than the sixteenth century.

The earliest sherds from the campaign to be dated with complete certainty belonged to blue-green storage jars. These fragments represent nearly all the characteristic decorations appearing on a well-known example from Susa dating from the seventh or eighth century A.D., but many of our sherds, of this type, seem to be later.

Another distinct group of sherds represents the Persian *sgraffiato* ware, a lead-glazed red earthenware with designs engraved through a white slip. Most of the Sohar examples have a pale green glaze, though light brown also appears. This ware, largely designed in imitation of engraved metalwork, belongs mostly to the twelfth and thirteenth centuries, although it was known several centuries earlier.

Underglaze painted sherds, on cream (almost white) clay, were found in very small quantities. The background of mottled turquoise is decorated with dark purple-brown (almost black) paint in rather broad, scribbly lines; the glaze is almost colourless. Underglaze painted ware gradually replaced the *sgraffiato* ware in the thirteenth and fourteenth centuries.

The most striking non-glazed pottery found at Sohar is a thin, well-levigated pink ware painted in white, brown and rusty red. The most elaborate design consists of an array of stylized flowers alternately done in a solid brown and red outlined in brown on a white field bordered by narrow brown bands, rows of brown dots and one broad red band. The context indicates an early Islamic date. As far as is known at present, this particular type of painted ware has been recorded from no other site, and thus the work at Sohar seems to have produced a completely original discovery.

A flat-bottomed dish with vertical walls affords an example of intricate moulded decoration. Although Islamic in date, this fragment bears the crescent surrounding the solar disc, a symbol common in pagan South Arabian religion. The bowl, of fine cream-coloured ware, is covered with a thin, pale yellow glaze which has been worn away in part. Three similar bowls (but with pale green glaze) were found more than half a century ago by the French expedition to Susa. The Sohar piece can be safely assigned to the ninth, tenth or eleventh century.

A singularly interesting pottery fragment from Sohar is the bottom of a mysterious pear-shaped pottery vessel. J. Sauvaget defended the theory that these objects were used in the Near East as weapons, and, in fact, contained the 'Greek fire', an incendiary naphtha compound (*naft* in Arabic sources) of mediaeval writers. Alternate theories, which would explain their use as exclusively containers for wine (one 'grenade' was discovered bearing a Kufic inscription implying that it was used as a container for wine[1]) or perfume, can also be taken seriously, even though some of the examples from Fustat (Old Cairo) actually contained *naft*, as the great Austrian scholar Adolf Grohmann pointed out some years ago in a letter. The grey ware in question is extremely hard and could not have been easily broken. The fragment is highly polished on the outside, and the inside has broad, shallow horizontal ribbing. Vessels of this type have been found in many parts of the Near East; a particularly varied group comes from Baalbek. Although most known examples are decorated with moulded or incised designs, the Sohar piece is plain, as is a brown one of almost identical form from Baalbek. Most sherds from Baalbek are from the thirteenth and fourteenth centuries, and this must indicate the general range of 'grenades' of this type. Dr. Richard Ettinghausen of the Freer Gallery of Art in Washington, a leading authority on the history of Islamic art and handicraft, has quite recently published evidence[1a] that these enigmatic vessels frequently were used for the transport of mercury, which played a wide role in Islamic medicine and industry.

Thus it was that no unequivocal trace of the postulated pre-Islamic city of Sohar was disclosed by our spade. If there was an early pre-sixth or pre-seventh century occupation at this site it was not substantial and the work of time and sea have removed all evidences.[2] Our findings are in direct conflict with historical traditions concerning the antiquity and former splendour of this one-time capital of Oman. Although there could have been a village in the vicinity, our excavations indicate that Sohar had no great wealth or importance before the third or fourth centuries after the time of the Prophet (ninth or tenth centuries of the Christian era). On the other hand, archaeological results confirm the reliability of the literary sources which describe the flourishing commercial life of the city and of its great size immediately before and after the tenth Christian century. The great *falajs*, or canal systems, which brought water from the mountains apparently belong to this period also.

In short, the findings of our expedition, the first archaeological reconnaissance undertaken in south-eastern Arabia, indicate that some of the past glories of Sohar have been exaggerated and that full-scale excavations in this area would not be as rewarding as originally hoped. At the time of Sohar's greatest dimensions in the Classical Islamic Period its large buildings and houses were never of the magnificence and splendour of a city like Baghdad or Basrah. Sohar, separated from the great civilizations of Mesopotamia, Persia and south-western Arabia by desert and sea, has at times enjoyed trade relations with those superior cultures, but has never matched them or successfully imitated them.

It was satisfactory to have come to a conclusion before being

obliged to close our digging season. Two days before our departure
for Muscat Jama fell on the narrow stone steps leading to our up-
stairs headquarters. At the time he was carrying a can of tomato
juice, two glasses, four knives and forks plus a large pan of boiling
water. All of the water fell on his right arm and shoulder. Like Africans in general and Somalis in particular when disaster overtakes
them, Jama's immediate reaction was 'I am finished.' They are easily
enthused and easily discouraged but they somehow never give up.
Dr Krause treated Jama on the spot with Bacitracin ointment, and
although it was a bad burn he would recover nicely.

Later in the day Sheikh Saqr arrived from Muscat with instructions from the Sultan for Sheikh Abdullah. They were to return
together to Buraimi. I had to smile as Sheikh Abdullah explained to
Sheikh Saqr in detail the advisability of taking the much longer
route via the Wadi Qur and not back up Wadi Jizi, the reversal of
our route.

As a *rukhsah*, 'parting gift', I gave Sheikh Abdullah a Colt .38
revolver plus 250 rounds of ammunition and to each of his men
twenty rupees. This presentation of gifts is an important and essential element of old-fashioned Arab manners, and it is as true today
as it was nearly a century ago when Guarmani noted, 'The gifts
most appreciated are firearms.' Everyone seemed delighted and we
were all more than sorry to see them leave. At our parting meeting
with Sheikh Ali, the Acting Wali of Sohar, I left him with two new
blankets and enough money to employ fifteen men for four days to
fill in the holes we had dug.

In addition to our two Land Rovers, Bill had hired a large lorry
from a local Indian merchant for 350 rupees to carry the bulk of our
equipment to Muscat. We bid a final farewell to Sohar at five in the
afternoon of Friday, 31 January 1958. The day before, I had received
a letter from the Sultan telling in detail of the great damage caused
throughout his country by the heavy rains. I only hoped things
were not as bad as they had been after the cyclonic storms of 1286
and 1325 which spread great havoc and destruction, or more recently
on 4 June 1890, when twelve inches of rain fell in twenty-four hours
throughout Oman, bringing death to some 700 people and uproot-
ing over 100,000 valuable date palms.

If anything, however, the Sultan had understated the seriousness of the present situation; time and again our lorry got badly stuck. Once Bill innocently cut some palm branches to put under the wheels. A moment later an officious-looking local resident rushed over threatening all sorts of things – complaining we were destroying the basic economy of the Batinah Coast. Without an instant's hesitation our own Talib flew into a rage and screamed back, 'Mr Wendell is the Sultan's dear friend – this is the Sultan's personal expedition and we will cut down all of the branches from Sohar to Muscat if it pleases us.'

Our convoy rolled towards Muscat throughout the night. Sometime around five in the morning the big lorry lost several leaves out of its left rear spring. While Bill remained behind with the small Land Rover I took Dr Krause, Ray, Jama, Talib and Ali aboard my Land Rover. Near the Azaiba airfield the road became a solid sheet of water. Although Jama wanted to stay on the road I insisted he drive off to the left out of the water. As usual, Jama was right, for this high ground proved an immediate trap. After wading around in the mud and putting what branches we could find under the wheels I finally had sense enough to head us back into the deep water. With my vehicle half submerged, the engine dead and water in the spark plugs I recalled the Quranic saying, *wa-ja'alna min al-ma kull shay'in hayy*, 'We have made from water everything living.'

After following the beach the long way round, we eventually reached headquarters at Fort Bait al-Falaj. Brigadier Waterfield kindly volunteered to send a Power Wagon back to rescue Bill if he did not turn up by noon. I breathed a welcoming sigh when an hour later Bill and lorry limped into Muscat. I was unkindly gratified to learn that he also had got stuck badly in leaving the road exactly where I had forced Jama to drive. Our former Muscat headquarters was at the moment full of assorted men counting out quantities of potatoes on the floor. This was nothing for Jama, who soon had the place livable. Jama also cleared our new shipment of film from customs. The film was in Bill's name and the Sultan's letter to customs in my name, which to Jama was a fair enough arrangement. The next morning was Sunday and started off with everyone getting his hair cut by a travelling Indian barber. Later in the day our two faithful associates Talib and Abd al-Karim came to bid us goodbye. They were most grateful to receive my parting gifts of money, for they were both on the Sultan's payroll and had expected nothing more. Then in recognition of his excellent cooking Bill raised Ali's salary from 200 to 300 rupees a month.

I asked Ali the Somali how the recent tribal war in Somaliland was progressing and learned that he had lost eight of his family and that one of Jama's family had also been killed. Some years before I had received a brief message from Jama's brother, Osman, 'Please loan me rifle my tribe having argument.' Somalis are very courageous, magnificent walkers and excellent scouts and have always been unenslavable or *hurr*, 'free'. The only time I ever suffered attack in Africa was late one night when a party of Somalis raided my Kenya hunting camp and stole our elephant tusks.

The Sultan was most interested to hear first-hand the details of our Sohar expedition. He very graciously approved my plan to have Bill, Ray, Jama and Ali excavate 640 miles to the west in his Dependency of Dhofar while I returned to New York City. In Dhofar in 1952–3 we had discovered and partially excavated the long-lost 2,300-year-old frankincense capital of Sumhuram and I believed much remained to be done at this site and Ray was just the archaeologist to undertake this work.

The next hour was devoted exclusively to making films in the palace. The Sultan ordered beautiful red Persian rugs to be placed outside his main reception room. Next came two chairs and a low table. His Majesty, being a first-class photographer himself, was fascinated watching Bill's masterful handling of our complex electrically-operated Arriflex movie camera with its 400-foot magazine.

In a relaxed mood the Sultan reflected on the obligations of a monarch himself and applied his conclusions to Oman in this way: 'Certain conditions in Oman inherited from the past are really not my fault, and if I do not have the funds to change these conditions where change is desired, it is still not my fault; if, however, I do have the means and do not improve my people and my country then I should be ashamed.' This follows the Prophet Mohammed's maxim that 'Verily a King is God's shadow upon the earth' and a 'Government is a trust from God.' His Majesty continued, 'If I had not been made a Sultan so early in life I would have been a professional historian, for another six years at a university was my real desire.'

In spite of the fact that the Sultan was brought up with relatively modern ideas he feels he must march forward slowly together with his people, ruling according to his people's ways and means and ensuring the preservation of certain traditions and customs; if he initiated drastic changes too quickly the Sultan feels he would soon become separated from his people. This does not apply to fields of medicine, communication, agriculture and the like where the Sultan insists that the latest developments should be immediately applied in his country as far as financial resources permit.

The Sultan's servants bowed low as they expertly poured coffee through a long bird-beaked ornate Omani pot followed by servings of Muscat *halwah* and a whiff of frankincense – all for the benefit of the picture. As we bid the Sultan goodbye I recalled one of his favourite sayings 'Never pour coffee from another man's pot.'

The land of the Qara people, next visited by the expedition, was something of a mystery in classical times. The writers of Greece and Rome, to whom most of Arabia was largely unknown, knew as a result of their contacts in Syria and Palestine that a large barren desert spread over a great area. They also had heard from seafarers and travellers that all of Arabia was not so. As a result, they divided the whole region, though not too precisely, into Arabia Deserta and Arabia Felix, that is Desert Arabia and Happy (or Prosperous) Arabia. In the second century A.D. Ptolemy listed, in his *Geography*, a third division of Arabia, Arabia Petraea, named after Petra, the capital city of the Nabataean Arabs, whose splendours may still be seen in the southern part of the modern Kingdom of Jordan. Arabia Petraea was the best known in the classical world, Arabia Deserta (the largest of the three areas by far) was uninviting and no one wanted to know much about it; but Arabia Felix (which was a somewhat vaguely located area between Arabia Deserta and the ocean to the south) was intriguing, reputed to be extremely wealthy and productive, the source of myrrh and frankincense.

The Greeks and Romans did not know, as we now do, that the part of Arabia where the trees and the plants grew thickest and tallest, the High Yemen, was not the source of the wealth-bringing spices, nor did most know that while myrrh came from regions immediately to the east of Yemen, the frankincense came from much farther to the east, from the region known at present as Dhofar, which in many ways deserves the epithet 'felix' nearly as much as does Yemen. Dhofar, when compared with most of the rest of Arabia, is a naturalist's paradise of vistas, glades, streams, lakes and waterfalls set in steep mountains clothed for part of the year in luxuriant vegetation with frequent groves of deciduous trees precluding any monotony.

Extreme contrast seems to be a feature of Asia as a whole, and of Dhofar in particular. This 38,000 square mile Dependency, which is part of the Kingdom of Oman, lies 640 sea miles west of Muscat, with a coastline extending approximately 200 miles between the points of land called Ras Darbat Ali and Ras Minji. The eastern boundary of Dhofar runs inland from Ras Minji for more than 170 miles to the north of Ramlat Mughshin. On the north, it runs along and into *ar-rimal*, 'the Sands', for about 200 miles as far west as Ramlat Shuait. Here the boundary turns south across Wadis Shuait, Khawat and Mitan, etc., from there to Jabal Sadakh at Wadi Habrut down to Ras Darbat Ali on the coast. This western boundary line roughly divides the tribes of Dhofar from those of the former Eastern Aden Protectorate.

In 1833 Andrew Crichton wrote, 'The whole of the southern coast is a wall of naked rocks, as dismal and barren as can well be conceived.' This statement was almost true except it overlooked the south-west monsoon (the word monsoon means season) from which Dhofar derives its unique climate, with its inflow of fog and drizzling summer rain yielding five inches on the coast and fifteen inches in the mountains. My first encounter with this monsoon was almost my last. In 1949, after bucking the monsoon winds for ninety minutes my fabric-covered Dragon Rapide was forced down to less than a hundred feet above the sea. At times I would barely make out through the mist and spray the huge vertical cliffs which we were following on our left, their tops invisible in the heavy clouds above. My pilot, whose only navigational instruments were a box compass and a wrist-watch, wisely turned around; we arrived back at Mukalla with our fuel supply at a very low ebb. Here we learned that the R.A.F. Dakota (DC-3) which we had bid goodbye that morning had struck a desolate, obscured hilltop, *Ras Himar*, 'Donkey's Headland', inland from Ras Sajar just west of Salalah with all lives lost. As these air currents which were nearly too much for my Rapide blow north-east along the Somaliland coast, they traverse no area of land (except the island of Socotra) and thus arrive saturated with moisture over Dhofar, causing a green carpet to arise from the earth. If ever this barrier of Somaliland were eliminated, all of south-west Arabia would climatically resemble Dhofar; and if Somaliland extended farther to the east the arid deserts would soon bury sweet-smelling Dhofar under the sands.

Here smiling plenty is found in the very bosom of desolation, for the narrow half-moon shaped coastal plain of Dhofar is an abnormal feature in this otherwise arid South Arabian coast, as it is the only major fertile region between Muscat and Aden. Erosion of alluvial soil from the Qara Mountains plus considerable water close to the surface enables everything that grows to flourish, including alfalfa, cotton, maize and other grains. The gardens produce papaya, chili peppers, melons, sweet potatoes and various vegetables, with coco-nut palms (the only local source of timber) occurring in abundance.

The Qara Mountains rise steeply to the north, limiting the coastal plain to a maximum width of ten miles. On occasion just before sunset these mountains look reddish from the seaward edge of the plain. Within these mountains lovely secluded little lakes and gorges are rich with tropical ferns and running streams. The slopes are honeycombed with fissures and caves partially covered with vegeta-tion. Sycamore, myrtle, white jasmine, and acacia trees abound. Above two thousand feet the undulating hills give a green park-like appearance during and after the rains. The upper reaches support large herds of cattle and are a noted breeding resort for Dhofar camels, which flourish not only on the abundant vegetation but also on a diet of dried bones and fish.

On the west side of Wadi Nihaz I once visited the remarkable cave of Sahaur, containing stalactites, bats, rock pigeons and (if local opinion is correct) assorted *jinn*. It is considered dangerously

unwise to wade in certain lakes for the *jinn* will give one a fever –
Mohammed's followers have never been able to eradicate these late
pre-Islamic cult survivals which one finds in various forms throughout the length and breadth of Islam.

As the Qara range slopes north from drizzle into the drab,
thirsty and greedy *najd*, or steppe, the vegetation becomes sparse and
aridity increases. To the south, hidden within this limestone wonder-
land of waving jungle and well-dressed green rolling meadows, is an
elevated Shangri-la valley, appearing to have been largely filled by
travertine or deposited calcareous tufa and containing beautiful
Lake Darbat. This long, narrow, deep and permanent body of water
curves north into the mountains for some two miles and branches
out to the south in various channels onto a pleasant meadow. These
channels are continually dammed up by the local Qara people for
irrigation purposes. Mimosa, willow, fig trees and luxuriant creepers
adorn the banks, which are lined with bullrushes, the natural habitat
for quantities of water hens, herons and ducks. Thus one reads with
surprise under the entry 'Arabia' of the 1959 edition of the *Encyclopaedia Britannica* the statement, 'There are no rivers and no forests
and, so far as is known, only four groups of permanent pools (Hasa,
Kharj, Aflaj and Najran), scarcely worthy to be called lakes.' The
Encyclopaedia of Islam Vol. I (Leiden, 1960), p. 538, is equally ill-
informed and misleading on this subject.

Our lovely lake terminates at Darbat Falls, a 500-foot vertical
drop over one of the world's magnificent natural phenomena, the
Dahaq. This huge horizontal limestone shelf, a veritable dam, represents over 'fifty million tons'[3] of precipitated travertine and stretches
for about a mile between Jabal Darbat on the west and Jabal Nashib
on the east. A feathery waterfall set in a background of long white
stalactites is unique in Arabia and must be seen to be believed. From
an observation post below on the soft white calcareous tufa deposit
at the foot of the misty falls and the sheer wall, the occasional Qara
tribesman peering down over the edge seems like a tiny midget.

Within and adjacent to these Qara Mountains a natural asylum
for primitive aborigines has existed where there are still nine illiterate
tribes[4] speaking four different Semitic tongues – Shahari, Mahri,
Batahri and Harsusi. These languages appear to be more closely

related to Ethiopic (first noted in 1834 by Wellsted and subsequently by Carter and Crittenden) than Arabic and are unintelligible to the Arab visitor. The people themselves (the Qara excepted) are referred to collectively by the neighbouring tribes as the *ahl al-hadara* and in spite of thirteen centuries of Islam one finds that many tribal, topographical and geographical terms and names in common use throughout Arabia are not Arabic at all, but derive from these four little-known tongues.

The small South Arabian with his strange blend of characters appears closely aligned to the Hamitic races of north-east Africa with strong Caucasian and minor Dravidian elements. In 1917, C. G. Seligman noted that the Southern Arabs were markedly round-headed, a surprising discovery as subsequently pointed out by my former University of California African Expedition anthropologist, Dr Henry Field, 'for the peoples of Africa from the *fallahin* of Egypt to the Bushmen of the Kalahari Desert are longheaded. The Northern Arabs are longheaded, as were the earliest inhabitants of Jemedet Nasr, Kish and Ur of the Chaldees in Mesopotamia.[5]

As long ago as the fourteenth century Ibn Battuta noted the physical and cultural 'African' affinities as regards the South Arabians. H. St. John B. Philby contended, though without any tangible evidence, that the present South Arabians are the direct descendants of the Sabaeans, Minaeans, Qatabanians, Himyarites, etc., and other ancient rulers of the south-west highlands of Arabia. Philby deduces that these people are early off-shoots of the 'pure' Semitic Arabs now considered lost or extinct.[6] Among the Qara and Mahrah the Hamitic influence is seen in the almost beardless face, fuzzy hair and dark skin pigmentation. Coupled with these characteristics the incongruous non-Hamitic brachycephaly must be attributed to miscegenation and migration. The delicately featured South Arabians may well represent a Hamitic residue left over from the dim past when the whole peninsula was possibly Hamitic. The large, tall, long-headed, hawk-featured North Arabians are Semitic Caucasian as exemplified by Abd al-Muttalib, the grandfather of Mohammed who had ten sons. 'Among the Arabs there were no more prominent and stately men, none of more noble profile. Their noses were so large that the nose drank before the lips.'

Tradition ascribes the impressive coastal ruins at Robat to the former Shahara capital and points to the primitive descendants of Shaddad bin Ad as the original and exclusive possessors of Dhofar. Subsequently the Qara invaded, overcame and partially absorbed them and in the process assimilate the Shahara culture and language.[7] Today some three hundred impoverished, disunited Shahara remain, serving their Qara lords as degraded menials. When a Shahari is confused or does not understand what is being said he usually sticks out his tongue. His speech was described by Theodore and Mrs Bent, who visited the Qara in the 1890s, as sounding like the 'language of birds'. A degree of forced racial purity has been maintained (they have less curly hair, comparatively light brown skins and higher cheekbones) in that only daughters of the tribe are taken to wife in the more noble tribes, and none will give vassals a daughter in marriage.

The people who inhabit the mountains of Dhofar, who in local Arabic are called *gabbali* (i.e. Classical Arabic *jabbali*; cf. the *jabaliya* of Sinai), 'mountainers', call themselves the Qara – singular, *qarawi*. They are among the most primitive people in all the Near East. It is conceivable they are a survival of the Abyssinian Christian conquerors that invaded south-west Arabia before Islam. According to Qara tradition they originally migrated from the west with the Mahrah, although it has been suggested that their lack of a camel *wasm*, 'tribal brand', points to a possible migration via the sea.

The numerous Qara are divided into some fifteen sub-tribes, sections or clans,[8] which are in turn divided among themselves by various blood feuds. Today, as in the past, they live in low mud dwellings and limestone caves. When relatives meet, they join hands, rub noses and kiss each other lightly on one cheek. Some carry straight flat swords and small peculiar circular wooden shields covered with skin. Although rather short of stature the Qara man possesses great powers of endurance and a good physique. He pierces his right ear lobe and more often than not hangs a silver ring in this rather elongated hole. He is almost beardless (although he never shaves his coarse chin-tuft), wears his greasy hair in long curly braids bound with a leather cord (called a *mahfif*) wound seven times around his head, has his dark body stained purple with the indigo dye of his garments, and for dress wears only a single, short black skirt reaching to the knees with a long end usually thrown over the left shoulder. A looped leather girdle circles his waist while under his armpit hangs, by way of shoulder straps, a leather bag for carrying a variety of miscellaneous items.

One of the remarkable occurrences of history is that although the religio-ethnic rite of circumcision, ultimately derived from ancient Egyptian practice, is not alluded to in the Quran, this custom is held to be founded upon the *sunna*, or customs of the Prophet, and is universal throughout Arabia and the Muslim world, where uncircumcision and impurity are synonymous terms.

Strangely enough, in Oman (but not in Dhofar where the operation is performed by a sheikh or man of note) this rite of excellence, goodness and purity is carried out in many instances by the lowest menial gypsy caste, the Zatut, who maintain themselves as a separate community and were originally (over 1,000 years ago) Hindus from Punjab. These unarmed wanderers whose sons and daughters (reputed to be very chaste and beautiful) are acceptable to the other tribes and who retain their own language among themselves, rank lower than the lowest slaves. They perform the operation for all of the tribes, using an old razor. The little boy endures acute pain, especially when the resulting wound turns septic and refuses to heal. Usually the mother is not present and another woman comforts the child who may be anything from three to eight years old at the time the operation is performed.

Among the Qara, as with the rest of the Oman tribes, the entire foreskin is removed from the male during the circumcision rites. The former nearly always perform adult circumcision at the age of fifteen (as a social recognition of sexual maturity) instead of at the usual five or six years, as practised in the rest of Oman. In Dhofar groups of young men undergo the operation together before a public gathering and with elaborate rites, as a test of personal courage and endurance.

Large numbers of men and women assemble around a large open space. On a rock in the centre sits a boy of fifteen, sword in hand. This sword, which has been blunted for the occasion, he throws into the air to catch it again in its descent, his palm clasping the naked blade. Before him sits the circumciser, an old man; behind him stands an unveiled virgin, usually a cousin or a sister, also sword in hand. She raises and lowers her sword vertically, and at the bottom of the stroke strikes it quiveringly with the palm of her left hand. The stage is now set. The boy sits, his left hand outstretched palm upwards, waiting for the actual operation. This made, he has promptly to rise bleeding and run around the assembly raising and lowering his sword as if oblivious of pain, the girl running after him. He must complete the circuit three times without being caught by his fair pursuer, and his manliness will be judged by his performance. If he fails, he will be regarded as a weakling. Success is attended by singing and firing of rifles.[9]

Bad as this seems it takes second place to the Mahrah who used to circumcise the male on the eve of his marriage, or the barbarous Hijaz 'flaying circumcision' where the skin was completely removed from the navel down to the inside of the legs.[10]

Among the Qara, radical clitoridectomy – or complete female circumcision, which is alluded to neither in the Bible nor the Quran (although common among the ancient Egyptians) is clumsily and brutally performed without ceremony at the birth of the female child. In the rest of Oman the little girl merely has the top of her clitoris, which is regarded as the prime centre of sexual excitability, incised at the age of ten, or soon after birth a bit of fine rock salt is placed on the clitoris which is then eliminated (rubbed away) by the insertion of a finger. This appears to be slight improvement over the Muntafiq shepherd tribes of the Euphrates where first a needle and thread is passed through the clitoris which is held by ash-dipped fingers in order that the parts may not slip from the grasp – the clitoris is then pulled outwards by means of the thread to its full length. The extended clitoris is then sliced off with one stroke of a rusty razor as close to the body as possible at the inner surface of the larger lips. The singular appearance of a gaping vulva occurs when the smooth walls indurate and retract after the removal of the lesser lips.

Qara women are small, attractive with fine features and quite active in a timid sort of way. Unlike the women of the *badu* (not all *badu* women veil even in the south), they wear no veils. On ceremonial occasions they use various colours (red and green are favourite) to paint their faces; for routine days striped black markings of antimony (*kuhl*) circle the nostrils running to each ear. The chin, jaw, cheeks and eyes are bordered in black.

About fifteen or a little older is the usual age at which Qara youths take wives, but if it appears that a Qara boy under fifteen is ready for marriage, he is supplied with a wife as soon as possible, and as long as one of the parties is reasonably mature, immaturity on the part of the other is not considered an obstacle to sexual relationship. In Qaraland expensive brides cost up to fifty cows – the cheap ones a mere five. For a girl's first marriage at about thirteen, the father concerned usually provides a husband without consulting his daughter. The rule, almost universal elsewhere in Arabia, that a young man has an automatic right to marry his *bint 'amn* 'daughter of a paternal uncle', while she is free to marry no one else without his permission, is not insisted upon among the Qara people. In her pre-betrothal state the Qara girl's pubic and axillary hair is either pulled out by hand or removed by using a type of wax made of frankincense and her head is shaven in alternate stripes. Just before marriage takes place she is allowed a full head of hair. Thirty days after her wedding night a woman will sometimes allow a long half-inch medial strip of scalp down to the actual skull from forehead to occiput to be removed with a razor, permanently parting her hair for life in an ugly irregular scar with occasional fatal results from the inevitable infection. In rare instances the woman performs this operation on herself. However, this whole procedure is happily becoming more or less a thing of the past. From then on her main object in life is to give birth to as many male children as possible. Childbearing is easy. She works up to the day of the birth and goes back to work the day after. It is the rare instance where the man will exclaim, 'My wife has had six bellies and she has failed to deliver even one alive!'

Divorce and remarriage are easy among most of the Qara people, and the two events frequently occur almost simultaneously, as an individual adult is not often willing to give up one spouse until another is available. It is reported that the desire to remarry is sometimes the cause of divorce. If a man and woman become acquainted in the pastures while tending flocks and decide that they would like to marry, the man can simply go to the woman's husband and ask how many cows he will take to release his wife. As sophisticated jealousy is rare among the Qara, the husband will usually come to a quick agreement rather than keep a wife who loves another. Besides, the ex-husband will have enough cows to obtain a new wife.

As with the Masai of East Africa and the Dinka in the Sudan (the Dinka are the greatest cattle breeders on the White Nile), the Qara people's life, thoughts, and existence are built around their cattle (sheep are almost non-existent in Dhofar and goats are the women's chore). Almost every Qarawi possesses some livestock and those who own fifty to sixty head are considered rich. It is estimated that there are about 25,000 cattle in Dhofar.[11] Here each cow (cows are very rare elsewhere among the Arabs) is given its own name and can be readily identified by the herdsman. Milk is an important item of food in the mountains, but fresh milk does not travel far from the herd. In Salalah the price, with minor fluctuations, is one M.T. dollar for one cupful of milk delivered each day for one month.

A fall in the production of milk is ascribed to the evil-eye and is usually cured by an elaborate frankincense rite. If this fails, the owner presses his lips to the cow's vagina, takes a deep breath and blows with all his might. After several repeat performances she is expected to respond to the irritation with the desired results; somewhat similar methods are employed by tribes in the southern Sudan. Another well-known Arabian practice is to stuff a calf skin and allow the cow to lick it at milking, thus increasing her yield through deception. The average yield is seven to nine pounds a day but exceptional cows will yield a gallon at each milking. No woman is ever allowed to milk a cow; this privilege rests entirely with the men.[12] In the rest of Oman the reverse is true. But the daughters, sisters and wives are permitted to draw the plough.

The Qara, steeped in superstition, attach importance to the avenging power of swearing by one of their local shrines (in diametrical opposition to the despised Wahhabi tenets) although on occasion they administer an oath on the Quran. When visiting the coast they go through the outward Muslim motions as customs demand; once back home in their mountains, however, some of them perform their own sacred tribal rites and do not observe the ablutions and prayers of Islam, for among these pastoral people many pagan and animistic cults still exist.

The Qara people harbour the most primitive attitudes towards sickness and death to be found in the entire Arabian Peninsula. When sickness comes, a cow or sheep is sacrificed and its blood sprinkled over the patient's shoulders and breast at high noon. Illness is usually ascribed to the evil-eye and applying the red-hot iron is a universal cure. A wife who has just lost her husband must never display grief – this would be considered shameful. Mothers, daughters and sisters cover their hair with dust and beat their heads. Death is often attributed to the spell of some poor suspected witch who is forthwith persecuted. When a man dies, creditors may claim up to one tenth of the estate, with the remainder divided among the sons, daughters and wives. Death sacrifices are wholesale and burnt offerings are commonplace. After a man's death, one half of his wealth (which reflects seven times greater virtue in cattle), consisting in this instance of young bulls and cows proven to be poor in milk, are sacrificed. Camels or sheep are also offered in blood offerings; similar customs are followed by the Wahibah tribe in eastern Oman. Multitudes of neighbouring tribesmen and visitors are attracted by this huge slaughter and resulting feast.

The dietary taboos of these distinctive inhabitants of the Qara Mountains also differ in some respects from those of other Arabians. While no one in Arabia will eat wolf meat or birds with a hooked beak suggesting a carrion eater, the striped hyena (the meat of the hyena is permissible in orthodox Islam) is eaten from Muscat to Aden. Contrary to accepted belief (published by Bertram Thomas)[13] the Qara people, to whom the hyena is a magical beast, consider the meat of the hyena *halal*, 'permissible', reporting that the powerful jaw muscles are a special delicacy. However, they refuse to eat foxes, birds, chickens and eggs.

The nearly universal Arabian law of sanctuary is meaningless to these people, and their social mores are almost reversed, for they pride themselves on the art of stealing and treachery. Murder, a common enough occurrence, is regarded as a wrong against the tribe rather than against an individual, and the taking of an innocent life from the guilty one's tribe is accepted in most instances as just revenge and retribution with the balance of power restored; it is also the easy way out, for blood-money in these mountains is assessed extremely high, sometimes taking a lifetime to pay off and impoverishing all the relatives concerned. If a man guilty of rape or even willing seduction escapes, the relatives of the wronged female may perform a like act on the guilty one's mother, wife or sister. Some years ago a teenage boy whose father was dead found his mother with child; the stigma of her immoral behaviour thus falling on her young son. To insure his untarnished name he brutally murdered her one night before she became an object of contempt, to the complete and full satisfaction and approval of his tribal elders.

FRANKINCENSE FROM DHOFAR

Spice wealth of Arabia – Frankincense trees – The myrrh trees
Dhofar in antiquity – The Marib Dam – Ruins at Hanun
Andhur Oasis

The prosperity of Dhofar through the ages has been based on its unexcelled incense which, in fact, formed the major economic pillar of all ancient South Arabia. The steppe region (*najd*) directly north of the Qara mountains, possessing the necessary special combination of geographic and climatic factors, has since ancient times been the major source of these fabulous aromatic riches which travelled across southern Arabia and up along the Red Sea to the Mediterranean world, giving rise to great Arabian kingdoms on the way and their capital cities of Shabwah, Timna' and Marib. There was never one incense road in the sense of Pliny's 'single narrow road' or 'high road' but always minor feeder routes and several major overland roads, and these routes shifted geographically with the rise and fall of the various South Arabian states. From its place of origin in Dhofar, part of the frankincense was shipped in coastal vessels from ports on the Bay of Sachalites. The rest was carried by caravan overland across the Wadi Mitan and the Wadi Fasad, where one route went directly across dreaded *ar-rub' al-khali* (the Empty Quarter), heading north-west. A second route skirted to the south of the sands to Hadhramaut, where the major land route to Timna', Marib, Ma'in, Yathrib (Madinah), Dedan (al-'Ula) and Gaza began at the city of Shabwah. This journey, according to Pliny, was made in sixty-five stages. A third route, requiring a forty-day camel journey, went north-east from Hadhramaut across the middle of the Arabian Peninsula to the Chaldean stronghold of Gerrha (the chief entrepot centre) on the shores of the Persian Gulf. Both Uqair and Salwa have been suggested as the site of Gerrha; from this centre incense was distributed to Mesopotamia and Palestine.

As my former expedition archaeologist, Dr Gus W. Van Beek, has recently pointed out, 'We do not know the details of the visit of the Queen of Sheba to Solomon, but there can be no doubt that it was an economic mission, the primary purpose of which was to secure an agreement concerning the distribution of frankincense and myrrh that would be beneficial to both parties. It is not improbable that arrangements were made covering the shipment of incense over both land and sea routes.'[1] This camel journey took place about the middle of the tenth century B.C., and followed the Marib-Dedan route.

In the course of his 1957 campaign at Beitin (Biblical Bethel), in Palestine, Professor James L. Kelso unearthed from debris outside the wall of the temple city a portion of a large, unique South Arabic clay stamp. This stamp, which is made of typically South Arabian straw-tempered clay is evidence of the incense trade between South Arabia and the chief royal temple of the Northern Kingdom, where Jeroboam I burned frankincense shortly after 922 B.C. This is the earliest, possibly even the first, South Arabian object found in Palestine and it indicates that contact had already been established between the Israelite Kingdom and South Arabia early in the first millennium B.C., possibly only a few years after the visit of the Queen of Sheba to Solomon.

The first users of incense are lost to us in the mists of antiquity, but we know that it was one of the most precious articles of commerce. Breasted, in his *History of Egypt*, tells us that myrrh was already used in considerable quantities at the time of the first dynasty, and the later Pharaohs (balls of incense were found in the tomb of Tutankhamen) employed it extensively in their embalming rites and as an unguent in perfumes; the ancient Israelites offered frankincense before the tabernacle; the Song of Solomon mentions the hill of frankincense and that this spice was used to scent the couch of Solomon.

It was also brought as a gift, along with myrrh, to the infant Jesus. 'They presented unto Him gifts; gold, frankincense and myrrh' (Matt. 2: 11), gifts worthy of a king. The meetings of the Roman

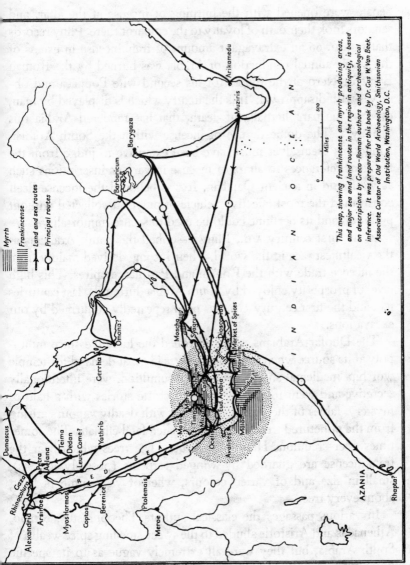

MAP 4. Frankincense and myrrh producing areas, and major sea and land routes of antiquity.

This map, showing frankincense and myrrh producing areas, and major sea and land routes in the region in antiquity, is based on descriptions by Greco-Roman authors and archaeological inference. It was prepared for this book by Dr. Gus W. Van Beek, Associate Curator of Old World Archaeology, Smithsonian Institution, Washington, D.C.

Myrrh
Frankincense
Land and sea routes
Principal routes

INDIAN OCEAN

Miles
0   500

Arikamedu
Muziris
Barygaza
Barbaricum
Omana?
Gerrha
Moscha
Syagrus
Dioscorida
Market of Spices
Mosca
Mambae
Main
Timna
Eud Arabia
Ocelis
Avalites
Malao
Damascus
Gaza
Rhinocolura
Petra
Aelana
Teima
Dedon
Leuce Come?
Yathrib
Alexandria
Arsinoe
Myos Hormos
Coptos?
Berenice
Ptolemais
Meroe
RED SEA
AZANIA
Rhapta?

Senate were opened with the burning of incense at the altar, and senators took their oath of loyalty to the emperor there. Pliny records that in A.D. 66 an extravagant amount of frankincense in excess of the whole annual production of Arabia was burned by the Roman Emperor Nero at the funeral of his second wife Poppaea and observes with disapproval, 'It is the luxury which is displayed by man, even in the paraphernalia of death, that has rendered Arabia this "happy".' The domestic use of incense within the South Arabian Kingdoms themselves must have been extensive to judge from the frequent references to altars of incense in various inscriptions such as we found in ancient Qataban. It was believed the incense itself constituted the most effective vehicle of prayer if collected without pollution and its perfume could be used to secure immortality.

In the first century A.D., Pliny described the South Arabians as the wealthiest race in the world. Their income derived mainly from the incense trade with the Roman and Parthian empires. This high level of prosperity enjoyed by South Arabia during the last centuries B.C. and the first century A.D. has been repeatedly confirmed by our excavations.

The Dhofar Arabians who controlled the lucrative spice monopoly at its source when frankincense was in great demand for temple worship, medicinal and household consumption, were intentionally secretive and went to great lengths to create stories with a halo of mystery: fables of the guardian dragon, with deadly vapours arising from the punctured trees and the associated fatal climate. The sometimes over-credulous Herodotus wrote, 'The trees which bear the frankincense are guarded by winged serpents (possibly locusts), small in size and of varied colours, whereof vast numbers hang about every tree.'

In various passages the classical authors Theophrastus, Strabo, Athenaeus and Aristotle alluded to the sweet-smelling spice wealth of South Arabia, but they were all extremely vague as to its specific point of origin. To the ancient world the Land of Incense was El Dorado, and one of the reasons why Augustus sent Aelius Gallus with that ill-fated expedition to Arabia Felix in 24 B.C. was 'to discover where Arabian gold and frankincense came from'. For nineteen centuries scores of travellers and geographers wrote more or less inaccurate accounts of the incense country, and it was not until the middle of the nineteenth century that the first intermittent rays ot light were thrown on Dhofar when Dr H. J. Carter, Assistant Surgeon, Honourable East India Company, travelling by means of the surveying brig *Palinurus* studied the frankincense along this coast, and Dhofar was definitely identified as Arabia's chief spice centre. Whereas in antiquity myrrh grew in the hills and mountains throughout south-west Arabia and west central Somaliland, frankincense appears to have been exclusive to Dhofar and to the eastern half of northern Somaliland. The scraggy picturesque frankincense shrub or tree, *Boswellia carterii*, grows wild and appears as a mass of ash-coloured branches with tiny leaves close to the ground and little central trunk. It rarely reaches over eight or nine feet in height. The fragrant gum-resin which contains a volatile oil flows best in March, April and May during the hot season before the onset of the humid summer monsoon rains, when the Qara Mountain trails are all but impassable. The frankincense tree itself requires little water, and the farther inland it is found, away from the damaging effects of the coastal monsoon, the better the quality of incense. Whereas the Qara people own frankincense trees around Hanun and also on the steppe, they never tap the trees or collect the resulting incense, for the Qara's number one objective in life is to look after their cattle, and water is scarce around the frankincense groves.

The chief responsibility for Dhofar's incense production rests with the Bait Kathir tribe, and each family marks its own frankincense trees. Repeated incisions are made after three or four years, with the young tree producing an odoriferous milky *luban*, 'olibanum', of delicate fragrance, which slowly oozes out to dry initially in pearly white beads (called milk-incense by the Chinese). These beads soon become pale yellow and more translucent. After three weeks the air-hardened *luban* globules or tears are harvested by the Bait Kathir, much of it from the Dhofar *najd* directly behind the Qara Mountains. This *najdi* or silver frankincense is the highest quality known, followed by the *shaẓri* from the Qara Mountains, then the *sha'bi* from the coastal plain. After collection the product is safely stored in dry caves until dispatch to the coast during winter to await the arrival of the wholesale merchants. Along the coastal plain at Khor Rori and Hasik[2] (Murbat and Sadh excepted) the frankincense trees are of a poorer quality and are tapped by the nomads or slaves who own no land, only goats, camels and cattle.

The Dhofar Steppe and Qara Mountains apparently do not actually produce any myrrh (*Balsamodendron myrrha*), although it is reported to grow there in proximity to the frankincense shrub. The myrrh tree differs in appearance in having a definite central trunk with a diameter reaching as much as one foot. In height it ranges from about four to fifteen feet, depending on the climate of the area. During the dry season the myrrh tree is leafless, bearing long thorns. In colour frankincense is reasonably white, whereas myrrh is quite red and tastes bitter, which is the meaning of *myrrh, murr* in Arabic. The analgesic or pain killer which was offered to Jesus just before the crucifixion (Mark 12: 23) was possibly a mixture of wine and myrrh. The Gospel of John (19: 39–40) states that Joseph of Arimathaea brought a mixture of myrrh and aloes, which was wrapped with the body of Jesus in linen. Such then, was the economic foundation of ancient Dhofar which, geographically and ethnologically, represents an isolated enclave. It has a limited oral history of anarchy and strife. Of its ancient history nothing except a few scattered and uncertain references were known before 1952, although the region had been described as a centre of Arabian civilization contemporary with the great days of Timna' and Marib by such ancient writers as Arrian and Claudius Ptolemy. The rare European visitors who touched on this coast before 1952 saw the scores of limestone ruins which dot the narrow, half-moon-shaped maritime plain, but they could only guess what cities and villages had once stood there. Although their appraisal sometimes came near the truth, they were more often wrong by many centuries.

My American Foundation archaeologists who entered Dhofar at the invitation of the King of Oman in March 1952 were the first to penetrate any part of south-eastern Arabia on a scientific archaeological mission.[3] The first ruinfield to attract our attention was Robat, about a mile inland and several miles east of Salalah, where there are acres of ancient remains characterized by standing black octagonal columns, usually six feet high, with square corbelled bases and capitals with fluted corners. On some of the columns one finds a curious fleur-de-lis pattern of an intricate design. Numerous shallow quarries of porous, shelly limestone (some of which are still worked) are left-overs from the past age of stone craftsmen. Cut into the bed-rock are watercourses and cisterns. Today parts of these ruins, including remains of numerous mosques, are overgrown by vegetation.

The largest and by far the most impressive single ruin in Dhofar, however, is located on the coast almost immediately east of Salalah. It is now called al-Balid, which to the local people means 'the city'.[4] Owing to its size and prominence, as well as to the fact that it was near our base of operation, al-Balid was the first site in Dhofar to be touched by the spade of the archaeologist. We were hoping to find traces of the same great South Arabian civilization we had been investigating only a few months before in Marib nearly 800 miles to the west. Expectations were followed by a degree of disappointment – but this was not altogether justified, for while al-Balid was slightly later than hoped, it still has an important history in the early Islamic period, if not earlier.

Al-Balid has been identified by some scholars as the Manteion Artimidos of the Greek geographer Ptolemy, and was a little later known as Zafar (i.e. Dhofar), ruled by an ancient prince who had an exclusive monopoly on the frankincense at its source and who put to death anyone who dared to infringe on his domain. During the reign of the Sassanian King Anushiriwan, around A.D. 570, his General at-Tabari Wahraz embarked at Ubulla, first seizing Bahrain, then a dependency of Oman, and disembarked his thousands of Persian troops at Sohar to overrun the country of Oman. The Persian fleet then continued west along the Oman coast, conquering Dhofar and Hadhramaut before taking Aden. This was the last notable incident in the history of Dhofar before the first convulsive throbs of Islam were to shake the Arabian Peninsula from end to end. At the beginning of the Islamic era the remarkable al-Manjawah family (presumably of Persian origin) is supposed to have ruled over Dhofar from Murbat, and to this day nearly all of the scattered ruins of Dhofar are pointed out as theirs.

The great Arab geographer Idrisi says that this family ruled

Dhofar in the middle of the twelfth century but that it was a dependency of Oman. In the thirteenth century it had (according to Yaqut) become subject to Bahrain. A city called Dhafar was later conquered by the rich Hadhrami ship owner Ahmed bin Mohammed al-Habudi who founded the Habudi dynasty and rebuilt the city in three years as Mansurah which was a prosperous city (now known as al-Balid) in middle Islamic times.

In the middle of the thirteenth century the Amir Mahmud bin Ahmed al-Kusi 'Lord of Hormuz' plundered Dhofar, killing many of the inhabitants; however, somewhere on the return journey disaster overtook the invaders causing the death of over five thousand by thirst and hunger. Soon after, Dhofar suffered another Hadhrami attack followed by an invasion by land and sea by the Rasulid King of Yemen. A few years later around 1285 Dhofar was visited and described by Marco Polo and, a half-century later or thereabouts, by Ibn Batuta who left a good description of what he calls 'the City of Dhafar', and noted that then as now sardines are an important part of the cattle-feed of the country. In the sixteenth century Dhofar, the city that is, was partly destroyed by a Portuguese squadron commanded by Hector da Silveria, on orders from the Governor of Goa. In short, the country has had many masters in its long history.

The Yemeni Saif al-Islam al-Ghassani of the sixteenth century was the last known occupant of al-Balid until 1952 when we excavated down through the highest mound and ran into sea water at the third or fourth century A.D. level. Few art objects of consequence were recovered; however, important archaeological information was obtained regarding this ancient city which was spread along the beach for a little more than a kilometre. As mentioned by Ibn Batuta (fourteenth century) there were numerous mosques in the city, all oriented about 210 degrees north of west, that is, almost exactly in the direction of Mecca, so that when the worshipper faced the *mihrab* or prayer niche he would be facing the *qiblah* (direction of Mecca). The accuracy of this orientation provides a good example of the practical sciences among the South Arabians of that time. The Palace and Great Mosque were found to be located not far apart, as described by Ibn Battuta, in the north-west part of the city. The main gateway of the city was found in the centre of the west wall. The ruins of al-Balid represent a great commercial centre of the period just before the beginning of the renaissance in Western Europe.

By the middle of April 1952 my American Foundation archaeologists finished their preliminary excavation at al-Balid and turned to other sites. A week's work clearing some of the small rooms on the tip of Ras Raisut[5] (eight miles west of Salalah) yielded no significant evidence of any kind. It was the third site dug – when discouragement was gaining momentum – which proved to be the outstanding city ruin of Dhofar in both antiquity and importance. Soon after the expedition had arrived in Dhofar and before any digging had been done, we had visited the coastal inlet of Khor Rori (actually pronounced locally more like 'Ruri') and noted that several rather uninteresting ruins stood on the east side of it. The main ruin, known as *al-kut*, 'the fort', to the local Arabs, had been well disguised by nature and from any distance appeared like a natural hill rising above the quiet waters of the inlet. It was only on a later survey of the area that it was noticed by my archaeologists, who decided with only little enthusiasm to give it a try, since the few pieces of pottery on the surface seemed to them to be 'relatively late Arabic'.

Excavations began on the site at Khor Rori on 26 April with workmen from the nearby town of Taqah (Tagat in the language of the Qara Mountain people). These men were either fishermen or herdsmen, and while they may have been very skilful at their natural professions, they stood in need of considerable training to do archaeological work. Dr Frank P. Albright, archaeological director, wrote in his field notebook: 'The 15 workmen we have are even worse than those we had at al-Balid. I did not think that possible. May as well use chimpanzees.' The next sentence in the record, however, completely changed the dark picture: 'In the room at J/K22 about 1 to 150m. below top surface we found six bronze coins and a complete inscribed tablet, Himyaritic!'

Thus on 27 April the story began to unfold, the story of this impregnable fortress city of forgotten renown which once guarded the best harbour on the Dhofar coast, and served ancient kings in their efforts to control the trade in frankincense. Near the northern gate we excavated an important temple in its entirety, the first time in Arabia that a pre-Islamic temple was completely unveiled. It contained an elaborate ablution system, two sacrificial altars, numerous bronze coins, and ancient frankincense.[6]

The discovery of the bronze tablet or plaque, deciphered by our expedition's chief South Arabian epigrapher, Dr Albert Jamme, was of major importance. This gave the name of the Hadhramaut moon god Sin accompanied by S M H R M (Sumhuram), the name of a long-lost city. The actual reading from right to left of this second-century A.D., six-line inscription was as follows: 'Shafsay and his mother Nadrat dedicated to their Lord Sin, Him of [the Temple of] Ilum, in [the city of] Sumhuram, for the protection of their persons, and of their king.'[7] Nearby a stone trough was uncovered bearing a strange writing running from left to right with peculiar forms of letters found previously only in inscriptions belonging to the biblical Chaldeans.

Carved on the walls of the inner city gate were seven inscriptions. Several mentioned King Ilazz of Hadhramaut, well-known in classical writings as Eleazus, King of the incense country. They included the name of the city of Shabwah and the local Hadhrami province and governor. Thus, here we had in this lost city of Sumhuram people who worshipped the moon god Sin and the first concrete evidence linking the Dhofar of antiquity with the capital city of Shabwah situated more than five hundred miles to the west. No wonder Hadhramaut had been renowned for its frankincense even though none of it has ever come from Wadi Hadhramaut itself. Just before the time of Christ, the kingdom of Hadhramaut had extended from near Beihan half-way across Arabia to include the greatest producer of incense, Dhofar, as a Hadhrami colony.

Frankincense never grew in the country of the Sabaeans.[8] The extensive forests described by Diodorus Siculus and Strabo (based on Artemidorus) were non-existent in the western mountains of South Arabia and only to be found far to the east in Dhofar. We know that Dhofar is to be identified with the land of the 'Sachalites' mentioned in Ptolemy's *Geography*, and other works of the period, for one of our inscriptions referred to the land as *S'KLHN* (Sa'kal) which would be rendered in Greek transcription 'Sachalites'. There seems little doubt that it was the huge Abyss or Dahaq that gave

Ptolemy his name of *Abyssapolis*, 'City of the Abyss', for our city of Sumhuram.

The Portus Moscha of the *Periplus* may well have been the port or harbour for the fortress of Sumhuram. The majority of the frankincense was shipped from Moscha during the winter north-east monsoon to the primary Hadhrami port of Cana for trans-shipment by sea to the outside world. At the same time the westward overland caravan routes were always important in the spice trade, especially when pirates imperilled the sea lanes. This traffic in incense was a most powerful force in determining the course of the political history of ancient South Arabia. The first century A.D. anonymous author of the *Periplus* describes how a certain Hippalus, 'a venturesome navigator whose name deserves as much honour in Roman annals as that of Columbus in modern history', first observed and recorded for the West the secret well known to eastern seamen of the use of the periodicity of the south-west and north-east Indian monsoon winds which enabled Arab and Indian ships to sail directly and thus more quickly from the Red Sea to India and back again virtually eliminating Arabia. This, in the opinion of numerous twentieth-century scholars, brought on the decline of the various South Arabian kingdoms. Although this was undoubtedly a factor, so also was the third-century fall-off on the import of oriental goods due to the Mediterranean region's economic woes plus the slackening of the demand for pagan spice odours as Christianity spread in all directions.

Arab historians have usually mistakenly blamed the breaking of the Marib dam for the downfall of all the South Arabian states.

As I recorded in my *Qataban and Sheba*:

The most famous ruin at Marib is the dam which was considered one of the wonders of the ancient world. It was probably constructed as Sheba approached its most powerful period, around the eighth century B.C. Lying a few miles from the old city, it is really a series of dams, sections of which are still standing. Even today, after centuries of lying in ruins, it is a spectacle beyond belief. . . .

We saw where whole sections of the mountainside had been carved away alongside the dam to form spillways to irrigate the adjacent fields. The dam had served as the central control for the mass of waters pouring down from the mountains of Yemen, the spot from which it was distributed to create mile upon mile of green fields.

Most amazing was the way the great stone walls had been put together. Huge boulders were so perfectly dressed that they fitted into each other like pieces in a jigsaw puzzle. We saw no trace of mortar of any kind, yet we looked at portions of the well that were more than fifty feet high, standing as they had when Sheba's great artisans built them about 2,700 years ago.

In the *Encyclopaedia of Islam* we read that, 'There is hardly any historical event in pre-Islamic history that has become embellished with so much that is fanciful, and related in so many versions, as the history of the bursting of the dam.' (In Arabic sources this event is called *sail al-'arim*.) Yet as I saw with my own eyes, the massive northern and southern sluices are remarkably well preserved to this day. As the dam was probably intact until the end of the rule of Abraha in A.D. 570, the final collapse took place within a few years and probably was caused by a social rather than a natural breakdown resulting in repairs being delayed until it was too late. Thus ended the most celebrated construction in pre-Islamic Arabian history.

At the present time Khor Rori consists of a long narrow expanse of water extending over a mile inland until lost in a dry, rocky *wadi* bed. A narrow sandbank has silted up the former outlet to the sea and now serves as the habitation of countless white burrowing crabs which grow to be about eight inches across. They can often be seen running along in enormous herds appearing from a distance to be giant spiders swarming up to establish a beachhead.

Besides the main city of Sumhuram on the east side of the *khor* there were a few other minor ruins in the vicinity. A table of rock locally named Inqitat, with an area of three or four acres, rises nearly a hundred feet above the sea on the east side of the mouth of the *khor*. As the formation juts out into the sea and has vertical cliffs rising out of the surging water, the only side accessible is on the north. Remains of a large wall run along the crest on this side. This wall cuts an imposing silhouette when viewed from below and must have been a very effective defence. It is, unfortunately, the most impressive feature of the site; a few houses once stood on the eastern end of the plateau, but remains of them are scanty and the thinness of the deposit indicates that archaeological excavations, if undertaken, could not be expected to reveal much of great importance. It is quite possible that the stones in this ruin were carried from the main city about half a mile inland on the same side of the *khor*; after that the site fell into disuse.

Other minor sites were briefly investigated by the 1952–3 expedition; Ghaur Fazl, a few miles north of the airport at Salalah, in the first week of May 1952; a small mosque at Khor Maghseil, a beautiful inlet some fifteen miles west of Raisut, late in August; Sadh, on the coast about sixty-five miles east of Salalah, in the middle of December; and some ruins just north of Murbat in February 1953 (two days).

The work at Khor Rori continued between these smaller efforts, of which Ghaur Fazl was the most interesting. In the Wadi Nihaz, which extends up into the Qara Mountains, we braved a swarm of locusts, butterflies, storks and an occasional puff-adder to investigate Ghaur Fazl, a large natural sink-hole about twenty feet in diameter and seventy-five feet deep. This somewhat awe-inspiring spot may possibly have been the site of the oracle Dianae Oraculum referred to by Ptolemy and attributed by the local Qara to Ahmed bin Mohammed al-Manjawi, their most celebrated early ruler. During rains and floods escaping air might conceivably emit sounds reminiscent of the oracle at Delphi. Although no evidence of former occupation was found on the bottom,[9] surrounding this cavity were ruins similar in aspect to those of al-Balid on the coast.

As part of the 1957–8 Expedition to Oman, a brief campaign of two weeks was undertaken at Khor Rori in February 1958. This was directed by Ray Cleveland and concentrated on one area along the south wall of Sumhuram, not far from the south-east corner. At this time the wind blowing from the south was a discomfort by day, but the one night it blew from the north was a catastrophe. It arose in the early hours of the morning and whipped the tents fiercely. Jama was awakened and called Ali to help him put more rocks around the tents to hold them down. This effort was successful in its immediate aim but the velocity of the wind was such that since it could not blow the tents away it ripped them and let them fall where they stood.

Earlier, when the two tents were first being pitched, Ali, the cook of the expedition, made the initial discovery, for while he was industriously collecting rocks to hold down the tent flaps he noticed one was a fragment of an inscription. Pulling a second and third stone loose from the soil he found that they were each fully inscribed and all fitted together into one. As subsequently translated by Dr Albert Jamme the five lines on the three pieces read:

1. 'Aziz, the Nacalite, has [hol]lowed and
2. emptied and helped in the city
3. Sumhuram; he has built in heavy materials for Thu'al,
4. He of 'Aslamum; he has promised to
5. Wadd'ab Ha['](an) Yardhikh.

In addition, two copper coins, both virtually illegible, and a few fragments of pottery were found among the top stones and loose earth. Where exposed to the elements (including the damp monsoon air) the cut stones of the ruins have turned black owing to a lichen growth on them; however, beneath the protecting surface of the soil and debris the rocks are light-coloured in appearance.

A trench two metres wide on the south side of the city wall at right angles to it showed that there the city wall rests directly on bedrock only a few feet back from the edge of the steep slope which drops away sharply to the level of the *khor*. An assault from this side would have been most difficult. If an enemy succeeded in scrambling up the side of the hill while various projectiles were being hurled at him, he would still be faced with a solid wall which was eight feet thick and must have been fifteen to twenty feet in height. With this situation existing on both the south and east of the city, the defenders could have concentrated their forces on the west and north where nearly level ground comes right up to the base of the walls.

Inside the wall at this point on the south a trial trench came down on a floor covered with lime plaster, which ran up on the inside face of the city wall. This trench was expanded toward the east to find the limit of the floor in that direction. A stone partition was just below the surface in this excavation area, but the untrained workmen removed a section of the top before Ray noticed it and was able to persuade them that they were removing a wall nearly a metre thick. Our Dhofaris refused to believe that a wall existed in the place indicated until Ray cleared a little of it on both sides and pointed out the lime plaster. This was the first lesson in archaeological technique for most of the men, and all feigned amazement and interest in what was shown them. Actually the workers at Dhofar were quite different from those in Sohar, who at times were in fact more meticulous than necessary and were always anxious to make a good showing for their efforts.

The rest of the wall, a fraction over three feet wide, was saved, and it was discovered to be the partition between a long narrow storage bin on the east and a larger room on the west. On the west side of this partition wall a damaged incense altar was unearthed. It possessed a raised inscription with the name of its owner in old South Arabian characters, combined with a tree motif supporting the crescent of the moon god Sin.

The narrow bin on the east was the fourth in a series, for three others had previously been uncovered parallel to it farther to the east. The larger room was more intriguing, especially after a plastered column base two feet high and nearly two feet square was discovered inside. Because of the incense altar and the square column base, it was suspected at first that something more important than a storage space had been found, but as clearing proceeded it became clear that this was merely another storage room, probably the ground floor of a house with living quarters above. In Muscat this arrangement is typical today and in Yemen granaries are often located beneath the houses. Like the long narrow bins to the east, this room certainly was once filled with frankincense awaiting shipment from the port.

The task at Khor Rori was lightened considerably by my good friend Sheikh Marhun bin Ali al-Ma'mari (i.e. a member of the Bani-'Umar tribe), who served as foreman. The Sheikh, who died in 1965, originated from Daqal in the hinterland of the Batinah Coast. He was typical of his class – pious, courteous, honest and dutiful. With his full, greying beard, Omani turban and ankle-length *thaub*, he added a great deal of dignity to the tone of the expedition. The manner of our first encounter was this:

Several years before, while *en route* from Muscat to Dhofar in the Sultan's motor launch, I had landed at Masirah Island. Late that evening at the R.A.F. base I chanced to overhear remarks among the airmen that a certain Sheikh Marhun would probably die in a few days. Investigating, I found that his hand and arm were grossly infected, and that the local commanding officer had ungallantly (and very untypically)[10] refused permission for him to fly to Aden because his arm smelled so bad it might offend the noses of the other passengers and contaminate the aircraft. Within hours we were at the Aden hospital where the doctors fought several days before finally saving the arm and hand in question. As it was his right hand, Sheikh Marhun would have died before allowing its removal, for in Arabia a missing right hand, rightly or wrongly, signifies thievery.

Public relations at Khor Rori involved a formal visit to the *nayib wali*, 'Deputy Governor', of the village of Taqah several miles to the west. The town elders and a handful of *askaris* joined in the solemn meeting at which spiced tea was offered and then small cups of bitter coffee. One of the old men present in the mud-plastered second-storey room was of little political consequence but had some social prominence accruing from the fact that the Sultan had married his daughter. This father-in-law of the Sultan and grandfather of Saiyid Qaboos bore the unimpressive name of Ahmed bin Ali and distinguished himself by dyeing the outer part of his full white beard with reddish-orange henna. This delightful rainbow mixture surrounded a browned, unemotional and wrinkled countenance which conveyed a certain sense of transcendent wisdom. The *nayib wali*, an agile middle-aged man named Sulaiman, was by contrast practical and efficient and rendered valuable services to the expedition.

The camp was augmented several days later, after Bill Terry had departed, by half-a-dozen regular soldiers sent out through the kindness of Major St. John B. Armitage to maintain wireless contact with Salalah for the expedition. Major Armitage, who then commanded the Sultan's Dhofar Force,[11] had previously served with the British Military Mission in Saudi Arabia and with the Arab Legion in Jordan under Glubb Pasha.

A quarter of a mile to the east of camp was surely one of the finest pools of running water available in all Arabia. A warm mineral spring flowed in a steady stream from beneath a ledge of rock, changing the water in the pool every few minutes as it flowed out into the *khor*. After a dusty day of excavating in the hot sun, fifteen minutes spent in this was extremely refreshing. Since water from the springs on the edge of the *khor* had a high mineral content and was quite distasteful, drinking water was obtained from the foot of Darbat Falls, located some four miles to the north of the camp. As always in Arabia, this stream water was boiled before being considered potable.

The diet at Khor Rori consisted mostly of tinned foods, occasionally supplemented by fresh fish, and in one case by a *dhabi*, 'gazelle', which Jama brought down with his rifle. The first meal from the gazelle was the liver, which has an excellent flavour when fresh, and then the cook proceeded to other cuts. In grace and speed the gazelle rates high among God's creation. Hunting, however, must eventually be prohibited by law if this beautiful antelope is to be preserved in Arabia. Fortunately, as it is, foreigners are not ordinarily permitted by the Sultan to do any shooting in Dhofar.

The third and final assault on the ruins of ancient Sumhuram was made in January 1962 when Ray Cleveland re-opened excavation there in a campaign which was to last throughout the winter. This was preceded, however, by a short campaign at Hanun, an isolated site, just north of the Qara Mountains on the borderlands of the Dhofar *najd*. Hanun is approximately thirty-six miles north of Salalah by the steep, winding road over the ridge of mountains, though about two-thirds of that distance as the crow flies. The spot is well known to the *badu*, for in the bottom of the deep wadi is a permanent water pool which can mean life instead of death to a camel driver and mount. The natives insist that the pool, a giant cup in solid limestone about twenty feet in diameter, is some thirty feet deep and will hold water for twelve years from a good rain; actually it is probably fed from underground in part, though it becomes very foul in the absence of fresh rain water.

The antiquity of Hanun had first been realized when Saif bin Bashir, a nephew of the Wali of Dhofar, reported to our Expedition in 1953 that he had seen a large inscription there. He had endeavoured to make a copy of it, and although he knew nothing of the ancient alphabet his copy was good enough to show at a glance that it was an Old South Arabic inscription. A Kodachrome photograph of it taken by palaeontologist Dr M. L. Natland and sent to the writer in 1955 reached Dr Jamme later in Washington D.C., and he was able

Ja 892

A sketch of the Hanum inscription from Dhofar.

to make out most of what it said. In addition to containing the name of the lunar god Sin, the patron of the Hadhrami Kingdom and the capital of Shabwah, it also names Sumhuram and gives the ancient names of Hanun as Sa'nân and of Dhofar as Sa'kalhan. The nine lines of the main text otherwise only tell us about a man who is dedicating three persons, presumably his sons, to services in the temple of the moon god.

The ruin at Hanun is a group of nine long narrow storage bins strikingly similar to those at the south-east corner of the city of Sumhuram. A small rectangular room stands detached opposite the entrance on the south. Another large room joins the main structure on the west. During the four days spent in actually digging, the detached rooms, the central corridor, one of the bins, and the large west room were cleared. Improbable as it may seem only one potsherd was found (of almost certain Mediterranean origin), and it seems that occupation here was only transient and that skin waterbags and pouches were used. The most important object found was a large incense altar (nearly a foot and a half high) with a short one-line inscription across the top of the face in the Old South Arabic alphabet; unfortunately this was mostly chipped away.

The purpose of this carefully planned stone structure in such an inaccessible place is to be found in the wadi-beds, in all directions from Hanun, in which grow the frankincense shrubs; this is in fact one of the very best frankincense-producing areas. The authority which built Sumhuram in order to control the export of the precious resin also built this seasonal collecting station at Hanun, whence it could either be carried to Sumhuram for shipment by sea or taken overland to Shisur and along the several camel caravan routes leading ultimately to the Mediterranean. There was no permanent occupation at Hanun, because the collectors, very likely supervised by a small group of soldiers, only went there in the harvest season, just as at the present time.

Excavations at Sumhuram, the main objective of the 1960 expedition, were resumed after closing down at Hanun as soon as equipment could be moved to Khor Rori and a camp set up. There is a superstition among many archaeologists that the best find will come on the last day or two of a season, but again Sumhuram violated this tradition. Scarcely thirty minutes after beginning work around a curious protruding wall just outside the east wall of the city, a large, flat offering table (about two feet long) appeared. On one end was the stylized head of a bull with a triangular leaf on the forehead. This head was quite different in style from examples previously known as it was without a groove (spout) over the head. This interesting object was the only important one found in this area, with the exception of the pottery, but the protruding wall proved to belong to a surprising feature of the defences of the city, an east tower twelve feet square, standing outside the city wall and six feet from it. A second tower, identical in plan, was later found outside the north city wall near the north-west corner of the city. Warriors stationed on top of them would seemingly be in a better position to pick off attackers attempting to scale the city wall.

The main scene of activity during this campaign was inside the north city wall not far from the north-west corner of the city. From the lie of the land outside the city, the archaeological director expected to find a considerable depth of occupation which would give the stratigraphic sequence still needed. The spot yielded that – and much more. Evidence of only one major building phase was found with remains of some rebuilding near the surface, although occupational debris, rubble and fine dust blown in by the wind had built up fifteen feet thick over bedrock. The surprises found were all in the collapse of one house and all within five yards of one another: parts of two bronze plaques with Old South Arabic dedicatory inscriptions (a total of seventy-two preserved characters); a unique, almost perfectly preserved, bronze bell about three inches high with the name of the moon god Sin on the side in three raised letters *SYN*, i.e. Sin, the patron deity of the city, and, three large fragments of a great bronze basin with vertical loop handles every six inches around the outside of its flanged rim.

An unusual, perhaps unique, object of solid metal (bronze, at least on the outside), a probably bronze weight (6½ lb. in its present state), was recovered with handle stumps on the top, and on the two sides a total of a dozen raised characters; on one side the characters are reversed. On the right the name of the Moon God Sin (reading from left to right), on the left (in normal Semitic order, right to left), the name of a man called Yashur-il, possibly the governor or other high official. The forms of the letters indicate a date of around the beginning of the Christian Era.

Especially significant pieces among the potsherds were several fragments of *terra sigillata*, handles and bases of amphorae from the

Greek Isles, and a section of a thin bowl somewhat similar to the Nabataean ware of southern Jordan. These small finds give more than adequate testimony of the trade relations between Dhofar and the Eastern Mediterranean Basin in the early centuries of the Christian Era.[12] The Greek amphorae also indicate that the ancient South Arabians had a taste for Greek wines and that they made enough profit on the export of frankincense to pay for them.

In spite of repeated investigations at Khor Rori over a period of eight years, one riddle still remains; where did the inhabitants of Sumhuram bury their dead? The visitor to the site can well wonder about the answer to this question, but the fact remains that no necropolis belonging to the city can be found, and thus many details about the beliefs and customs of the people remain unknown.

On his trip to Dhofar in 1928, Bertram Thomas visited an oasis approximately fifty-seven miles north-east of Salalah in the broad Wadi Andhur at the southern edge of the *najd*. Andhur is nominally considered a possession of the ignoble Batahirah tribe but is actually used exclusively by the Mahrah as represented by the Thuar section. The dwindling wild Batahirah with an exclusive language at present dwell along the coast and mainly engage in shark fishing by swimming on inflated skins. At Andhur Thomas noticed and recorded some 'archaic ground monuments', north of the oasis in the wadi bottom, but he made no reference to the ruins at the oasis in his writings. In late 1945 Wilfred Thesiger arrived at Andhur and briefly described the ruins,[13] having set out from Mughshin seven days before, following the Wadi Katibit through the barren Jaddat al-Harasis. In 1954 I located this site from the air; however, it was 21 March 1960 before my small exploratory party consisting of archaeologist Ray Cleveland, Jama, geologist T. E. ('Ted') Stanzel of the University of Texas, geologist R. S. ('Bob') Williams of Beloit College, Wisconsin, and Seif bin Bashir set out to reach this ruin from the ground. Due to the recent heavy rains, the *wadis* north of the Qara Mountains dissecting the relatively rugged plateau[14] were partially flooded and our Power Wagons, after crossing the Qara range, were bounced and badly knocked about as we drove in a reverse direction, south-southeast, up the *wadi* floor over a thick cover of rounded pebbles, cobbles and loose limestone boulders.

Approximately one hour from our objective we stopped and examined in amazement a curious installation which gave testimony to now forgotten cultic practices of the past. Here nearly a dozen low heaps of stone, certainly burials, lay in a straight line running approximately north and south. A parallel line to the west consisted of open fireplaces, one for each of the burial mounds. More exciting still – at least seven of the stones lying about, some in the heaps, some at random on the ground, bore marks which could be nothing but writing, but in a mysterious script.

A final twenty-minute breathless walk brought us to our objective, the remains of masonry and walls on top of a roughly circular plateau with an area of approximately an acre standing like an island on the east side of the broad *wadi*, offset by almost impenetrable groves of palm trees to the west and north. This precipitous, cliff-bound plateau, roughly fifty yards in diameter, had a defensive wall on the north side where it was least steep and most vulnerable.

This was not the main ruin, which was situated on a relatively high peak extending to the north and joined to the flat circular plateau by a narrow saddle ridge. In the centre of this ridge a basin a foot and a half in diameter had been hollowed in the solid rock; its age and purpose remain obscure. The small north peak was vaguely oval in shape, possessing well-built walls which would have offered adequate protection against nomadic attackers. Along the south-east edge of the oval inside the wall (and partly built into it) were three large stone troughs placed end to end. The northern part of the oval was occupied by a rectangular building of curious plan, seemingly one tiny room inside a larger. Narrow stone steps ascended from the inner room up towards the north, suggesting that the structure had possessed an upper storey in its original state. Here the stones of the masonry were cut and placed in a fashion reminiscent of the original masonry at Sumhuram (Khor Ruri), and the identical lime mortar, as used in the gateway and square towers of Sumhuram, are clear indications that this building belongs to the same general period (first century B.C.–fourth century A.D.).

The most likely interpretation of these ruins is that a fort had stood here to guard and control the collection of frankincense from the large and important surrounding incense area; actually this is the very heart of the best frankincense-producing area of South Arabia. An alternative view is that a combination temple and fort is represented by the ruins. In any case, Andhur Oasis was a highly important stopping place on the old caravan routes, leading northward to the Persian Gulf and westward to Hadhramaut. The ancient kings of Hadhramaut had to secure Andhur Oasis to control the vital frankincense trade; the fortress on the ridge was designed to accomplish this objective. Even today camel trails can be seen leading out to the north-west in the direction of Shisur; another route leads west-southwest to the post of Hanun, where the frankincense collection centre described above was partially cleared by the expedition. Murbat is only forty miles due south of Andhur Oasis, but a direct route is rendered impossible by the precipitous southern face of the intervening Jabal Samhan. The writer interviewed two Mahrah who live under the overhanging cliffs and in caves. They spoke Arabic and stated that it took three to four days' camel journey to reach Salalah, thus confirming the difficulties of this passage.

Hanun, Khor Ruri and Andhur, are the only sites in the entire Province of Dhofar which can be assigned with any degree of certainty to pre-Islamic times. The extensive ruins on the Dhofar Plain other than Sumhuram, including the unusually impressive site of el-Belid, all belong to Islamic times. Thus the several seasons of archaeological exploration and excavation undertaken in Dhofar by the American Foundation for the Study of Man lead us to conclude that sedentary occupation of any importance came rather late to this part of Arabia. The notable exception to this generalization is the city of Sumhuram on Khor Ruri, built by outsiders as a colony, probably not long before the Christian Era.[15]

SALALAH TO SHABWAH

Dhofar Negroes – Land tenure – Exploring ruined Hasik
The Empty Quarter – The Sands – Khasfah Well – The
Bait Kathir – Atlantis of the Sands – Looking for Ubar
On to Shabwah

In the past the main characteristic of any ruling regime in tribal Arabia has been instability; however, today Dhofar enjoys peace and prosperity with friendly, relaxed, unafraid people. It is immediately apparent to all upon arrival that the Sultan treats Dhofar as his own personal Royal Domain, unhampered by other Omani considerations emanating from the capital at Muscat. The Council of Ministers created in 1921 by Sultan Taimur is immediately responsible to the Sultan for all Oman affairs, with the exception of the Omani Dependency of Dhofar, whose Wali is directly responsible to the Sultan. Thus the Council of Ministers and the Wali of Dhofar operate on the same level, reporting directly to the Sultan, from whom all authority is derived.

Salalah, the capital, is relatively clean, its streets wider than those of most Arab towns. The waterfront of Salalah is dominated by the Sultan's impressive palace with air-conditioned rooms and the modern Saidi Primary School. Early in 1961 a new hospital containing the most modern equipment was completed, with half of its twenty-two beds reserved for women. The plan for this hospital has been with the Sultan for fourteen years, but only recently has he possessed the means to finance the project.

On an Aramco map of Arabia published in 1952 (also in the *Aramco Handbook*, 1960, p. 62), Salalah is omitted completely and instead prominence is given to the tiny, insignificant Dhofar fishing village of Murbat. In local Dhofari usage the term Dhofar is restricted to the capital Salalah, al-Husn ('the Palace'), al-Hafah, 'Auqid, Dahaliz and Razat (near al-Ma'murah). Thus when in Taqah or Murbat one should not be surprised when a local Dhofari requests a ride to Dhofar (which to him means the general area of the capital); if you reply, 'But this is Dhofar', he will exclaim, 'Oh no, this is Taqah', or 'This is Murbat.'

Locally the seashore community in which the palace and school are located is regarded as a separate town and is called al-Husn, while the name Salalah is restricted to the old town of high houses about a mile inland. To the Dhofari, who depends entirely on his own feet or his donkey for transportation, the distinction is not an academic one.

At Salalah the Negro community is almost completely self-contained and represents the largest single non-Arab element in the city's population. Most of Dhofar's indigenous Negroes think of themselves as being Arabs, while one who has recent or obvious connections with East Africa is called *sambo*. Well-fed and well-dressed, they look better and seem happier than many of the tribesmen. Accompanied by chanting and the beating of drums, the Negro women dance on any and all possible occasions. They exorcise the devil at funerals and bring happiness to weddings, where they appear in long processions sensuously swaying to and fro with full water jugs miraculously balanced on their heads. The small number of Somalis in Dhofar are distinguished from both Arabs and Negroes.

Until 1922, when these practices were stopped by order of Sultan Taimur, the Dhofar Negroes would first bury their dead, then level the ground and dance on top of the grave to drive out the evil spirits. After this the tomb was completed in the proper Dhofar fashion. Also stopped by Sultan Taimur was the practice of having the whole community gather in front of the house of a woman who was to bear an illegitimate child. With shouting and dancing she was exposed before her fellow countrymen; then the woman in question would of her own accord join in the festivities and dance with the others.

A twenty-five-minute drive brings one to Ma'murah, the Sultan's beautiful experimental agricultural gardens in the midst of graceful palm trees. The first to mention coconut palms in Dhofar was Ibn al-Mujawir, who visited the area around 1221. In this region the coconut and not the date, as in the rest of Oman, is the dominant palm. There is enormous wastage, as most of the coconuts are picked green for the 'milk', leaving the discarded 'meat' to be consumed by ants. As building material the coconut palm is far more enduring than the date palm. An unusual addition in al-Ma'murah are the four hundred flourishing frankincense trees which the Sultan has transplanted from the Dhofar steppe. Here, for extensive irrigation as well as for the Sultan's swimming pool, fresh water is conducted from a lined channel originating from a large spring in the Wadi Razat located in the foothills, which at source flows at an estimated 400,000 gallons an hour, year in and year out.

Three types of land-tenure are recognized by the Sultan in the irrigated parts of Dhofar: private ownership with written title; long-term rental from the state, for plantation crop farming; short-term rental from the state for annual crop farming. Farms vary in size from five to ten acres, and as irrigation is from wells they are known by the name of *bir*, 'well'. Freeholders have no right of alienation without Government permission. Fragmentation is avoided by the law which makes all the heirs of a farmer inherit the farm in common, with obligation to work it in common, although one or more heirs can buy out the rest. In the extremely rare case of a sale of a farm, the price would be about M.T. $1,000 per acre, without any improvements or machinery. Farms can be mortgaged to raise money for improvement; and they can be confiscated for non-payment of taxes. The beast of draft for ploughing is the camel, but most of the work of cultivation is done with heavy hoes.[1]

One morning late in 1954 while I was staying at the Sultan's palace at Salalah, His Majesty casually mentioned the ruins of Hasik (*hasik*, or a word similar to it, in Sabaean means 'incense') lying on the west side of Kuria Muria Bay. In 1929 his father, accompanied by Bertram Thomas while travelling by sea to Salalah, had run into unexpectedly rough weather and had anchored and briefly inspected this ruined city which overlooks the ocean in eastern Dhofar. The Sultan's description whetted my ready appetite for exploration, and a week later, on 11 November, I sailed out from Murbat,[2] eastwards along the gneissic coastal plain with the Jabal Samhan scarp in the background.

This was truly the Sultan's expedition, for in addition to a dhow and personnel he had also supplied me with everything from food, water and arms to a quantity of silver Maria Theresa dollars[3] for use as *bakhshish* when needed. (The South Arabians from Yemen to Oman always think in terms of silver). His Majesty's snow-white motor dhow[4] had a high stern and poop projecting considerably over the rudder. It was armed with ten *askaris* and tribesmen, including Barik, son of the Wali of Dhofar, who was manfully struggling to learn English; he became my temporary professor of Arabic. It was on this trip that I first realized the fruits of Jama's endless patience with me and began to understand the local dialect. One's Arabic simply has to improve when it is the only language available.

Along this 'barren, bare, unsightly, unadorned' coast, from Salalah eastward to Sur, a distance of five hundred miles, there is not one real bazaar. All supplies are bartered for from passing dhows. In the Gulf of Masirah the insignificant island of Mahot formed the chief trading station for this part of the coast, second only to Sur, during the flourishing slaving period of the eighteenth and nineteenth centuries. Slaves in batches of one to two dozen were landed from Zanzibar and trafficked inland to Adam and Nazwa. Exports were mainly dates, shark-fins and tortoise-shell. We sailed slowly along accompanied by dozens of spouting whales and arrived at the fishing village of Sadh at three in the afternoon. Sadh had a reasonably good harbour with extensive mountains of pre-Cambrian granite cut with numerous dykes and sills forming a picturesque background. After a reception governed by Arab hospitality at its best, it was agreed we would anchor in this small harbour until two the following morning. This would allow just the right time for our arrival at Hasik in the early daylight, if all went according to plan.

At nine o'clock the next morning, while pulling in a four-foot barracuda, Barik pointed out Hasik to me. The buildings were constructed on the side of a mountain and entirely exposed to the sea, yet the blend of dark ruin and dark surface rock was so perfect that an unsuspecting enemy sailing by could well miss the city completely.

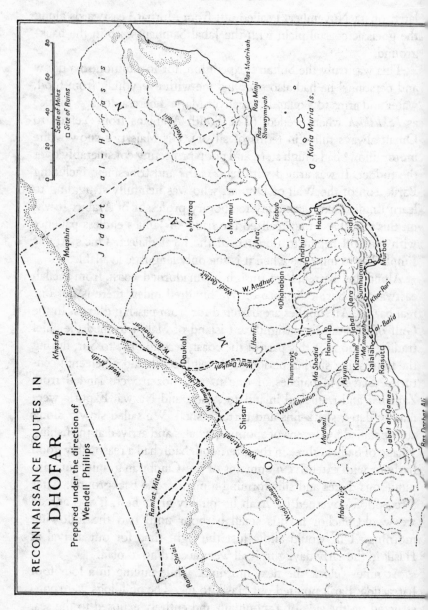

RECONNAISSANCE ROUTES IN
DHOFAR

Prepared under the direction of Wendell Phillips

Scale of Miles

□ Site of Ruins

A major unbroken mass of the sheer and precipitous Samhan range rose solemnly to a probable height of four thousand feet in the background. My Arab captain lowered the small *huri*, 'canoe', in which one balances and paddles at the same time. It was extremely hot and seemed even more so by reason of a bad cold and the need to serve in the dual capacity of motion picture and still photographer.

The extensive unwalled ruins comprised numerous small houses with no protective covering of sand and no dressed limestone block. After setting everyone to work collecting surface pottery fragments, I made three trial trenches in different locations, uncovering a quantity of pottery with little else of interest. Hasik (according to purely local legend it is one of the traditional locations of the tomb of the prophet Hud, the fourth in descent from Shem, the son of Noah), although believed to be referred to by Ptolemy and quite unusual in many aspects, did not appear to me to be over a thousand years old, and if it was occupied in pre-Islamic times, no evidence of this was forthcoming from my brief examination.

Al-Bakri, a native of Spain who died in A.D. 1094, mentions Hasik as the western boundary of Oman, while Idrisi, writing in the first half of the twelfth century, described this site from material collected by other travellers: 'The town is now quite ruined. It is called Suq Hasik, and is inhabited by the Korah (or Qorah) and other tribes, of the frankincense country.' Two centuries later Ibn Batuta disembarked at Hasik, which he found to be 'inhabited by Arab fishermen'. He reported with astonishment that the people built their houses of 'fish bones using camel skin for roofs.' In 1835 Captain S. B. Haines observed, 'Some of the people here were entirely without clothing, living exclusively on fish, and wretched in the extreme.'[5]

Within the present ruins was a Muslim graveyard with tombs bearing dates as recent as two hundred years ago.[6] Somehow I could not gather sufficient energy to investigate the large stone fort on the *jabal* overlooking the city. Guided by several of the local Batahirah fishermen I did, in order to view a ruined dwelling, reach a point two-thirds of a mile up the *wadi*, which contained scattered, stunted date trees, tamarisks and acacias. Before sailing away from this wretched coast I left our local hosts happy with one M.T. dollar apiece, given in the name of the Sultan.

The world of many early Muslim geographers was shaped like a ball floating in the eternal sea, half in and half out. Of the two quarters exposed, one constituted the 'Inhabited Quarter', the other the 'Scorched Quarter', *ar-rub' al-muhtaraq* or the 'Ruined Quarter', *ar-rub' al-kharab*. If Professor Nabih Amin Faris is correct in his recent suggestion, this idea of a great region of desolation only in fairly late times was applied to the great lifeless desert of south-central Arabia (although Ibn Majid[7] in the sixteenth century uses a very similar name while commenting on a verse which may be considerably older) and it was Doughty who for the first time introduced the term *ar-rub' al-khali*, 'the Empty Quarter', into western literature on the Arabian Peninsula – a name which has stuck in Western circles, although the area is still known under a variety of other names, including *ar-rimal*, 'the sands', and *dahna*, '(sandy) desert', by the *badu* who live on its circumference. On D'Anville's map of 1775 it was shown as the 'Great Space' and on Palgrave's map of 1862 as the 'Great Sandy Desert'.

Burton had observed, 'Of the Ruba el Khali I have heard enough, from credible relators, to conclude that its horrid depths swarm with a large and half-starving population.'[8] In the latter part of the nineteenth century the matchless Doughty had stated, 'I never found any Arabian who had aught to tell, even by hearsay, of that dreadful country.' While Miles wrote, 'As regards the physical features of this immense tract we are almost in entire ignorance, as no European traveller has hitherto explored its recesses, and we have only the vague and uncertain accounts of the Bedouins to rely upon.'[9] In 1904 Hogarth summed up *ar-rub' al-khali* as 'A virgin tract, obscure enough to give a geographer pause ere he argue of its unknown content from the other parts of the peninsula.'

In 1930 St John Philby's thoughts were as always focused on *ar-rub' al-khali*: 'I had not forgotten, moreover, that Bertram Thomas was at Masqat which, as I myself had told him in Amman some years before, was the best possible starting point for an attack on the uncrossable sands. The subject came up during conversation at one of the private sessions of the king; and Abdullah Sulaiman had expressed the opinion that the area should be explored at once, if only to obviate the possibility of claims to sovereignty by foreign Powers on the strength of prior penetration.'[10]

The almost impenetrable veil over this Empty Quarter, which obsessed Wellsted and Burton as 'a teasing mistress, that beckons only to forbid', was finally lifted from the south following the easiest route by Bertram Thomas in 1931 on behalf of Crown Prince Said of Oman and from the north in an epic of desert travel by St John Philby[11] in 1932 (during the month of Ramadhan) on behalf of King Abd al-Aziz of Saudi Arabia. Thus Omani sponsored penetration took precedence over Saudi-sponsored penetration in one of the last of the world's unexplored areas.

Like Jacob, who waited and worked for Rachel for fourteen years, Philby worked and waited fourteen years to cross the Rub' al-Khali, only to lose the laurels due the pioneer to Bertram Thomas, by one year. 'Few men,' wrote Lawrence, 'are able to close an epoch. We cannot know the first man who walked the inviolate earth for newness' sake: but Thomas is the last; and he did his journey in the antique way, by pain of his camel's legs, single-handed, at his own time and cost,'[12] and thus earned the title bestowed upon him by Lowell Thomas as 'The Greatest living Explorer.'

The Empty Quarter occupies an area of nearly 250,000 square miles in the south central portion of the Arabian Peninsula. In the most extensive definition of the name, it is bounded on the east by the Oman Mountains, on the south by the Qara Mountains and the Hadhramaut Arch, on the west by the mountains of Yemen and Hijaz, and on the north by the windswept steppe of Saudi Arabia and the flat gravel plains of Trucial Oman. This giant shadeless basin is the *locus* of interior drainage and receives the meagre run-off which may occasionally occur on the flanks of the surrounding highlands. Many large *wadis* drain into *ar-rub' al-khali*, but lost all definition on their contact with the great mass of sand. Although rainfall is almost entirely lacking, brief showers (averaging two to three inches a year) have been recorded and have formed many small *khubras*, 'playas' ('beaches'); there is no run-off to the sea. Within the quietude of *ar-rubʿ al-khali* itself, the specific pattern of the sand dunes and type of dune systems varies considerably due to the strength, direction and variation of the local winds.

The southern edge of the sand area is represented by a variety of dune forms which almost completely blanket the bedrock, are not affected by its shape, and do not lend themselves to conventional analysis. Further to the north, the dunes become larger and are aligned in a north-northeast direction. This alignment is a result of the prevailing winds from the south-southwest. This prevailing wind direction is further evident in other places in Dhofar. Strong winds from the south-southwest have picked up loose sand from the *wadis* and have abraded the nearby countryside, causing 'deflation streaks'. The chaotic assemblages of mounds and scarps on these dunes also indicate some transverse winds from the east and south-east. Due to the strong prevailing winds, the sand has been swept into long parallel sharp-crested ridges, exposing broad, flat strips of bedrock of low-lying, deflated areas called *shuqqan*, flanked on each side by towering linear or longitudinal dunes called *ʿuruq* which may extend for many miles in an unbroken line. The unmistakable dune massif or pyramid dunes differs from the crest-level of the dune chain in having a far higher summit. In the expressive words of the British authority Ralph A. Bagnold, 'In places vast accumulations of sand weighing millions of tons move inexorably, in regular formation over the surface of the country, growing, retaining their shape, even breeding, in a manner which, by its grotesque imitation of life, is vaguely disturbing to an imaginative mind.[13]

These dunes reflect an intense individualism and change colour with each hour of the day. They are composed predominantly of rose-red tinted, well sorted and rounded quartz sand, although in the southern regions the lighter colour reflects an increasing limestone content. The source of this sand is not definitely known, but it is believed to have been derived from the clastic sediments outcropping along the flank of the Arabian Shield. 'Some of it [*ar-rubʿ al-khali*] may have moved inland from the floor of the Persian Gulf during the Pleistocene Period when much of the Gulf was dry. Some may have migrated long distances from sandstone outcrops in the north-west. More likely the Rub al Khali sands have been derived from transitory streams which over the millennia have flowed out of the encircling highlands of Yemen, Hadhramaut, and Oman.'[14]

After being deposited in a late Tertiary sea by fluvial action, the sand became exposed to the arid climate and the winds have created the pattern of dunes visible today. Actually, approximately eighty per cent of *ar-rub' al-khali* is sand-covered, making it the largest body of sand in the world.

In 1926 the noted ornithologist and explorer Major R. E. Cheesman observed, 'In Hasa the northern part of the Great South Desert is spoken of an Al Raml, and the southern as Ahqaf, and the Rub al-Khali is not even understood.'

Actually the term *ar-rub' al-khali* is only known generally to outsiders. I have never found the term used in a geographical sense by the southern tribes of this ocean of sand. Thesiger writes, 'I have heard townsmen and villagers in the Najd and the Hajaz refer to it as the Rub al Khali, but never Bedu who lived upon its borders.'[16] They do use *barr khali*, 'empty land', for any area of desert without pastures, and the sands are known collectively as *ar-raml*, 'the Sands'.

It is often difficult to define the limits of *ar-rub' al-khali*, since in numerous instances the sands themselves are not as barren and waterless as the surrounding desert areas. Those who dwell essentially in these Great Sands are the Rashid, Bait Imani (a section of the Rashid) and Murra. As C. D. Matthews has pointed out, '. . . not a single complete tribe of Arabia, with all its divisions and sections, lives continuously, through all the seasons, year in and year out, in any sandy desert, whether in the Empty Quarter, or the Great Nafūd in the northwest, or any of the smaller *nafūds* more in the centre of Saudi Arabia.'[17] The Manahil among others not only inhabit the Great Sands but also the desert plain and border sand region with seasonal shifting. The Bait Kathir hardly ever enter the Great Sands proper, only around Mughshin in Dhofar. Nomadic life in *ar-rub' al-khali* is precarious, unstable and inadequate; brackish water, brief pastures and the quantity and quality of camels and raiders are the main factors of tribal survival. It is chiefly the undefeatable, thin, half-starved *badu* of these sands who use tents and employ camel litters for carrying their women and children.

On Saturday, 3 March 1956, in the late afternoon I set out with four desert-equipped Dodge Power Wagons, one Land Rover and a party numbering twenty-seven. It was the beginning of a successful attempt to penetrate by motor vehicle farther north into the Empty Quarter than had ever previously been accomplished starting from the Dhofar coast. My purpose was twofold; to mark clearly the Sultan's water-hole at Khasfah, which had been visited by Wilfred Thesiger by camel in 1945, and to search for the legendary lost city of Ubar. My partners in exploration were Sheikh Hamud bin Hamid (the Wali of Dhofar), my former field director Charles McCollum, geologist Hal Knudsen, Dr Gunther ('Nick') Schaefer (our physician), and Jama. In addition we had an Adenese cook, five bedouin sheikhs, two Arab drivers and twelve of the Sultan's *askaris*. Our guide to Khasfah was the notorious camel raider Sheikh Janazil bin Said of the Bait Musan section of the Bait Kathir tribe.

While *en route* north, in several of the upper Qara *wadis* we examined triliths, or systems of three elongated undressed blocks of stone approximately two feet high set on end forming a triangle at the base, then leaning inward with their tops together. As observed by Bertram Thomas[18] in 1928, as a major group they seemed to lack orientation as to a point of reference although generally aligned with the axis of the *wadi*. Several bore badly eroded inscriptions of a probably pre-Islamic date. This writer agrees with Wilfred Thesiger[19] that these triliths are commemorative monuments and that they do not seem to mark the site of graves.

Our final assembly point before striking into the great sands themselves was at Daukah, which lay over one hundred miles inland from the coast. As my time allotted for this undertaking was limited, we set out during the height of a sandstorm which made it almost impossible for those behind to follow the tracks left by my lead vehicle. Heading generally north-west, we crossed the Wadi Bin Khautar and travelled north along the east flank of the Wadi Umm al-Hait (which signifies 'Mother of Life' to the local *badu*). This great trunk drainage system becomes Wadi 'Atinah to the south. A few miles farther on, the *wadi* was crossed and immediately our trucks were stuck in the deep sand. Progress was slow, and camp was set up on the south-east bank of the Wadi al-'Aridh. This *wadi* has a north-easterly course and varies in width from one-half to two miles. Here among the dreary, monotonous *marakh* bushes and the *ghaf* acacias live several extremely poor Bedouin families, their goats and camels feeding on the scant vegetation.

That night around the fire we temporarily forgot the Prophet's admonition, 'Singing and singing songs cause hypocrisy to grow in the heart; like as water promoteth the growth of corn', and sang songs, the Arabs replying with far better renditions of their own. 'Braying forcedly in the nose' was Doughty's unkind description of the singing of the Arabs, and to the unaccustomed ear these *badawi* melodies all sound the same, but they definitely are not. The most popular of our songs was 'Old MacDonald Had a Farm' with the *badu* instantly recognizing our best efforts at animal sounds. One song was kindly dedicated to me as 'the American sheikh of the Bal-Harith' and another praised 'the American oil company for doing more than the British oil company in Dhofar'. To my cheerful prophecy that if no oil was located, 'the Americans would surely find them water', they replied in unison '*allahu akbar* [God is Great], please give us oil not water.' As the expressed thoughts of the desert *badu* are normally limited to camels, rifles and virgins in this order of importance, I was delighted to hear how their scope had broadened. I remembered to remind them of their earnest lack of desire for water during the course of this journey, for one always has trouble in apportioning water to these sons of the desert. Those who haven't said a decent prayer in a year suddenly become ultra-religious on convoy, demanding huge quantities of water for their ablutions. They love to drink up a week's allowance the first night with the knowledge that if God fails to provide more, I will. However, when a party of *badu* reaches a well, custom rules that no one drinks no matter how thirsty he may be until all have arrived to partake together. The same custom holds true for food.

The next morning I picked up a lovely, extremely thin flint spearhead in mint condition, displaying beautiful pressure-flaked workmanship combined with delicate retouching technique.[20] Several of my sheikhs said that they had seen others 'used by our forefathers'. This South Arabian Neolithic (these implements are classed as 'neolithic' in the very broadest technological sense) is probably derived from 'African West', as nothing similar is known from India.

To cross Wadi al-'Aridh, Charlie reduced tyre pressure to gain more surface over the difficult sand. Farther north, the dunes, some over four hundred feet high, had a definite north-northeast alignment, and driving in the deep valley freeways between these mountains of sand was a joy, with many gazelles and an occasional oryx racing ahead as though to keep us company. The oryx avoid the sands when possible, preferring the gravelly deserts. Unfortunately, the route to Khasfah necessitated our cutting across this dune alignment a number of times. Thanks, however, to the foresight of the Sultan, we carried special traction strips consisting of canvas with tough wooden crossbars. These were employed repeatedly throughout the day to get us across the soft and sometimes precipitous dunes where the angle of repose may be up to 60 degrees. At one point it took us over three hours to move less than 200 yards.

After an uneventful night's camp we awoke with our clothes soaking wet from the early morning dew. The days were very hot and the nights equally cold. The previous evening after dinner we had joined the Wali, who was seated on the corner of a huge blanket spread out in the sand. White-bearded, sixty-four year old Sheikh Hamud was a delightful companion, never complaining no matter how hard the going. It was at the end of our expedition that I learned that the Wali had brought along a tent for his own comfort, but seeing I had none he promptly forgot to use his own. Sheikh Hamud, of the Bani Ghafir tribe, originally came from Sanaa in Oman. His large tribe has always been very loyal to the Sultan. Sheikh Hamud's father was a Qadhi, who had sent his son to Muscat at the age of eighteen to work for Sultan Taimur. In 1922 when the Sultan dispatched his twelve-year-old son Said (the present Sultan) for schooling in India, Hamud, then about thirty, went along as his companion.

This particular morning, except for occasional traverses to the west to cross the sand ridges and hollows, our direction of travel was north-northeast. From here on the isolated dunes became larger and more numerous, finally resolving into almost continuous sand. At 9.40 a.m. our guide Sheikh Janazil pointed ahead to absolutely nothing with a triumphal *Wallah*, 'By God', and sure enough we were at Khasfah, over seventy miles inside *ar-rub' al-khali*. The surrounding area was a very white lime carbonate or caliche entirely devoid of vegetation and with only a few scattered bushes growing on the nearby dunes. The water-hole itself lies completely within the sand dunes and is almost impossible to recognize from either the air or the ground. This solution cavity was approximately two and a half feet in diameter at the surface with several pieces of wood forming a protective circle. The slightly brackish water stands at a depth of five feet below the sand.

In thirsty Arabia, water is truly the supreme consideration, and in the southern part of *ar-rub' al-khali* and borderland steppe the name Khasfah is given to water-holes believed by the *badu* to have been formed by a falling star, with no help from the Sons of Adam. For many of the Faithful the sands answer questions and the stars at night exercise a direct influence to be considered along with the interpretation of prophecy and dreams. According to the Prophet, 'Good dreams are from God; and false dreams from the Devil'; some Muslims still observe the rule, 'When anyone of you has a bad dream spit three times over your left shoulder, and seek protection with God from the Devil thrice; and turn from the side on which the dream was, to the other.'

I had previously arranged for a Dakota (DC-3) to spot us from the air, but had not counted on the difficulties involved. The plane first flew in from the north and east, then continued to search to the east and south. Charlie burned two tyres but the smoke would not go above the high sand. Next he climbed the highest dune and set off a series of flares. Eventually the pilot took a heading of N. 45° W. and, approaching low, found our tracks which led him to Khasfah. We kept in contact at all times with Salalah by radio in our trucks, as one of the problems was to locate this specific Khasfah accurately on our maps. As we worked out later on the basis of aerial mosaic control and traverse bearing, the location of Khasfah is eighty-nine miles north of Daukah and fifty-four miles west-northwest from

Mughshin, at a distance of approximately 200 miles from Salalah on the coast.

The well of Khasfah was so enclosed in the dunes that as soon as the plane turned after locating our trucks it promptly lost us again.

Our business now was the erection of an official monument at the well. This was constructed on the spot in the best Muslim taste, for anything that partakes of 'the graven image' is against the divine ordinance of Islam. While Jama covered this historic event with the movie camera, stones were mixed with cement and the *askaris* lined up as the guard of honour to fire a salute in the air as the Sultan's flag was raised. Next, the Wali, using a bullet as a stylus, wrote in the fast drying cement the Sultan's name and signed his own in Arabic. I followed in English with, 'H.M. Sultan Said bin Taimur Sultan of Oman Khasfah March 5, 1956, Wendell Phillips.'

Although the Arab is a firm believer in the noon nap, I settled for a shooting match in which all participated. We departed at three in the afternoon. As if the trip to Khasfah had not been bad enough, now, as we attempted to retrace our tracks back to Daukah, the steep or northwest side of each dune barred our way. Some forty-eight miles from Khasfah we detoured three miles searching for a better route. It was our thirty-two year old geologist, Hal Knudsen, using his aerial photos, who put the guide Janazil to shame and eventually found a passable exit; however, in all fairness it must be remembered that guiding vehicles is quite different from guiding camels.

Before long we stopped to buy a goat from some members of Sheikh Janazil's family, who eagerly enquired for the latest news after having hurriedly rubbed noses with everyone within reach. With these Bait Kathir the rubbing of the nose takes the place of hand-shaking when the *badu* greet each other in the desert. This southern desert bordering *ar-rub' al-khali* has remained a forbidding wilderness, intolerably hot and waterless, peopled only by a few illiterate and more or less barbarous nomads whose world consists of two parts, Muslim and non-Muslim, and who have lowered their needs to the irreducible minimum. The principal Arabian travellers have all described these people: Burckhardt admired them, Palgrave loathed them, and Doughty understood them; it was of them that

Lawrence wrote in the *Seven Pillars*, 'Bedouin ways were hard even for those brought up in them and for strangers terrible; a death in life.'

Although mainly inhabiting the desert and steppe regions of northern Dhofar, one section of the Bait Kathir known as the Al-Kathir live in the Qara Mountains, where like the Qara people they look after their cattle, goats and camels. As a tribe the Bait Kathir can probably man 600 rifles in an emergency. On this occasion I was surprised by chance to find a bullet in the rifle chamber of one of Sheikh Janazil's bareheaded young relatives. This is quite unusual, for the desert Arab's rifle is almost always carried empty unless he is expecting trouble.

These Bait Kathir commonly tattoo their upper and lower gums in black lines to strengthen their teeth in the sockets and have their straight black hair in long braids. They wear their beards to suit their taste and many smoke a small pipe, whereas the Ibadhis from the interior Oman mountains do not smoke and teach that the beard must remain untouched. They will, however, cut their nails and trim the moustache. The Bait Kathir subsist mainly on milk from their goats and camels which in turn derive their respective moisture requirements from the available vegetation. Impossibly brackish water can be made quite drinkable with the addition of a little milk. Very rare showers are collected in pools.

The Bait Kathir, as with *badu* in general, are blind to most natural beauty and view all scenery and landscape in terms of good and bad grazing. Two to three hours of heavy rain a year means a good year in the melancholy steppe, where water measures life, whereas farther north in the dunes thirty to forty minutes of rain in one solid shower will moisten the sands sufficiently to produce adequate grazing for a period of twelve months. Actually, here on the steppe the lack of sufficient grazing presents a more constant problem to these desert-adjusted *badu* than water which is always very scarce, for food is a daily requirement of the camel whereas water is not. A camel is very bad at changing his diet and camels which are moved from the desert to the coast, or vice versa, have to be taught what they can eat and what they cannot. The Caliph Omar once said, 'The Arab prospers only where the camel prospers.' Thus the health and welfare of one's camel is of supreme importance and set above all other considerations. Most Bait Kathir own six to eight camels apiece. They ride sitting behind the hump in a kneeling position and usually prefer the female camel for a long journey; they hardly possess any bull camels. In winter these *badu* can last seven or eight days without water or food provided that their camels hold out. They will pour the last precious drop of water down the nostrils of their mounts rather than down their own throats. This is known as 'snuffing' the camel. (Goats will go longer without water than camels.)

The Arab proverb 'Allah created the Bedouin for the camel, and the camel for the Bedouin' is certainly true regarding the Bait Kathir, whose ever-patient camel is his foster-parent, his *alter ego*, and in times of stress he rates his camel above his women. His camel is *ata Allah*, 'the gift of God', and in monetary value a good camel may sell for double the price of his daughter. Few can afford the expedient of more than one wife. Like Burckhardt,[21] I cannot recall even hearing of a *bedawi* who had four wives in his tent. The wife is allowed to milk the camel, in marked contrast to the Qara. If a camel is milked with unwashed hands it is believed it will go dry.

There is no 'age of consent' as such among the female Bait Kathir where a little, half-washed girl is not entitled to consent to anything. The following general statement given by Thesiger to the writer holds true for the Bait Kathir, but is not applicable to the coastal regions of Dhofar: 'A Bedu lad who wishes to seduce a girl sits near her at a party; he then pushes his camel stick through the sand until the hook is beneath her, and turns it over. If she jumps up he knows he is rejected but if she sits still he can count on her accommodating him.' A girl's unsoiled virtue and honour as marketable assets belong to her father. Most are disposed of as opening flowers by the adolescent age of thirteen or fourteen. Few reach eighteen unmarried. A girl of twenty is considered *passée* and referred to as old. Here the hand of the girl in question is always reserved for the son of her paternal uncle. 'He who is ashamed of his *bint ʿamm* will get no boy from her.'[22] If this first cousin rejects his claim, she is disposed of to the highest bidder, who may be an old man, with no consideration given to physiological or psychic incompatibility.

The Bait Kathir do not marry during Safar, the second month of the year, or in Dhu-Qa'dah, the eleventh month. The marriage price of a virgin bride may vary from 50 to 500 dollars. Half goes to the father and the rest is divided among the brothers, mother, uncles, aunts, etc. In theory the half to the father is an advance payment for the bride's personal effects.

At Daukah the Wali bid us goodbye, for he was returning with two vehicles directly to Salalah to report to the Sultan. Before leaving he kindly bestowed on me his water tank plus two welcome jerry cans. That evening fresh supplies were loaded onto our two remaining Power Wagons and Land Rover for the trip in search of Ubar.

According to legend Ubar, 'the Atlantis of the sands', was a many-castled marble city of fabulous riches that possessed a fort of red silver encrusted with rubies; the fabled city is purported to have been situated in the middle of a fertile oasis in what is now the sand of the great *ar-rub' al-khali*. Its inhabitants belonged to the tribe of Ad and flourished for centuries in wealth and wickedness (its wonderful gardens were known as *jannat 'ad*, 'the Paradise of Ad') until as punishment for their sins they were turned into *nisnas*, one-eyed, one-armed half monkeys.

The story of the *nisnas* goes roughly as follows, according to Yaqut's thirteenth-century *Geographical Dictionary*. An Arab traveller arrived at Shihr and was taken in as a guest by one of the Mahrah who lived there. The Arab stayed with the Mahri some days; when he raised the subject of the *nisnas* (a creature known in early Arab legend), the host told him, 'We hunt it and eat it, and it is a beast with one arm and one leg, and it has no other members.' The Arab replied, 'By God, I want to see.' The obliging host thereupon instructed some of the young men he had to go hunt one of the creatures, and sure enough the next day they came bringing a creature with a 'face like the face of a man except that it was only half a face', with one arm attached to the chest, and with one leg. When the *nisnas* saw the Arab it said, 'By God and by you.' So the Arab told the young men to release it. They replied, 'Mister, don't be deceived by its words, for it is our food.' The Arab insisted until they released it, whereupon it ran away as swiftly as the wind. When it came time for the Mahri's meal he asked the young men if he hadn't sent them out to hunt something for them. They said they did, but the guest released it. The story drags on with the Arab going out to hunt with the others, who use dogs, and they come upon more of the creatures. The Arab is very sure that the Mahrah are doing wrong to kill and eat the *nisnas*, as it can talk, but they don't agree. The Quran says that these creatures were formerly men who were transformed into beasts by an early prophet as a punishment. Professor W. F. Albright has facetiously termed this creature 'the abominable sand man'.

My present effort was not my first attempt to locate this elusive lost city. On 26 October 1953 I had made my first Ubar expedition setting out from Shisur, the only permanent watering-place in these central steppes, located about 100 miles inland from Salalah at an elevation of 1,300 feet. This famous natural well, the scene of many a deadly engagement, is remarkably hidden deep down in a narrow crevice in the limestone rocks undercutting the hill. Even after climbing down the steep passage of drifted sand it was difficult to see the actual water. I reached far in with one hand and sure enough it was there. The scene here was dominated by a rocky highland crowned with an old ruined fort flying the Sultan's flag and manned by Bait Kathir tribesmen who serve six-month periods. Legend attributed the construction of this stone fort to the early sixteenth-century Hadhrami ruler Badr bin Tuwairiq. In 1955 the Sultan built a new tower alongside this crude old one and equipped it with a machine-gun, wireless and eight *askaris* in addition to the Bait Kathir.

From Shisur it is six to seven days by camel to Mughshin, where the Sultan has a detachment of men plus a wireless set, and eight days to water in the Eastern Aden Protectorate (now called 'Protectorate of South Arabia').

A few miles west of Shisur a 400-lb drum of petrol bounced up in the back of my second Power Wagon and landed on the bare feet of Sheikh Muhsin, smashing both of his big toes. He never made a sound while our physician, Dr Martin Gavin, shot him full of morphine. As a violent sandstorm was blowing, I decided we should not stop here in the unprotected open dunes. Again and again over the next two hours our trucks stuck in the deep sand. By now, in spite of his proverbial endurance, this uncomplaining sheikh was in a bad way. Even though the sand was blowing hard from high dunes off to the west and north the tent was set up in the first level area reached. I explained to Sheikh Muhsin that one of his toes would have to come off and that the doctor might possibly save the other. Our sheikh replied with a genuine smile that he was in the hands of the doctor and God; the desert is truly a maker of self-controlled, magnificent men.

At this moment one of the other Bait Kathir sheikhs entered the tent, which was already filled with swirling sand, and stated in positive terms that the toe must remain, that he could fix it. Keeping in mind that among these people a woman's ailments may be diagnosed by smelling one of her hairs, and that sheets of iron or tin are tied over open sores, I reluctantly showed him the crushed toe in question with the bone in tiny bits lying on the surface. Then, before I could interfere, he bent low over our injured sheikh chanting some curious sacred formula, a possible rite of spirit exorcism for the evil-eye, in his typically high reedy voice of the desert. When he reached a semi-hysterical climax he bent low and gently spat upon the poor crushed toe, actually blowing several pieces of bone into the sand. This was too much even for me and I removed our well-meaning friend without further discussion. During the next half-hour, while geologist John Meier held the instruments and I held the sheikh's foot, Dr Gavin performed in the highest tradition of his calling, saving the second toe. Sheikh Muhsin smiled his gratitude to all concerned and in particular to palaeontologist Dr M. L. Natland who had just presented him with a magnificent Finnish hunting knife as a salute to bravery.

From here on my party included Charlie McCollum, Dick Bussey, Jama's brother Osman, our guide Sheikh Musallam bin Tafil, Said bin Mohammed and the Sultan's *askari* Awadh bin Subaiti. We had food and water for two days only and petrol for some 200 miles. This, plus my fellow explorers, made a considerable load for one stake-bed Power Wagon.

In numerous instances it is far more risky to explore in South

Arabia by motor transport or by air, where a mechanical failure may spell total disaster, than by camel caravan where God designed the perfect desert mechanism and failures are exceedingly rare.

Wilfred Thesiger maintains that the day of 'real' Arabian exploration ended with the appearance of the wheeled vehicle. He has told me personally that he feels that 'it is not a question of danger but of atmosphere. With camels the traveller is in harmony with his surroundings while moving at three m.p.h. (the proper pace) and in a car he is an intruder, self-sufficient and insulated from the real life of the desert.' So be it; but with the exception of my brief camel journey in 1951 from Beihan through the Mablaqah Pass to the ruins of Hajar Hinu az-Zurir in the Wadi Harib, I have always relied on Power Wagons and Land Rovers where time was essential and it was necessary to transport heavy equipment and large numbers of people over considerable distances. Now, one mile out, Charlie threw up his hands in despair at what lay ahead. He turned us round, and back at camp we replaced the normal tyres with two big sand ones for the front wheels. That evening we slept as best we could in the hard, very cold sand. The Arabs huddled all night around the fire, each taking turns at keeping a lookout for uninvited guests. We were off by 5.30 a.m. and after a very difficult stretch of sand entered a *sih*, 'gravel plain'. The major portion of this *najd* or hinterland of Dhofar is a relatively flat gravelly plain gently tilted to the north. Topographic relief of the bedrock rarely exceeds thirty-five feet. Over most of the northern Dhofar the Dammam formation, probably of the Middle Eocene age, is exposed at the surface between the dunes. On the basis of microfauna identification this same stratigraphic unit extends northward under the sands for a distance of at least seventy-five miles. Several samples collected in or near *wadi* courses suggest a later Miocene or possible Pliocene age, although the evidence is not yet conclusive.

At around 10.00 a.m. I stopped a lone Bait Kathir Bedouin with several camels. His rifle remained on his shoulder while he held on to the muzzle. Another common sight is the rifle slung from the shoulder hanging at waist level parallel to the ground. When I enquired if he knew the location of Ubar he shouted into my ear *faqat ash-shaitan yaʻrif,* 'Only the devil knows.' I shouted back *wallahi sahih,* 'True, by God.'

Our guide, the noted hunter Sheikh Musallam bin Tafil of the Masalihah, was very evasive as to just where we were. He had previously described to me in graphic detail the ruins of this sand-covered city, and said that he had once led Wilfred Thesiger into the area by camel but they had missed the actual ruins for reasons he could not or would not explain. Thesiger had noted at the time, 'Musallam could not come with us because we should be travelling through Mahrah country and, having killed one of them, had a blood-feud with that tribe.'[23]

I believed we had passed the Wadi Mitan and were now on the Ramlat Mitan, i.e. 'the Sands of Mitan'. In December 1930 Bertram Thomas had crossed Wadi Mitan by camel on to this same hard steppe, when his Arabs unexpectedly pointed to the ground. 'Look, Sahib,' they cried. 'There is the road to Ubar.' Here were 'well-worn tracks, about a hundred yards in cross section, graven in the plain.' One of his Rashidi tribesmen said that as a boy somewhere between Mitan and Fasad he had come upon 'two large white rounded blocks of stone, notched at the edge and both alike, but each so big as to require two men to lift it.'[24]

Desert Arabs are obsessed with wild stories of buried *dhahab,* 'gold', but these blocks of stone might represent the drums of a temple column and would hardly have contributed in my opinion to this boy's imagination if he had not actually seen them. It was on this journey that Bertram Thomas became the first explorer to cross *ar-rubʻ al-khali,* proving that this desert was not impassable, and thereby to close an epoch of exploration.

Charlie now cut back several miles and turned north up the *wadi.* The dunes on all sides were enormous mountains of massed sand, the largest I had ever seen. We were forced to halt for lunch simply because proceeding farther was impossible, especially with only one vehicle. Regretfully we had turned back, heading east just south of the great dunes, when suddenly Charlie exclaimed, 'There are the tracks!' It was California Charlie, not my desert-bred guide, who located these rows of parallel tracks incised deep in the hard surface and covered with glazed pebbles. I counted eighty-four tracks running side by side. They had every appearance of being very old and must have represented a time when there were countless camel caravans in transit through this uninhabited region of today.

Shortly after Bertram Thomas originally described these tracks Philby had written, 'The Caravan tracks – if they are more than camel paths leading from the steppe pastures to waterings in the sands, which are numerous in the neighbourhood in question – are intriguing enough and merit consideration.'[25] In my opinion these deeply-incised parallel tracks are certainly more than mere camel paths which could not lead to numerous waterings in the sand, for such waterings are either non-existent or extremely rare in this neighbourhood. I felt they could well lead to Ubar or several Ubars. (In July 1960 Philby expressed his opinion to this writer that these tracks may be part of the Pilgrim road to Mecca, beginning in Carmathian times in the tenth century.)

Eleven months after Thomas had crossed from south to north, Philby became the second man to cross *ar-rub' al-khali*, only his route was the more difficult one from north to south. One of his objectives was Ubar, or as he spelled it, 'Wabar'.[26] He was led to the city's supposed location only to find two sand-filled craters surrounded by high walls of slag. But, in my opinion the numerous Arab legends about Ubar are based on more than meteorite craters alone. Philby certainly solved a local riddle but not necessarily the mystery of Ubar, for the broad belt of tracks we had examined lay approximately two hundred miles to the south-west of his craters, and are definitely believed by our *badu* to have been made centuries ago by caravans bearing incense from the Qara Mountains to Ubar. In Kuwait during 1943 Colonel H. R. P. Dickson, who possessed an unrivalled knowledge of desert life and desert dwellers, questioned Muhammad Salim ibn Drahim al-Murri concerning Ad ibn Gin'ad, the mythical King of Ubar. He was told that many ancient tracks still exist in the desert, especially over rocky parts that have been exposed, and all converge on the area where the buried city lies.[27]

Now, two and a half years later, I was set for another major effort to locate Ubar, this time fully prepared. The month before, the Wali, on orders from the Sultan, dispatched a Bait Kathir by camel to locate two Bait Imanis who some time earlier had brought in several very poor fragments of pottery which might represent the location of Ubar. While the Sultan and I planned the Khasfah trip, one of these sought-after Bait Imanis arrived at Salalah unexpectedly. Thus the Sultan kindly agreed to my request to change guides at Daukah and explore west from Khasfah in an effort to find Ubar.

Before leaving Salalah the Wali, Jama and I interviewed this Bait Imani who volunteered, 'There are stones in the sand with pottery fragments scattered over a considerable area.' When I asked if he could lead us to the site, the Bait Imani replied *Na'am*, 'yes', but that he was not sure whether he could from a truck. He described the region in question as being 'four to five days by camel west from Shisur,' or eighty to a hundred miles. This was 'in the biggest of the big dunes and I do not know if your trucks can make it.' He was also worried for fear he would get car-sick. Jama asked if he had ever ridden on a motor vehicle before and he replied *abadan*, 'never'.

Then the trouble began, for he added that, 'If even one man from Bait Kathir goes along, I will not show you the place.' He was obviously afraid that his expert services would only be utilized this once. The Wali, far from pleased, stated in positive terms that a Bait Kathir would be sent out immediately to explore the area and find the pottery site. This was just what I did not want for it might take months or years and our clever Bait Imani knew it. In my poor efforts at persuasion I got down on the floor to draw pictures *badawi* style and offered our obstinate future guide 100 M.T. dollars plus a new American rifle and ammunition. He replied that the Sultan's *askaris* were welcome but not one of the Bait Kathir. The meeting ended in total failure.

Two years before there had been trouble between these tribes when the Bait Imani occupied Shisur. Although this was definitely Bait Kathiri tribal territory only two of them were present at the time. After a few days the Bait Imanis left in a hurry when a large group of Bait Kathirs were reported *en route*. In spite of the on and off antagonism between these two tribes they both acknowledge a common ancestor called 'Kathir'.

The following morning Jama again met with the Wali and the Bait Imani while I purposely stayed away to give Jama a better chance to perform on my behalf. It was suggested that I would give our hoped-for guide 120 M.T.'s, a rifle and ammunition with thirty additional dollars coming from the Wali. Jama wisely added that only if this turned out to be Ubar would the rifle and ammunition change hands; the money would be paid in any case. The Bait Imani countered with the proposal that he should accompany me on all my trips into the area and that if a military post was established by the Sultan it was to be manned only by Bait Imanis. Later that afternoon the Sultan said, 'No', regarding the second request, as this was not Bait Imani territory, but that if it was agreeable with me the Bait Imani could be my lifetime companion to Ubar.

The next day our new guide accompanied by Sheikh Janazil stopped Jama and urgently asked him to repeat in front of this witness what had been promised him. Jama was annoyed and walked away with the guide holding on to his hand. Jama finally said, 'Don't worry, whatever Mr Wendell offered you – you will get – no less and maybe more.' That night the Wali remarked, 'In over twenty years as Governor I have never seen such a one as this Bait Imani.' Now, as we left Daukah for Ubar, my party numbered sixteen with four Bait Kathirs including Sheikh Janazil plus our Bait Imani guide and one other of his tribesmen. In addition to what the Wali had left us we carried four drums of petrol, three drums of water, five days' supply of food, assorted rifles and ammunition plus the essential canvas strips.

Initially geologist Hal Knudsen navigated the party by aerial photos westward over Wadi Daukah and Wadi Ghudun towards the sand-filled Wadi Atinah. From here on, the Bait Imani took over. Somehow he seemed to know where he was at all times as he led us across the hard, white, apparently unfossiliferous surface limestone and conglomerates. His Arabic was almost impossible to follow; even fluent Arabic-speaking Jama had difficulty. At times our guide appeared far more interested in the whereabouts of gazelle and oryx than Ubar; however, I relied on the good old American bonus motive of a new rifle plus a fortune in bullets to give the necessary incentive.

This desert region of sand and stones and then sand and sand and sand is starved without water, but it is far from dead. The fauna is restricted to those which can in the main survive on moisture derived from the scant vegetation, for the sun is the chief enemy of all desert life. 'Being sterile herself, she is jealous of all life and would spoil it while yet in the embryo.' Vultures (Thesiger never saw a vulture in the Empty Quarter itself), eagles, ravens and owls still occur; also pale, sandy-coloured scorpions, lizards (certain types, with the exception of the large, vicious monitor, are considered a choice delicacy by the *badu*) and a variety of snakes, including the sand-coloured horned viper.

Arabia is the only land bridge connecting the Palaeartic, Oriental and Ethiopian regions and there is a strong relic Ethiopian element in the fauna of Dhofar, where, to cite just one example, one of the common snakes is the deadly African puff-adder. Wolves, badgers, hedgehogs, leopards, foxes, the hyrax (the 'coney' of the Bible), hyenas and gazelle[28] abound on the coastal plains and in the mountains; while the lovely shy and rare ibex (Arabic, *wa'il*) with its large recurved horns, which was frequently represented in the art of the Arabians of antiquity, is mainly restricted to the less accessible rocky fastnesses of the mountains, and the oryx (known to the Omanis as *bin sola*, 'son of the aloes tree') is found beyond the mountains in the inhospitable *najd* south of *ar-rub' al-khali* and also in the sands, especially the south-western section.

Now, under a tamarisk in Wadi Atinah, Charlie shot an elusive *Oryx leucoryx*, the size of a cow, to give us fresh meat. I can well believe the assertion that the mere sight of a man's footprint in the sand would send the oryx over the skyline. Before this large female antelope, which was equipped with long, slightly curved, needle-point horns (the bulls are short-horned like their African relations) had stopped kicking, our *badu* rushed up and cut the throat in the prescribed Islamic manner, and then sliced open the stomach and took turns drinking the warm gastric juices. The glistening white (silvery) oryx is known to the *badu* as *baqar al-wahsh*, 'wild cows', and was originally described in 1528 by Tenreiro under this name for its tracks are almost round like those of a cow, in addition to which it has a cow-like feathered tail and small hump. The oryx may well have given rise to the myth of the unicorn,[29] for when seen in profile its twin horns appear as one. They are used as flutes by the local *badawi* girls.

Suddenly, in the midst of this absolute desolation and tremendous quietude where year by year everything remains almost entirely unchanged, we came upon the highway of deeply cut parallel camel tracks over 100 yards wide. They followed a north-northwest course. Four miles farther to the north the tracks entered the high sand, but as the ridges were not continuous in this area we were able to follow the parallel grooves in the intervening open spaces for another twenty miles. In certain places we could observe through the bright quivering air where large dunes, like a sea of fiery glass, had slowly migrated or grown over the tracks, partially obliterating them until they disappeared from view. The canvas strips were not enough and we were forced to winch our way over several of the dunes. Actually one of the keys to getting over these areas is unlimited muscle power, which thanks to the Sultan's slaves we had in abundance. One has no depth perception when going down a steep slope and correctly to estimate distances is almost impossible as nothing exists to supply a standard of measurement.

Many of the dunes surrounding us were over 600 feet high, a sparkling rose-red of exquisite purity of colour and fantastically beautiful. Although appearing absolutely smooth from a distance the surface of these mountains of sand is covered with tiny parallel waves or ripple marks indicating upward movements of sand. Much to their embarrassment our guide and his fellow tribesmen became quite car-sick as we crossed this troubled sea of sand with its immense undulations previously traversed only by camel. There was a total lack of concept of motion among our Arab companions and on several occasions a tragedy was barely averted as one would calmly step off a fast-moving car into the desert.

Just before dark, we came upon an open space in the centre of a large depression completely surrounded by dunes, one of which was at least 800 feet high. Our guide waved us to a halt and, as though by magic, walked over a few feet and picked up several pieces of relatively modern pottery.[30] This was our Bait Imani's Ubar, but to me it was the remains of an old nomad camp. There was nothing to trench; everything lay exposed on the surface of the sand. There were no words to describe my disappointment and in all fairness our guide was honestly upset as well.

All at once I was very tired and while Charlie set up camp on the spot I sat and marvelled at the streaky blood-red sunset. It was a windy, sand-filled night with several unpleasant encounters with huge desert spiders reminiscent of our days in Beihan. To demonstrate to all that I had recovered my sense of humour, I playfully shot a giant flare from my Very pistol into the ground in front of the assembled party seated around the camp-fire. Before the flare died or my associates recovered from their shock, I was able to capture an excellent night sequence for our film. In his excitement Sheikh Janazil fired off a round in the air and then demanded an immediate replacement, which I gave him or he would have suffered remorse for days over this wasted cartridge.

The next morning, confronted by a vast expanse of immense dunes, a wild wilderness landscape, I decided to risk only one vehicle, the Land Rover, in a search for the renewal of the highway. We loaded on only essential rifles, food and water. Our guide had never been beyond this point. After proceeding several miles north-west, it was Dr Schaefer who located the tracks again with his field-glasses, but from here on I knew we were all through. Not only could we go no farther without becoming hopelessly entrapped but, as it was, Charlie almost lost our Land Rover in the impossible continuous dunes, for there is no barrier so great as a complete desert. The last we saw of the ancient tracks, they were bearing N. 75° W. in the direction of Saudi Arabia within a mighty mountain system of billowing immeasurable sands stretching like a vast ocean as far as the eye could see in its cruel and sublime grandeur.

The mystery of Ubar remains unsolved. In a completely inaccessible area where today there is little or no camel traffic, a well-marked highway centuries old, made by thousands of camel caravans, leads west for many miles from the famous spice lands of Dhofar and then mysteriously disappears in the north-west without a trace in the great sands. A dozen Ubars could well be lost among these high dunes, unknown even to the present-day *badu*. I firmly believe some day some explorer will solve the mystery of Ubar, Arabia's most intriguing lost city.

Our return trip was marred by carburettor trouble, and at 7.00 p.m. only twenty-six miles had been covered. After dinner I decided to chance some night driving, which can be fatal in this limestone terrain if one drives unexpectedly into a bottomless sink-hole.

Later we reached a high scarp that was absolutely impossible to cross. The theory that if you can make it in, you can make it out, does not hold at all in *ar-rub' al-khali*, and in this instance we fell back on the old traveller's maxim, 'Return by another path in a doubtful land.' Charlie led the way for four miles to see if we could get round this barrier, and this we eventually did. Here Sheikh Janazil became almost hysterical when he thought we might enter Mahrah country where he was a much wanted man and we were not armed with a *rabi'*. In South Arabia a traveller requiring protection through an uncertain tribal area secures in advance a blood-member representative of the section of the tribe in question, known as a *rabi'*, whose escort in theory ensures protection. Here in borderland Mahrah[31] territory, a member of the Bilhaf, a rather nondescript non-Arab, Mahri-speaking tribe (which neither raids nor is raided) is accepted as a *rabi'* by the Mahrah as though a member of their own tribe. Some of the Mahri sections will also accept a Somali. It has only been within the last fifty years that the Batahirah recognize a *rabi'* at all. A slave[32] of the Qara will usually suffice in Qara country. In 1950 while *en route* to Beihan with a fourteen-truck convoy, I had secured two local sheikhs as added insurance around disputed Shabwah.

An approaching party is always assumed to be an enemy until proven otherwise. When the alarm is given, the *rabi'*s rush ahead waving their headcloths and shouting out their names and tribes for identification. Of course this only works if the raiders are of the tribe or accepted faction of the *rabi'*s. To indicate his peaceful intentions, a *badawi* will shout *al-afiyah*, 'health'. If caught alone or out-numbered one's only hope is to immediately hold up one's rifle above one's head or throw it into the sand and surrender to the nearest enemy. Camels and arms are always forfeit, and if a blood-feud exists your life is forfeit as well.

These purely nomadic Mahrah that Sheikh Janazil so feared are a powerful tribe divided into twenty-six major sections. They in-habit and overlap the little-known coastal area between the western border of Dhofar and the mouth of Wadi Hadhramaut. This huge area between Wadi Masilah and the Qara Mountains extending to the Arabian Sea (from Musainah to Ras Dərbat Ali) was first explored by Major T. Altounyan.[33] Two exiled sections of the Mahrah are also found in eastern Dhofar where they have no land rights, for this area belongs to the Batahirah tribe around Ras Shuwaimiyah.

Sheikh Janazil explained hurriedly that between his Bait Kathir tribe and the Mahrah there was almost always a state of war. Many of the Bait Kathir can understand the Mahri language, which is quite a different Semitic tongue from Arabic. It is common for the Mahrah[34] men to wear their curly hair long with a single earring in the right ear. I regretted we did not see some Mahrah women with their green and blue striped noses, chins and cheeks.

With the safe return of all participants in the Ubar expedition to Salalah and our King, my story of Oman and its people comes to an end. The story of our subsequent adventures in Arabia requires some introductory remarks.

Carved on the walls of the inner city gate of the ruins of Sumhuram were several inscriptions which mentioned King Ilazz of Hadhramaut and the city of Shabwah from which he ruled. Shabwah was also mentioned in the Hanun inscription discovered in 1953 just north of the Qara Mountains on the borderlands of the Dhofar *najd*. Thus here was real evidence linking our lost city of Sumhuram in Dhofar with Shabwah, capital of the ancient kingdom of Hadhramaut, situated more than five hundred miles to the west, completely outside twentieth-century Dhofar and Oman. In 1955 I wrote, 'Shabwa, the mysterious "Sabota" of sixty temples mentioned by Pliny [*circa* A.D. 23 to 79], had been the secret objective of almost every explorer to penetrate South Arabia. Traditions of sand-covered temples, palaces, and buried treasures have made this one of the best-known and most sought-after spots.'[35]

Strabo (*circa* 54 B.C. to A.D. 24), was more cautious than Pliny. After cataloguing three out of the five kingdoms of south-western Arabia – the Minaeans, Sabaeans and Qatabanians – Strabo mentions a fourth: 'The Chatramotitae are the farthest of the nations toward the east. Their city is Sabota. All these cities are governed by one monarch and are flourishing, they are adorned with beautiful temples and palaces. Their houses, in the mode of binding the timbers together, are like those of Egypt.' And further, the unknown author of *The Periplus of the Erythraean Sea*, also writing in the first century A.D., notes that 'inland from this place Cana [probably the modern Bir Ali on the Coast of the Gulf of Aden] lies the metropolis Sabbatha [Shabwah] in which the King lives. All the frankincense produced in the country is brought by camels to that place to be stored. . . .'[36]

In 1939 Colonel D. van der Meulen, a pioneer Dutch explorer of Hadhramaut, noted 'Shabwa was an important town in the time of the Sabaeans and it is not impossible that it is the "Sabota" of the ancient geographers, or "Sheba", the home of the queen, who through her visit to King Solomon in Jerusalem, won immortal fame.'[37] In 1954 Richard H. Sanger, one of the Department of State's leading authorities on Arabia, wrote, 'Although the Ethiopians claim that the Queen of Sheba was an Abyssinian princess, while others, such as Philby, claim she came from northern Arabia [Philby is wrong here], there is reason to believe that she came either from the ancient town of Saba (Sheba) or from Shabwa in the Hadhramaut.'[38] In 1955, the writer attempted to clear up the confusion between the names 'Shabwah' and 'Sheba'.

In antiquity, Shabwa was probably the least important and the youngest of the capitals of the four great South Arabian kingdoms [excluding Ausan], and had nothing to do with the Queen of Sheba. It was located in an arid country incapable of supporting a large population, which is not the case with Timna or Marib. [This statement may not be correct as there must have been a great deal of irrigation in the Shabwah area in pre-Islamic times.] Its possession of salt-mines and above all its key position on the old incense road made it important. That position also explains why the capital of Hadhramaut lay so far west of the main wadi. It could catch all the trade coming north from the ancient seaport of Cana as well as that coming along the valley.[39]

It was not until 18 February 1963 that the writer became the first American to study the fabled ruins of Shabwah.[40] My all-Arab party included Jama, greyer but still the wonderful Jama of old; Mohammed Akil Abbasi, a twenty-seven-year-old Arab and Aden's finest professional photographer; and a heavily armed escort of seven hand-picked Arabs, long-haired desert veterans of the famed crack Hadhrami Bedouin Legion. From the Haura airstrip in Hadhramaut we drove in two specially equipped Land Rovers sixty-seven miles west over the sands to the gleaming white fort of Bir Asakir, with its 270-foot deep well, where we had spent the night in 1950 during our first pioneering expedition to Wadi Beihan to excavate Timna, capital of the ancient kingdom of Qataban.

My original plan, made in Mukalla with Arthur Watts, South Arabia's foremost Arabist, was to spend the night at Bir Asakir and reach Shabwah the next day. I changed my mind at the last minute and decided to keep moving and drive the distance of approximately forty-five miles to Shabwah to insure that our visit was a surprise and to enable us to take pictures with the late afternoon shadows.

In a recent personal communication to the writer Professor W. F. Albright stated:

The Valley of Hadhramaut is by far the most suitable region in the whole of South Arabia for sedentary occupation in the Bronze Age. The Valley is much wider than any other valley and water is nearer the surface than almost anywhere else, except in a few oases. It was therefore possible for settlers to raise fine crops in the rich alluvial soil with easy access to a perennial supply of water. It is therefore probable that this Valley was settled long before there was any sedentary occupation further west. When camel caravans came into use toward the end of the second millennium B.C., there was probably a brisk trade with Babylonia; it was not apparently until somewhat later (perhaps in the tenth century B.C.) that caravan trade between South Arabia and Syria-Palestine developed to any extent. The earliest capital we know, called Shabwat in the inscriptions, undoubtedly dates from much later than the settlement of the Valley of Hadhramaut proper.

In 1950 I had observed how 'Wadi Hadhramaut grew so broad that it scarcely resembled a wadi any more, and we entered upon the eastern edge of the Ramlet Sabatein, a vast sandy plain extending from near Marib in Yemen on the west almost 200 miles into the opening of the Wadi Hadhramaut on the east, and from Timna in Beihan northward to some vague point at which it merged almost imperceptibly into a huge desert, Rub' al Khali.'[41] We now recrossed this hard-packed sand and gravel at speeds up to over fifty miles an hour. Along the way we stopped in the sands to photograph an old *badawi* woman with a beautiful daughter. The mother promptly offered her fifteen-year-old girl both to Mohammed and me as a wife for 100 shillings. She seemed truly heartbroken when we regretfully drove away. We camped a couple of miles from Shabwah at an altitude of approximately 3,000 feet. It was still invisible, for in the words of Lord Belhaven (*The Kingdom of Melchior*, p. 54), 'It is surrounded by low hills, except to the east, where it is hidden by a flat-topped berg.' I left one Land Rover and most of our escort behind, as this was the month of Ramadhan and time to break the fast. This, of course, was a sad mistake. I should have mounted every rifle we carried. Upon arriving at the first ruins we parked and started our inspection on foot.

I, with all due respect, could not agree with Philby's[42] observation in *Sheba's Daughters*, p. 85: 'The whole ruin-field lay before us, disappointingly small and insignificant. . . . Not a single ancient building stood intact, not a pillar of the sixty temples erect. The ancient capital of the Himyarites ['Himyar' is the Classical Arabic name for the ancient South Arabians] was just a jumble of fallen debris.' To me the ruins appeared quite extensive and containing beautifully cut stones, many with marginal drafting and pecked centres. I noticed the average cut stone was larger than at Timna, although of the same style, dressed in front and crude and rough in the rear. This archaeological site was certainly more impressive than Timna in Beihan and appeared to be in the main unlooted.

While we were looking at these ruins, almost without warning a considerable number of the local population appeared out of no-where led by a very dirty white-bearded old man who said he was Sheikh Saleh and screamed, 'Where is your *rukhsah*, "permission"?'

No rifle bullets were fired over our heads in the customary desert greeting of Southern Arabia such as we had first experienced in 1950 at Bir Asakir. Nor were we accorded the greeting given to Philby when he visited Shabwah in 1935. 'As they passed, each man shook each of us by the hand, placing palm against palm with the fingers curving round in a loose clasp rather than a grip, and kissing the intervening air with an audible intake of the breath.'[43] In spite of Jama's masterful handling of the situation, it became tense in the extreme. Numerous rifles covered us. We kept walking on, talking and joking. I was worried about our photographer Mohammed, who was nowhere to be seen. Later I learned he had cleverly been taking pictures from behind a wall. After a near tragedy, when I was saved by quick-witted Jama as one of the local Arabs took aim to shoot me while I was balanced on an ancient narrow wall, we decided to withdraw for the night. No one sheikh appeared to exercise any real control over Shabwah – the city was divided between the Buraiki tribe and the Karab tribe.[44] Each hated the other and at this moment both hated us.

We were invited to return that night to talk but I said no – I wanted no part of a dark, strange and unfriendly village. At the suggestion of my chief Askari, Lance-Corporal Ali Bahamer Bahkarwan, we shifted our camp some 200 yards to a high area crowned with an ancient ruined fortress on the summit. I remembered Philby's comment as I lay down to sleep. 'The place seemed to be full of snakes. Two were brought to me that afternoon, and in the evening a Horned Viper came from under the car and wriggled across my bed.' Half a dozen *badu* joined us the next morning and an angry fight developed between them as to who would ride in our Land Rovers. One man promised that he would show us an inscription and thus assured himself a ride. We approached Shabwah from the right, or west, and were immediately assailed on all sides by angry armed citizens. Our escorts first pleaded on our behalf, then spread out to cover the scene from the high places. We were hopelessly outnumbered.

I knew once we were really stopped we would be stopped for good. I left the Land Rovers and walked slowly ahead. The Arabs were puzzled because I carried no rifle, only a western style holstered .357 Magnum Colt 'Single Action Army' or 'Peacemaker'. We found the large and very excellent inscription our voluntary guide had promised us. It was too big to move for a better angle to photograph. We now drove the Land Rovers for a short distance. The road curved up a steep hill; on all sides were buildings built over the huge foundation stones of antiquity. Ahead our way was blocked solid with rifles levelled at point blank range. I again walked forward, trusting our hosts would be ashamed to aim all their fire at me alone. Jama rushed up to go in front of me and Sheikh Saleh pulled out his *jambiyah* and thrust the curved blade in Jama's face. I relaxed for trouble and carefully watched this hysterical old man. But Jama's easy, ever smiling manner, plus his rapid-fire Arabic (Jama is never at a loss over a local dialect) won the day.

Several heated fights now developed between the Shabwah population – some for us, some against us. We moved ahead slowly. Much of the old city of Shabwah has been rebuilt over and over – using the ancient foundations plus numerous ancient hewn stones in their ugly present dwellings.

I took Sheikh Saleh by the hand and we led the mob – my sheikh was for the moment delighted at so much attention being directed his way. As we continued towards the high part of Shabwah – the city is in a shallow sandy bowl with a high back rim of ruins and dwellings – the people were screaming for gifts of money. Jama finally promised to give money to the chief sheikhs when we departed, if – and he emphasized *if* – we were happy.

As Philby had more time for observation and was not faced with urgent security considerations, I am borrowing some of his excellent detailed descriptive material.

There is little enough left of its ruins, but just enough perhaps to give one an idea of what the temple may have been in the days when Shabwa was a capital city of the Himyarites. . . . Along the north side lie four square column-bases of limestone separated by intervals of two and a half feet. Each of these bases is two and a half feet square with a central circular depression about two feet in diameter, which would seem to prove that the columns must have been round. To the south of each base, and separated from it by a space of six inches, lies a rectangular block of limestone two and a half feet long (E to W) and one foot wide immediately impinging on the roadway, but of obscure meaning, though they may have supported an arched wall standing immediately behind the pillars. The space between the first two pillar-bases (at the east end) is filled in with steps, while there are vague signs of similar steps between the central pair. . . . Finally, in alignment with the northern edge of the column-bases about six feet to eastward of them, and projecting forward from the lines, is a massive block of limestone six feet wide (from E to W) and ten feet long, forming apparently a ramp – there must have been a similar block on the other side – at the head of a broad stairway leading down the slope to the southern end of the main street of the city. This staircase, of which nothing now remains, must have been about thirty-four feet wide with a drop of about fifty feet to the head of the street. Two large, rectangular markings on the upper surface of the ramp suggested very strongly that there may have been a colossal statue or other massive decoration on each of the ramps, flanking the line of columns to form an imposing approach to the temple. . . .

Such, in as much detail as I was able to secure, is the great temple of Astarte [?] as it is to-day. I cannot doubt that it was the most important building in Shabwa, dominating the whole city and impressing the visitors who, on entering by the main gate in the north-west wall, would look straight up the main street to the great stairway leading up to the pillared entrance flanked on either side by imposing statues or pylons. Beyond them rose the main temple building running up to the sky-line of the ridge, with the holy of holies and its ancillary chambers on the flat platform of the summit.[45]

Our situation had been deteriorating and I finally made an impromptu speech in my best Arabic, with Jama's fluent help. While old Sheikh Saleh kept interrupting and trying to stop me I explained as loudly as possible that 'I had not expected to come to Shabwah and thus was not properly equipped. I am a veteran of the Aden Protectorates, Yemen, Dhofar and Oman; the only individual ever to see the major ancient capital cities of Timna, Marib, Sumhuram, Sohar and now Shabwah. Every one of you should truly be ashamed of yourselves as noble Arabs, for your gross lack of hospitality, the worst I have experienced. Some day, *inshallah*, "God willing", I might return with an expedition and a *hakim*, 'doctor', set up a field hospital to treat the sick, bring archaeologists and employ many Arabs of Shabwah in a series of excavations. Then and only then will you know the truth about your forefathers.'

My little talk had a definitely quieting effect on all concerned. One might ask why I waited so long, but I had to stop moving to speak; by now we had our pictures and the people of Shabwah knew we had won the day, so they had no recourse but to listen.

It was clear to me that a major and long-term archaeological project should be undertaken at Shabwah. Leaving aside, for the moment, the ever-present problems of security, protection from the

sun in this 'land without shade', and the training of the local disease-
ridden population as archaeological workmen, my thoughts kept
reverting to the urgent future problem of drinkable water and eat-
able food for my party. The Buraiki have nothing. Their only well is
fouled by the urine of their flocks. Poor arable land yields a little
millet. They get milk and meat from their goats, but only by grazing
them at great distances from their village, and meat is seldom more
than a twice-yearly treat.

On our return back across the city, we inspected a very fine large
inscription placed as a support over the door of the local mosque.
This inscription belongs to Yada"il Bayyin, King of Hadhramaut;
this may be the king of the first century B.C. or another of the same
name. We next visited the famous salt mines of Shabwah which were
similar in the method of mining to Aiyadin in Beihan, but smaller in
extent. Just before leaving Jama gave 200 shillings to the Sheikhs and
I gave a revolver exhibition, shooting tin cans we had with us, while
everyone applauded wildly. I let one of the chief local trouble
makers shoot my .357 magnum and as he fired he held the heavy colt
close to his face, so that the 5½-inch barrel flew back and hit his
forehead a terrific blow with the front sight, as I guessed it would.
This instantly won over the crowd, including my blood-stained
victim, who proved a magnificent sport. We shook hands all round
and left the best of friends, with the local citizens of Shabwah, led
by Sheikh Saleh, begging us someday to return *inshallah*.

I vaguely remember one of the enthusiastic citizens of Shabwah
pressing a dirty cloth into my hand containing something heavy,
while I was shooting. I handed it to Jama and in the problems of the
days that followed, after keeling over in the sand with a high fever,
I forgot all about the incident. Jama packed my belongings in Aden
and thus I was pleasantly surprised to find upon my return home to
Honolulu a small collection of coins from ancient Shabwah wrapped
in a dirty rag. I immediately dispatched the five most readable coins
to Dr Albert Jamme, who noted that one of them was a Sabaean
coin, the other four Hadhrami coins of unique design in regard to
detail. If such archaeological evidence could be obtained on the
briefest of visits to Shabwah, what would systematic excavation
reveal beneath the surface? That is something the future holds in

reserve for the adventuresome archaeologists who will some day penetrate this inhospitable wilderness with a scientific expedition.

In the phraseology of Oman, the unworthy author of this account beseeches in conclusion all his pious and generous brethren, if they should detect in the said work defects or errors, that they will cover these blots with the straightforward hand of sincerity, and not probe as a surgeon does a wound; for the only narrative which is above criticism is that related in the words of God alone, the Sovereign of men.

'May Allah show mercy to the tongues of travellers.'

OIL

Today, America has a major oil stake in the Sultan's strategic country which controls the entrance to the Persian Gulf. It is a long way from my profession of archaeological exploration to the subject of oil, but an unfortunate turn of events in the Spring of 1952 made it necessary for me to withdraw my expedition to Yemen and led me temporarily from one to the other.

During the many pleasant hours spent discussing various topics with the Sultan, including the problems of economics and his great desire to benefit his people, the question of the lack of oil in this country arose. His Majesty explained, with the quiet air of one who accepts God's will in all matters, that on 2 January 1951, he had received an official notice in writing from the manager of the Petroleum Development (Oman and Dhofar) Limited, a subsidiary of the Iraq Petroleum Company (I.P.C.), one of the world's great oil combines, which said in part that 'we have the honour to refer to article 19A of the Dhofar concession agreement dated the 24th of June, 1937' and 'that it is the company's desire and intention to terminate that concession six months from the date of this letter of declaration, that is, the 20th December, 1950', that 'We shall be pleased if your Majesty will confirm as soon as convenient that the above arrangement is in order and meets with your approval'.

'What happened next?' I inquired.

The Sultan smiled and said he had replied in less than twenty-four hours in five lines which, summarized, said, 'Your letter received – we were delighted to note its contents – the arrangement is in order and meets with our approval.'

I was slightly taken aback over the word 'delighted'. The Sultan explained that I.P.C. had held this large area under concession for some fourteen years. Outside of one or two brief survey parties travelling by camel, nothing had been done – no test wells drilled, in fact no well sites even located. From 21 February until 2 April 1948 my friend Major T. Altounyan had conducted the final I.P.C. geological party into Dhofar. The written report of their 500-mile survey with a caravan of

76 camels states in part 'as a whole the survey was conducted in enough detail for recommendations to be made as to oil possibilities' and under 'Conclusion' the report said, 'the absence of sufficient thickness of source and cover rocks and of suitable structure precludes the possibility of finding any commercial accumulation in Dhofar'.

'Not too encouraging, is it?' said the Sultan. 'No', I replied, 'but why were you delighted when I.P.C. finally gave up their concession? They must have been making you annual payments.' 'Yes, that is true', said the Sultan, 'but we need oil in Dhofar, not yearly payments', and without changing his tone of voice, he continued:

'And by the Will of God we shall have oil, for I am granting you the oil concession for Dhofar.'

Completely astounded, I asked in order to regain my composure, how big an area Dhofar was. The Sultan replied that if he remembered correctly it was approximately the size of the American State of Indiana. It gradually dawned on me that the Sultan was actually offering the oil rights on this huge piece of the earth's surface to me! As though in a dream, I thanked His Majesty for his gracious gesture and for his continued kindness to me, but, as I hastened to add, I knew absolutely nothing about concessions in general, and Arabian oil concessions in particular. The Sultan nodded and replied that he was certain I would learn fast enough if I tried very hard.

'Shall we begin to work on our oil agreement now, or would you prefer to begin tomorrow morning?' continued the Sultan. Like all good University of California graduates, I agreed there was no time like the present.

For the next few days we laboured together over the first draft. The Sultan, combining an expert knowledge of international law with his flawless English, soon had a workable oil concession agreement which he typed himself (I never learned to type).

The Sultan issued the concession in the name of my Philpryor Corporation, which had engaged in various activities in East Africa, Egypt, etc., without thought to Omani oil.

The concession document headed by the Sultan's impressive coat-of-arms began 'By these presents Sultan Said bin Taimur, King of Oman, grants unto the Philpryor Corporation, a company incorporated in the State of Delaware, in the United States of America, and hereinafter referred to as "the company" through their president, Doctor Wendell Phillips, the exclusive license and permission to explore and prospect for natural gas, crude petroleum and cognate substances, including asphalt, bitumen and ozokerite, in the Dependency of Dhofar in South Arabia, including the territorial waters thereof, subject to the following terms and conditions': – etc.

In three and a half pages we listed twenty-one major points – for example, 'Point (5) – The following areas shall be regarded as beyond the scope of this grant – cultivatable land; areas reserved by the Sultan for barracks, defence purposes and the like; aerodromes; burial grounds, graveyards, shrines and mosques and other places of worship or sanctity; and ancient ruins of archaeological interest such as Al Baleed and Ar Robat, 'Point (12) – The currency to be used in Dhofar shall be Maria Theresa Dollars and Dhofar Baizas'.

It was agreed that several items needed further study and comparison with the established Kuwait-Saudi Arabian oil agreements, and therefore the Sultan would mail me my concession in the near future *insha'alla* 'God Willing.'

It was weeks later, back in Manhattan's mid-town Hotel Van Cortlandt, when an impressive envelope arrived covered with red sealing wax. Inside was the concession with this covering letter dated Muscat, 29 May 1952.

Dear Wendell:

I am sending with this two grants, one of which concerns oil, and the other, most other minerals.

I hope that you and your friends will find them satisfactory in form, and that the operations which we hope will result, will be to our mutual benefit.

With best wishes.

Said.

When you are a penniless explorer and have no knowledge of the oil business, the possession of an oil concession presents certain problems. Where does one go from here?

To begin with, Dhofar Province had two strikes against it. The great I.P.C. had condemned the area and had given it up after fourteen years. (Certainly I.P.C. possessed more geological knowledge of Dhofar than anyone else).

And who in America had ever heard of Oman – let alone the Dependency of Dhofar? What about the Sultan – what kind of a king was he? What about supply, maintenance, health and security? These were all major problems even if something favourable could be protrayed geologically.

This area of Arabia was remote from American thinking which was, in the main, oriented by Aramco toward Saudi Arabia. No oil ever had been produced within hundreds of miles of Dhofar. The cost of preliminary exploration alone would be millions of dollars – there was no place for ships to dock, no ports, no facilities. Everything must either be flown in or unloaded offshore and floated in by dhow, lighter or Arab swimmer. There were no roads into the interior and only a handful of us from the outside world had ever been into the Qara Mountains, much less across them where the oil, if any, would probably be.

In Oman, however, I had one great advantage – an intelligent, friendly, co-operative and very pro-western ruler. During the many months that followed I devoted what time I could spare from archaeology to being escorted to the door of many of America's most illustrious oil companies. No one it seemed wanted the oil rights to some place where there would be no oil anyway. Thus my concession remained merely an interesting historical document destined for an eventual place of honour in my mother's scrapbook.

Then, after a rapid fire meeting with my long-time friend and associate, Sam Pryor, Vice-President of Pan American World Airways and Alton Jones, President of Cities Service Oil Company at New York's 29 Club, we were finally on our way. Next followed a period of detailed meetings with Vice-President George Hill and other Cities Service officials. During these preliminary discussions two things were immediately apparent: I knew absolutely nothing about the oil business and Cities Service knew even less about South Arabia. Thus, Vic Whetsel, Cities' Manager of Foreign Operations, his Staff Executive John Ristori and I made a perfect team. Without Vic's far-sighted imagination and understanding, backed by some forty years of foreign experience Cities Service would never have initiated work in Dhofar.

With the Sultan's approval I agreed on behalf of the Philpryor Corporation (Phil for Phillips and Pryor for Sam Pryor) to assign the oil concession to the newly formed Dhofar-Cities Service Petroleum Corporation, a 100 per cent owned subsidiary of Cities Service, with 50 per cent of Dhofar-Cities interest to be held by the Richfield Oil Corporation of California.

Before this final assignment was made, various interesting problems had to be settled. Cities Service is strictly a holding company. In other words, it has no operations itself, but owns the stock in numerous operating subsidiaries. All operations in the United States and elsewhere are carried out through subsidiary operating companies and all contracts are made in the name of the subsidiary companies.

Now the problem was that I had sold the Sultan on the merits of Cities Service, not on the merits of the Zulia Petroleum Corporation, a wholly owned subsidiary into which Cities wanted to put the concession. Zulia, named for a state in Venezuela, was immediately available for the assignment of the Dhofar concession. Zulia was to be only a temporary expedient, explained Executive Vice-President Burl Watson (now Chairman), until Cities Service could get a new corporation comparable to Aramco properly organized and staffed.

The Sultan had other views however; he had granted this concession to Philpryor Corporation and to Philpryor alone. He was agreeable to my assigning it to Cities Service or to a wholly owned Cities Service Company formed specifically for Dhofar but not this Zulia. In any case, the name Zulia reminded the Sultan of the Zulus in Africa.

On 29 January 1954, I received the following letter from the Sultan.

Dear Wendell:

I am herewith enclosing my permission for you to assign the oil concession to the newly formed 'Dhofar-Cities Service Petroleum Corporation. I am not pleased with the typing of this letter but it can be re-typed on some future date.

By the Grace of God I have been keeping in good health and hope you to be the same.

I shall write you more next week Inshallah.

With best wishes,

Said.

Another major problem – major at least for Philpryor Corporation was the royalty to be paid on any oil produced by Dhofar-Cities Service from the concession area.

There was little precedent to go on for situations like this were very rare. The most famous overriding royalty was the 5 per cent paid to the late C. S. Gulbenkian by I.P.C. many years ago. This made a multi-billionaire out of the brilliant Armenian, who had once been very kind to me in Lisbon, Portugal. With Dhofar I couldn't ask for too much because Cities and Richfield would have to spend many millions in exploration and even if they should finally prove I.P.C. to be wrong and find oil, many more millions in drilling and development would have to be spent. So I drew the line through the middle of Gulbenkian's 5 per cent and asked for a $2\frac{1}{2}$ per cent royalty, equivalent to the monetary value of $2\frac{1}{2}$ per cent of all the oil produced saved and sold from Dhofar. Then the bargaining started.

Cities Service officials countered with various proposals, none of which were satisfactory to me. I was never good at arithmetic and by then I was really getting confused. I understood $2\frac{1}{4}$ per cent. I wanted $2\frac{1}{2}$ per cent. I didn't want any other arrangement and said so plainly. After days of apparently futile negotiations, when it was finally clear that it was $2\frac{1}{2}$ per cent or nothing, I received what I had asked for in the first place. Thus it paid me not to be too clever in arithmetic.

In the months to come Vic Whetsel and I made repeated trips to see the Sultan. A temporary headquarters for the oil company was established first at the airfield near Salalah, Dhofar, and then moved through the courtesy of the Sultan to a lovely setting along the beach in the centre of a large palm grove.

First we undertook a programme of aerial reconnaissance in our search for oil, flying hundreds of miles in the interior often up to the edge of the *ar-rub' al-khali* 'Empty Quarter'.

Once I had assured the Sultan that the oil company was really serious, he ordered his Arab engineers and tribesmen to work night and day building the first road across the little-known Qara Mountains which rise over 4,000 feet above the Arabian Sea.

Using the most primitive tools imaginable, the Arab workmen sang their way ahead at an unbelievable speed. When limestone boulders had to be broken up, fires were built to force the rocks apart by heat alone. This steep and winding road over the mountains eventually reached the 3,000 foot elevation mark during its 30-mile course. We were working against a deadline – the annual arrival of the south-west monsoon. Once the monsoon started, no wheeled vehicle could traverse the Qara Mountains. Even the sure-footed mountain camel would slip and fall in the mud. However, as soon as the heavy drilling equipment reached safety on the other side, the monsoon was no longer a problem, for it ended abruptly in a wall of sunshine and deadly heat just north of the mountains.

At all times a quiet audience of Qara tribesmen stood by watching the proceedings with the keenest of interest, for this new road was cutting right through the centre of their mountain homeland. Every day they would bring large buckets of goat's and camel's milk for the refreshment of the Sultan's weary workmen.

Many wonders were performed and miracles created out in the interior sandy wastes. Small air-conditioned cities began to function where only months before camels grazed. Monstrous Kenworth trucks roared over the mountain highway, pulling giant collapsible derricks, to the wide-eyed wonder of the primitive Qara people. Hundreds of Arabs from Aden, Yemen, and Dhofar had steady employment and medical services for the first time in their lives.

In the fall of 1953 exploration began, the equipment was moved in during the spring of 1954 and drilling commenced in the spring of 1955. On 2 August 1957 a short statement appeared on the front pages of New York's newspapers announcing the discovery of the Marmul structure (11 miles long by 5 miles wide). Marmul was a textbook surface anticline, however, the first two wells soon fell off in their flow of low-gravity crude and much to our disappointment well number three produced only water.

By the late 1961 Cities Service together with Richfield had drilled 23 wells, 6 over 10,000 feet in depth, employed up to 983 Americans, Europeans, Indians, Adenese, and Omanis at one time and had spent between thirty to forty million dollars in their valiant attempt to establish commercial production.

Early in 1962 Cities Service in its last effort entered into an agreement with the great Texas Independent, John W. Mecom and Pure Oil Company, in which they were to drill one well at their own expense and after which Cities Service was to decide whether to continue operating in Dhofar. Thereafter, with the consent and approval of the Sultan and Philpryor Corporation, Dhofar-Cities Service Petroleum Corporation assigned to John W. Mecom and Pure Oil Company, effective 18 October 1962, all of its interest in the concession subject to the $2\frac{1}{2}$ per cent overriding royalty reserved by Philpryor Corporation at tne time of its original assignment of the concession on 17 January 1953.

Fifty-three-year-old John W. Mecom is among tne first five of the world's greatest independent oil producers. He operates as a plain individual, not as a corporation, and has extensive production in South Texas and Southern Louisiana with overseas concessions in addition to Dhofar in Columbia, Yemen, Jordan, and three of the Trucial States (Sharjah, Ajman, and Umm al-Qaiwain). In addition to holding the world's record for drilling the deepest producing oil well at 25,000 feet in Louisiana, he owns numerous major hotels, several large manufacturing companies, boat companies, construction companies, and drug stores.

In the spring of 1963 Shell Oil Company of Oman made its initial discovery east of Dhofar in east central Oman. By 1965 Shell had established commercial production and soon a pipeline was to be laid through a pass in Jabal Akhdar coming out to the Gulf of Oman just north of Muscat. By early in 1965 Mecom and Pure had drilled five wells in Dhofar ranging from 3,000 to 11,600 feet with oil shows in three of the wells. At this time Continental Oil Company entered the Dhofar concession as a third partner with a one-third interest with Mecom remaining as the operator and with Union Oil Company of California taking over Pure Oil Company's share.

On October 12, 1965, His Majesty gave the writer, in his own name, an offshore concession extending from the high-water mark out to a depth of one thousand feet covering approximately 300 miles of coastline at the entrance to the Persian Gulf from Khatmat Milahah to Ras al-Hadd. On December 12, 1965, the writer assigned the major interest in this offshore concession to one of the leading West German oil companies, Wintershall Aktiengesellschaft of Kassel, with the writer retaining a 5% interest in the concession following in the footsteps of the late great Gulbenkian.

On December 12, 1965, His Majesty bestowed upon the writer a second offshore area covering approximately 450 miles from Ras al-Hadd to Ras Minji facing the Indian Ocean.

I remember well how on long treks through the desert, the Sultan's face would light up as he would exclaim, 'Wendell, just think what I can do for my people when we have oil'.

ARCHAEOLOGY

with special reference to the Arab East[1]

Archaeology, that branch of science which is concerned with earlier phases of human culture, proceeds from the evidence of the present to reconstruct a picture of the past. The basis of archaeology's investigation is technology, the word culture being defined as 'that complex whole which includes knowledge, belief, art, morals, custom, and any other capabilities and habits acquired by man as a member of society'. Culture is an intermittent time phenomenon and archaeology is anthropology in the past tense.

Inductive archaeology reigned supreme in the pre-nineteenth century era of non-scientific approach. Observed facts were adjusted to fit the traditional accounts of writers such as Homer and Herodotus, and the philosophies of Plato and Aristotle. Only in the last hundred years has archaeology set out to discover rather than to confirm and substituted truth for proof as its ultimate objective.

In the first half of the nineteenth century archaeology was dominated by collectors whose chief desire was to fill their hungry cabinets with treasures. Modern archaeology began in the latter half of the nineteenth century when the past works of man were enabled to speak their own story. The key was a knowledge of typology or 'the classification of the various types of objects which are discovered and the study of their history'. The invention of modern methods of excavation is in the main credited to General Pitt-Rivers in England, and to Heinrich Schliemann at Troy, Mycenae and Tiryns, the first of the immortal archaeologists who recognized that a truncated mound represented an accumulation of layers of occupation.

Progressive refinement of technique was developed under Sir Flinders Petrie in Egypt, who stated, 'once settle the pottery of a country, and the key is in our hands for all future explorations'. It was he who introduced

[1] The author wishes to express his indebtedness to his former expedition archaeologist Dr Gus W. Van Beek of the Smithsonian Institution for extensive assistance in the preparation of this appendix.

systematic recording and the use of pottery for dating. He was followed by those outstanding geniuses who developed the archaeological techniques which have since become standard: Sir Arthur Evans, who found in Crete a completely forgotten civilization, Dr George A. Reisner, whose expertly trained Egyptians of Guft are still among our foremost excavation foremen, and Professor William F. Albright, the Dean of Palestinian archaeologists, who has stated, 'There can be no doubt that archaeology has confirmed the substantial historicity of Old Testament tradition'.

Exploration and excavation, the primary methods of scientific archaeology, do not end where written records begin. They cover a wide field not only in subject matter but in time as well. One would never attempt to construct a map without visiting the country concerned nor should archaeological conclusions be attempted without adequate field work. It is sometimes possible to date on surface evidence without the use of excavation; however, if we are to understand the methods and techniques used in excavating an ancient site, we must have some knowledge of the different kinds of archaeological remains and of the manner in which they are formed.

The most common remains in the Near East are those of ancient towns and tombs. Of the latter there are a number of varieties, the most common of which are mausolea built of masonry, natural caves, various types of chamber tombs cut in the earth, jar burials, and artificial heaps such as tumuli and cairns. Tombs are important in archaeology because they provide information about the burial customs of a culture, and they yield whole or restorable objects that fill in gaps in our knowledge of the objects of a culture.

The great problem with tombs is finding them. Sometimes they are discovered accidentally by farmers tilling the soil; occasionally erosion exposes the roof or entrance of a tomb; frequently they come to light during the excavation of a site; sometimes they are found when an archaeologist digs an entire area, completely stripping the surface in search of tombs.

Once a tomb has been located, the excavation of it is a straightforward matter. If it is a chamber tomb, both the entrance to the chamber and the chamber itself are cleared of their filling of stones or earth. Since no filling is ever as compact as undisturbed soil, and since it is usually of a different colour, the excavator can easily discover the edge of the filling by scraping the surface smooth with a mason's trowel or by carefully digging the filling from the centre outwards. If the filling is softly packed, it will fall away from the undisturbed soil, leaving the original cutting exposed. Mausolea are excavated in much the same way as any other building, the technique of which will be discussed below.

Inside the tomb, all objects and bones are carefully cleaned in position. In some instances they must be specially treated with chemicals to prevent disintegration. A plan and photographs are made of the burial chamber. Extreme care and limitless patience as well as enough physical endurance to work in cramped, dust-filled, and dark chambers is required of the tomb excavator.

The remains of ancient towns and cities are usually found in the form of occupation mounds in the Near East. These artificial mounds, one of which is called a *tell* in most Semitic languages (beginning with the Babylonian *tillu* or 'ruin heap'), are commonly shaped like truncated cones, with flat tops and sloping sides. Their area depends on the size of the ancient settlement, and usually varies from two or three to several hundred acres; one of our Arabian sites, Hajar Bin Humeid, comprises an area of about four acres: Timna' measures about fifty-two acres; Marib covers about two hundred acres.

The height of the mound depends on a number of factors: the kinds of building materials used, the length and character of the occupation, the number of times the site was occupied, and the rate of erosion to the site after abandonment. Thus in sites where sun-dried mud bricks were the primary building materials, the accumulation of debris is normally greater than in sites where stone construction was used. Mud-brick construction deteriorates rapidly as a result of erosion by rain, making frequent repairs necessary. When the mud-bricks eroded or crumbled, they were not swept up and carried away, but were trodden under foot, thereby raising the level of the street, court, or floor. Stone construction, on the other hand, is more permanent and requires less frequent repair than mudbricks. But when a stone building was destroyed, the blocks were often reused in building the structure, or were carried off and used in constructing buildings elsewhere. Thus the accumulation of debris in sites with stone construction is usually much less than in sites where mud-brick were used.

An example of this is at Tell al-Maskhutah in lower Egypt near Tell el-Kebir in the Biblical 'Land of Goshen'. This site was reputed to be the Stone city of Pithom which was built by the Israelites in slavery in Egypt before the Exodus. The city is built of mud bricks made with chopped straw and the walls are still well preserved. The mud must have come from the Pelusiac branch of the Nile.

Furthermore, if an occupation of a site was peaceful and lasted for several centuries, relatively little debris accumulated. But if a town was destroyed either by natural disaster, such as an earthquake, or by war several times in the course of a century or two, the accumulation of debris was relatively great. Similarly, a site that was only occupied for a few hundred years will have a small amount of debris as compared with a site that was occupied for several thousand years. Thus Teleilat el-Ghassul, a chalcolithic site in Palestine which was occupied less than a thousand years, stands only about four to six feet high. Old Testament Jericho, on the other hand, was inhabited for more than six thousand years, and in spite of considerable erosion, it reaches a height of more than seventy feet.

Whatever the size, mounds are made up of the debris of at least one and usually a number of occupations. The debris and remains of each occupation form a stratum of the mound. Several successive occupations of a site result in a series of superimposed strata in the mound; the debris of the earliest occupation comprises the lowest stratum, and the debris of the latest forms the top stratum. In turn, each stratum may be made up of a number of layers, each of which may represent a different kind of debris. Each type of debris has its own texture and colour. For example, the colour and texture of occupational debris, which is usually greyish-brown and packed hard, differs from destruction debris, which – in a site where mud-bricks were used – is more loosely packed and may be an orange-brown or reddish-brown with bits of fallen and disintegrated brick or, if the buildings were burned with fire, a grey or sometimes a white layer of ash. The differences in colour and texture of the debris enables the archaeologist to disintinguish the various layers of debris.

Obviously these layers are not absolutely level nor uniformly thick over the mound. In low areas they tend to be thicker as a rule; toward the sides of the mound, they dip sharply downward; in a fill, they tend to rise to a point in the centre or slope along one side depending on where the labourers who filled the area stood and dumped the dirt. Frequently layers are cut by pits sunk from layers above, by foundation trenches for later buildings or by robber trenches. In such instances, later deposits are found at the same absolute level as the layers which have been cut and in part destroyed.

In the first area opened on the north of Sohar, for example, a number of superimposed hard clay surfaces were found in conjunction with a stone wall. In each of these surfaces from one to half a dozen circular pits about a foot in diameter had been dug. In keeping with scientific methodology it was necessary to clean out the contents of all the pits associated with a single surface before that surface itself was completely removed. The workmen caught on almost immediately and were soon vying with one another to see who could exhibit the greatest skill in locating and clearing a *giflah* 'pit'.

Since the archaeologist is primarily interested in recovering the culture of each occupation, he must deal with the remains of each occupation as a unit. Thus each stratum must be excavated as a unit; it must not be contaminated by later material from strata above or by earlier objects from strata below. Furthermore, each stratum is made up of a number of layers of different kinds of debris, and it is of the utmost importance that each layer is removed as a unit and uncontaminated by material from other layers. For example, sometimes within an occupation period there are several phases of building. If we are to gain an accurate picture of the history of the site, it is important that we distinguish these phases, determining which is the earliest and which is the latest. These phases, of course, are associated with certain layers of debris. If, therefore, we are to separate the phases from one another, we must strip off the layers with which they are associated one by one.

With this understanding of stratigraphy in archaeological remains, we can now turn our attention to the art of excavating. The first problem confronting the archaeologist is where to dig. The choice of a site and the selection of an area or areas of the site usually depend on a number of factors. The most important of these is the archaeologist's purpose in digging. If he wishes to develop a pottery chronology for an area, he will select a site that has been occupied over a long period of time, and he will dig in the domestic quarter of the town, since that is the area where pottery was most commonly used. If he is interested in investigating the fortifications and gateway of a site, he will excavate along the perimeter of the mound near the place or places where the approach to the top of the mound is the most gradual, since ancient man often sought the most gentle grade for climbing to his city, just as we do today. If he is interested in determining the chronological range of the occupation of a site with a view to future excavations as we were at Sohar, he will dig a number of small test sections at different places on the mound.

Practical considerations also determine the choice. The amount of money at the excavator's disposal, the distance of the site from a good market town where supplies can be obtained, the availability of the site for excavation, the regulations governing excavations in a country, and the security of the area in which the site is located are factors that play a role in the selection of the site.

At Sohar, a large part of the ancient mound is covered by present-day dwellings and another part is strewn with inviolable Muslim burials. Excavation was therefore limited to unoccupied areas on the fringes of the city or to vacant lots. For one of our exploratory trenches, we were fortunate in finding a large open area near the centre of the mound where the greatest deposit had accumulated.

The size of the area excavated is usually determined by balancing the objective of the dig with the amount of time at the excavator's disposal and by the number of trained archaeological supervisors and workmen available. Generally it should be small enough to control, but sufficiently large to provide ample working room. If the excavator plans to go deep, he must dig a larger area to allow for stairways or ramps for getting in and out of the area, and for ample light and work space as the excavation deepens. A good rule of the thumb for determining the size of the area is to make the width and length of the area equal the probable depth of the excavation. Thus if the archaeologist foresees digging to a depth of 15 feet, the surface area should be no less than 15 feet long by 15 feet wide. When the site has been selected, it is surveyed and contour plan is made. The area or areas chosen for excavation are drawn on the plan. Camp is set up; tools are purchased; workmen are hired; excavation begins.

I have emphasized that each stratum and, in fact, each layer must be removed if one is to get an accurate view of the culture and history of an occupation. Obviously one cannot dig an arbitrary depth over the area, since this would normally cut through several layers and mix their contents together, with the result that it would be impossible to determine the culture characteristics or date of any one layer. In excavation, then, each layer must be stripped off as a unit regardless of its unevenness and varied depth. Except in instances where the colour and texture of a layer of reddish-brown decomposed mud-brick, the colour and texture of the layers are difficult and generally impossible to distinguish when digging from above, owing to the slight differences in colour tone and relative hardness of packing. But while these distinctions are difficult to make when digging from above, they are generally easy to see when viewed in vertical section from the side. For this reason, the excavator digs a small control or test trench, measuring about three feet wide to a depth of two or three feet along one or two sides or perhaps through the middle of the area. This trench is carefully excavated from above, and its sides are kept vertical and smooth during the digging. When a depth of two or three feet is reached, the excavation is stopped and the archaeologist examines the two profiles of his area on each side of the cut. Thus the test trench places at his disposal a key to the stratification of the area showing the depth, direction, colour and texture of each layer, and the relationship of one layer to another.

On the basis of this key, the excavator peels off the layers in the remaining unexcavated portion of the area. If possible, it is desirable to dig two control trenches at right angles to one another, in order to obtain stratigraphic control throughout both the length and breadth of the area. As the layers appear, they are numbered and fully described in the excavator's notebook; for quick reference, these numbers are written on tags which are attached by means of long nails to the layers showing in the vertical section.

The control trench is also used for investigating special problems, such as locating earthen floors and determining the relationship of walls to layers of debris and to other walls. Even if the test trench is poorly excavated and the layers from it are hopelessly mixed, its sides still preserve a key for the accurate removal of layers over the remainder of the section. It is better to destroy three feet of an area in a test trench and thereby gain a means of controlling the remainder, than to spoil the entire area by digging without stratigraphic control. In short, the control trench is the heart of stratigraphic excavation. Without it, accurate stratigraphic excavation is impossible to attain. It is to archaeology what the X-ray is to medical diagnosis.

When walls of buildings or fortifications appear, they are investigated to determine the layers with which their construction and destruction are associated. They are cleaned, photographed, and planned, and they are also carefully studied for architectural features. When all possible information has been gleaned from them, they are carefully dismantled so that lower strata can be excavated, since they are frequently reused from earlier deposits, and fragments of sculpture and inscriptions are sometimes found built into later walls. For example, in 1952 at Dhiban (Biblical Dibon), Jordan, a capital was discovered of the Byzantine period reused upside down as a springer for an arch in an Arab house. We discovered a similar instance of a reused block at Hajar Bin Humeid in 1951. In a house wall of the Islamic period, a long and very important pre-Islamic inscription had been built into the wall upside down.

In sites where stone was used as the primary building material, walls were frequently destroyed for their ready-cut blocks by later builders at the site. With a careful study of the layers, the archaeologist can usually find and trace the trench left by the removal of the walls which we call a robber trench. In this way, the plan of the foundations of the building can often be reconstructed even though the blocks have long since been removed. He can usually ascertain the period of the removal of the blocks by determining the date of the layer which is associated with the digging of the robber trench.

In the last area dug at Sohar, a robber trench was found not far below the present surface. It was about three feet wide, over three feet deep, and ran the full fifteen feet across the area of the excavation. It is easy to see how seriously the results of a careful stratigraphic excavation could be affected if the contents of such a large intrusion from above, as represented by the fill of the robber trench, were mixed unknowingly with the finds from the layers on either side of it. In this particular case, the difference in age was hardly significant, but there are many cases in which the date of a robber trench and the stratum around it vary many centuries.

This process of excavation is continued until the end of the campaign or until the purpose of the excavations has been achieved. At the end of the season, the sides or vertical sections of the trench are drawn to scale showing the exact position and characteristics of each layer and the relationship of it to surrounding layers; this task is greatly facilitated by the descriptive tags attached to the section as noted above. Black-and-white and colour photographs, the former for publication and the latter for the excavator's further study, are also made of the sides of the trench. In addition, the excavator also has a series of plans and photographs of the building remains of each excavated stratum. By using both kinds of drawings and photographs, he can reconstruct the stratigraphy of the excavated area. This is the real test of a technique of excavation.

All excavation is destruction; once an area has been dug, it can never be reconstructed except by the excavator from his notebook and drawings. No two areas, not even when they adjoin one another, have identical stratification. This means that archaeology is one of the few disciplines in which the opportunity to duplicate an experiment exactly is not found. Because of this, archaeological excavation is critical work, and each area must be dug and recorded as carefully as possible.

From this description of excavation technique, it should be clear that archaeological digging is hard work. Power tools are never used, although a small bulldozer could be used to good advantage for tasks like removing a dump left on top of a mound by an earlier excavator, or moving large stones and blocks. Picks, hoes, mason's trowels, and knives are the best all-round tools for excavation; but sometimes a nut pick, a toothbrush, or even a camel-hair brush is the only implement that can be safely employed.

Thus far we have concerned ourselves with the nature of archaeological deposits and methods of excavation. Now we must turn to the objects, and consider their nature and importance, and the methods of handling them in the field. Many kinds of objects are found in the excavation of Near Eastern sites: stone reliefs, sculpture, inscriptions, and small objects such as bowls, jars, ladles, seals, beads, and incense burners; clay vessels of all kinds, inscribed tablets, and figurines; metal (usually bronze or iron) tools, weapons, and personal objects such as fibulae; occasionally objects of bone and ivory such as pins, plaques, inlay panels, and rings; rarely wooden objects such as furniture or bowls. By far the most common finds are pottery. Every ancient mound is littered with 'sherds' (broken fragments of pottery), and astonishing numbers are found in every excavation. For example, in one campaign of slightly less than three months' duration at Dothan in Palestine, more than 145,000 sherds were found. Generally speaking, objects found in Arabia lack intrinsic worth apart from exceptional finds such as the bronze lions and the gold necklace from Timna'. Objects are of importance to the archaeologist because they shed light on various aspects of a culture, and are useful for purposes of dating and comparing cultures. To understand these areas of importance, one must know something about objects themselves.

All human institutions and everything that man makes undergo change. This is true of language and government on the one hand, and of architecture, tools, weapons, pottery, and other objects on the other. The rate of change (some things change more quickly and more frequently than others) and the direction of change (some things improve; others degenerate; still others disappear) vary with different classes of objects and with different members of the same class. No fixed rule governs the operation of change; we only know that all things change in the course of time. This is of the utmost importance to the archaeologist.

In excavating a mound of many strata, he finds objects in the different layers of debris that make up each stratum. He knows that the objects from the lowest stratum are earliest, that those from the stratum immediately above are later, and that those from the next stratum and the next one above it are successively later in time. Thus from stratigraphy the archaeologist knows the correct order of objects in the scale of time. With this information he can arrange any class of objects in their stratigraphic sequence from the earliest to the latest, isolate the important characteristics of each class of objects in each stratum, and determine when the objects underwent change. In other words, by knowing the correct sequence of objects from his stratigraphic excavations, he develops a history of the objects, i.e. he discovers the layer in which a particular kind of object first appears, each layer in which change took place, and the layer in which it last appears. This presupposes, of course, that good stratigraphic excavation has been done, i.e. that each layer has been carefully stripped off the mound; otherwise the layers and their contents will be hopelessly mixed, and it will be impossible to determine with any degree of accuracy the layers in which changes took place.

Once the characteristics of the objects of each occupation at a site are established, many kinds of useful information can be gathered from the objects. Since all sites in a given culture share similar kinds of objects, many of the characteristics of the entire cultural area in which the site is located can be learned from these objects. Furthermore, once the characteristics of the objects have been determined, it is easy to establish which objects were made locally and which were imported from other lands.

With regard to imports, by using similar typological analyses from other cultural areas, the region from which the imported object came and the probable date of the import can also be discovered. In some instances, archaeologists recognize foreign characteristics in locally-made objects, and thus are able to show that local craftsmen imitated imported objects, even though the foreign prototype may never be found in the area. Both imports and imitations of imports prove the existence of contracts between cultures, and are of the greatest importance for an understanding of ancient economic life.

With these possibilities in mind, the excavator is extremely careful in his handling of objects in the field. If they are to be useful in describing an occupation, they must obviously be kept separate from objects of earlier or later occupations. In practice, this means that all objects found in a layer are kept together in baskets, each of which is identified by a tag on which is written the description of the layer and, whenever possible, the part of the area, e.g. the number of the room, in which the objects were found. When the excavator reaches a new layer, he sets aside the previous baskets containing objects of the layer just excavated, and he uses other baskets and tags for the objects of the new layer. The tag remains with the objects from the layer through cleaning and recording, and is attached to the bag or box containing the objects of two or more layers of the same date. The contents of those layers can be combined in the reconstruction of the cultural history of the site. But if the objects of each layer were not kept separate in the excavation and it is later recognized that they belong to two different periods, they cannot be separated into their proper respective layers. It is an obvious, but frequently overlooked, principle of excavation that layers and their objects can always be combined if later study proves that they belong to one period; but two or more layers and their contents cannot be separated into individual components if they were excavated as if they belonged to one period.

Most objects found in an Arabian excavation can be safely cleaned by washing, but the cleaning of clay tablets, metal, wooden, ivory, and bone objects usually require special methods and equipment not ordinarily available in the field. Such objects are carefully packed and shipped to a laboratory as soon as possible. When objects have been cleaned, they are sorted and studied. Many objects, usually sherds, are discarded by the excavator, owing to the high cost of shipment and storage space, and it is in the sorting operation that he determines which objects must be kept and which ones can be discarded. All objects that are kept are recorded in the field catalogue, and whole or restored objects, together with all objects of exceptional interest, are drawn and photographed in the field if time permits. They are then packed for transport to the national museum of the country in which the excavation took place or to some other centre for more thorough study and detailed analysis.

What I have briefly described here is good excavation technique in this decade of the twentieth century. We have come far from the treasure-hunting days of archaeology, though this is still the view of archaeological work held by many laymen. We have every reason to expect greatly improved methods during the coming decades. With each improvement in technique, we are able to squeeze more information from our material, and as a result to make greater contributions to knowledge of man's past.

Notes and Bibliography

CHAPTER I: AKHDHAR AND MUSCAT

1. P. Aucher Eloy, *Relations de voyages en Orient de 1830 à 1838* (Paris 1843). In his journal, which was edited by M. Jaubert in 1838, Eloy gives a graphic account of his sufferings and adventures.

2. J. R. Wellsted, *Travels in Arabia*, Vol. I (London, 1838), pp. 115–16.

3. William Burks Terry, famed photographer who flew the longest photo-reconnaissance missions of World War II, mapped Tarawa Island for the invasion, developed radar cameras, depth-charge locating cameras, automatic bomb-spotting cameras and the colour comparison method of depth determination for the Central Pacific atolls.

4. S. B. Miles, 'Across the Green Mountain of Oman', *Geographical Journal*, Vol. XVIII (1901), p. 482.

5. See Ray L. Cleveland, 'Muscat: Capital City of Oman', *Middle East Forum*, November 1959, pp. 27ff.

6. J. G. Lorimer, *Gazetteer of the Persian Gulf, Oman and Central Arabia*, Vol. I (Calcutta, 1915), p. 214.

7. *The Voyages and Travels of John Struys* (London, 1684), p. 353.

8. A. Hamilton, *A New Account of the East Indies* (1727), ed. Sir William Foster (London, 1930), Vol. I, pp. 44, 46.

9. In 1853 Richard Burton noted that 'there is a standing order in the chief cities of Egypt, that all who stir abroad after dark without a lantern shall pass the night in the station-house'. *Pilgrimage to Al-Madinah and Meccah*, Vol. I (London, 1893), p. 119. This custom was also introduced into Aden by Captain S. B. Haines.

10. In spite of his authority as an eyewitness it is difficult to accept the figure given by Sheikh Mansur: 'In the want of correct data, I shall not probably exceed the reality by stating the number of inhabitants, in 1802, to have been near 60,000.' *History of Seyd Said* (London, 1819), p. 23. In 1816, Lieutenant William Heude observed, 'The population of Maskat has

been variously estimated; a constant bustle and activity, and a great influx of strangers making it appear far greater than it is. . . . I think that with resident strangers, it falls not short of 30,000 souls.' *A Voyage up the Persian Gulf and a Journey Overland from India to England in 1817* (London, 1819), p. 31.

11. Lieutenant T. Lumsden, *A Journey from Merut to India* (London, 1822), p. 68.

12. See her *A Woman's Journey Round the World* (London, 1852), p. 236.

13. J. R. Wellsted, *Travels im Arabia*, Vol. I, p. 352-3.

14. J. S. Buckingham, *Travels in Assyria, Media and Persia*, Vol II (London, 1830), pp. 408, 413 and 428.

15. *See* William Foxwell Albright, 'The Chronology of Ancient South Arabia in the Light of the First Campaign of Excavation in Qataban', *Bulletin of the American Schools of Oriental Research*, No. 119 (1950), pp. 5–15. Gus van Beek, 'Recovering the Ancient Civilization of Arabia', *The Biblical Archaeologist*, Vol. XV (1952), pp. 2–18.

Berta Segall, 'Sculpture from Arabia Felix: The Hellenistic Period', *American Journal of Archaeology*, Vol. 59 (1955), pp. 207-14.

Gus van Beek, 'A Radio Carbon Date for Early South Arabia', *Bulletin of the American Schools of Oriental Research*, No. 143 (1956), pp. 6–9.

Berta Segall, 'Sculpture from Arabia Felix: The Earliest Phase', *Ars Orientalis* II (1957), pp. 35–42.

Richard LeBaron Bowen, Jr., and Frank P. Albright, *Archaeological Discoveries in South Arabia*, in *Publication of the American Foundation for the Study of Man*, Vol. II (Baltimore, 1958).

Frank P. Albright, 'The Excavation of the Temple of the Moon at Marib (Yemen)', *Bulletin of the American Schools of Oriental Research*, No. 128 (1952), p. 25ff.

A. Jamme, 'Les expéditions archéologiques américaines en Arabie du Sud (1950–1953), *Oriente Moderno*, Vol. 33 (1953), pp. 133ff.

Frank P. Albright and Albert Jamme, 'A Bronze Statue from Mareb, Yemen', *The Scientific Monthly*, Vol. LXXVI, No. 1 (January 1953), pp. 33–35.

Berta Segall, 'The Arts and King Nabonidus', *American Journal of Archaeology*, No. 59 (1955), pp. 315–18.

Berta Segall, 'Problems of Copy and Adaptation in the Second Quarter of the First Millennium, B.C.', *American Journal of Archaeology*, Vol. 60 (1956), pp. 165–70.

Albert Jamme, *Sabaean Inscriptions from Mahram Bilqîs (Mârib)*, in *Publications of the American Foundation for the Study of Man*, Vol. III (Baltimore, 1962).

Ray L. Cleveland, *An Ancient South Arabian Necropolis*, in *Publications of the American Foundation for the Study of Man*, Vol. IV (Baltimore, 1965).

16. R. B. Serjeant, *The Portuguese off the South Arabian Coast* (Oxford, 1963), p. 164.

17. With regard to inscription number three Professor A. M. Honeyman remarks, 'Has the first part of the inscription been recarved?' The photograph seems to show that the lettering of the upper part has been crushed into a space slightly too small for it. One wonders if the inscription may have been deliberately altered after Portugal became independent of Spain again in 1640. Professor R. B. Serjeant comments, 'My only suggestion is that, as Philip III was a Spaniard, he might have sent a Spaniard as captain of the fortress, and the Portuguese commander after 1640, disliking his probably proud inscription, changed the first part. What suggests this to me is that in the 1588 inscription, Philip II of Spain is styled as Philip I of Portugal, but Philip III of Spain, his successor, is so styled in this inscription without reference to his being Philip II of Portugal.' R. B. Serjeant, *op. cit.*, p. 165.

18. On September 21, 1933, President Franklin D. Roosevelt wrote to the present Sultan, 'Great and Good Friend: One hundred years ago on this date Edmund Roberts, Esquire, an agent of the Government of the United States, signed a treaty of Amity and Commerce with your illustrious great-great-grandfather. . . . It is a satisfaction to record that this Treaty, one of the oldest agreements still in effect between the United States and any other country, has continued uninterruptedly for a century to form the basis of relations between the two nations.'

CHAPTER 2: RELIGION IN OMAN

1. T. P. Hughes, *A Dictionary of Islam* (London, 1895), p. 377.
2. R. Patai, *Golden River to Golden Road* (Philadelphia, 1962), p. 347.
3. D. van der Meulen, *The Wells of Ibn Saud* (London, 1957), p. 147.
4. R. Owen, *The Golden Bubble* (London, 1957), pp. 171–2.

5. E. A. Salem, *Political Theory and Institutions of the Khawarij* (Baltimore, 1956), pp. 31–2.

6. Mohammed ibn Abdu-l-Kerim esh Sharistany, *Kitab-el-Milal wa'n-Nihal* [*Religions and Sects*]. Taken from *History of the Imams and Seyyids of Oman* (London, 1871), Appendix B, p. 392.

7. E. A. Salem, *op. cit.*, p. 34.

8. S. M. Zwemer, *Arabia: The Cradle of Islam* (New York, 1900), p. 78.

9. Other pioneer American missionaries are to be numbered among the outstanding explorers of Arabia, many of whose names are legendary: Nearchus, Gallus, Ibn Battuta, de Couillan, di Varthema, de Quadra, Paez, Montserrate, Jourdain, Middleton, D'Arvieux, Pitts, De la Grelaudiere, Barbier, Niebuhr, Forskall, Cramer, Von Haven, Baurenfeind, Badia (Ali Bey), Seetzen, Burckhardt, Sadlier, Maurizi (Mansur), Ehrenberg, Hemprich, Tamisier, Wellsted, Cruttenden, Carter, Whitelock, Combes, Hulton, Schimper, Botta, Wolff, Eloy, Passama, Hamerton, Playfair, Arnaud, von-Wrede, Wallin, Stern, Burton, Palgrave, Disbrowe, Guarmani, Pelly, Miles, Halévy, Keane, Van Maltzan, Koch, Doughty, Hunter, Blunts, Huber, Euting, Manzoni, Caprotti, Glaser, Hurgronje, Defler, Bents, Nolde, Hirsch, Harris, Zwemer, Malcolm, Tate, Wahab, Harrington, Bury, Haig, French, Jacob, Cox, Schweinfurth, Beneyton, Musil, Wavell, Bell, Shakespear, Leachman, Raunkier, Raswan, Philby, Holt, Van Ess, Carruthers, Lee-Warner, Forbes, Little, Dickson, Rutter, Cheeseman, Lees, Williamson, Eccles, Boscawan, Thomas, Cobbold, Muller, Landberg, Rathjens, Harrison, van der Meulen, von Wissmann, Helfritz, Storm, Hamilton, Twitchell, Gardner, Stark, Ingrams, Caton-Thompson, Perowne, Fakhry, Thoms, Dykstra, Meinerthagen, Fox, Altounyan, Serjeant, Thesiger. (To the best of this writer's knowledge this is the first approximately complete list of notable Arabian explorers ever assembled on one page).

10. Joseph Pitts, *A Faithful Account of the Religion and Manners of the Mohometans*, Fourth Edition (Exon. 1731), p. 259. This was originally published in 1704 and contains the first authentic account by an Englishman of the Pilgrimage to Mecca.

Works also consulted for this chapter

E. W. Lane, *Manners and Customs of the Modern Egyptians* (London, 1954), p. 111.

S. W. Koelle, *Mohammed and Mohammedanism* (London, 1899), p. 474.

A Life of Ramon Lull, written by an unknown hand around 1311, translated from the Catalan by E. H. Peers (London, 1927).

P. Thomas, *Christians and Christianity in India and Pakistan* (London, 1954), p. 172.

George Smith, *Henry Martyn Saint and Scholar* (London, 1892), p. 552.

John Sargent, *Memoir of the Rev. Henry Martyn* (London, 1819), p. 497.

Edward J. Juri, *The Middle East: Its Religion and Culture* (Philadelphia, 1956) p. 119.

James Robson, *Ian Keith-Falconer of Arabia* (New York), p. 30.

Rev. Robert Sinker, *Memorials of the Hon. Ian Keith-Falconer* (Cambridge, 1888), preface, p. 1.

Rev. Robert Birks, *Life and Correspondence of T. V. French* (London, 1895).

CHAPTER 3: TO SOHAR

1. See G. J. Eccles, 'The Sultanate of Muscat and Oman, with a Description of a Journey into the Interior undertaken in 1925', *Journal of the Central Asian Society*, Vol. XIV (1927), pp. 21–2. See also Bertram Thomas, *The Arabs* (London, 1937), p. 251.

2. The contention of Walter Dostal ('The Evolution of Bedouin Life', in *L'antica società beduina*, ed. Francesco Gabrieli [Studi semitici 2, Rome, 1959], pp. 11–33) that riding on the hump represents significant progress over riding behind the hump can only provoke ridicule among those intimately familiar with camel nomadism. Dostal's very original hypothesis that a camel herder riding on the crupper could not keep large herds of camels (*op. cit.*, p. 27) is not to be taken seriously; the writer has frequently seen enormous herds of camels in various parts of Oman, and the camel drivers have always been riding behind the hump.

3. See Carl R. Raswan, *Drinkers of the Wind* (New York, 1942).

4. R. F. Burton, *The Gold Mines of Midian* (London, 1878), pp. 120–1. The story has been slightly modified by the writer.

5. P. Ponafidine, *Life in the Moslem East* (London, 1911), p. 129.

6. John Lewis Burckhardt, *Notes on the Bedouins and Wahabys* (London, 1830), pp. 260–1.

7. Harry E. Wedeck, *Dictionary of Aphrodisiacs* (New York, 1951), p. 54.

8. H. St. J. B. Philby, *The Heart of Arabia*, Vol. II (London, 1922), pp. 215–16.

9. *The History and Description of Africa and the Notable Things Therein Contained* (1526).

10. 'The rejection of camel flesh . . . goes back far into the past: the prohibition was included in the Levitican code of the Jews; it was observed at ancient Haran in Mesopotamia; and it was enforced by the Syrian Christian hermit St. Simeon Stylites (d. 459?) who forbade camel flesh to his Saracen converts in an effort to rid them of their heathen ways. . . . Though the Moslems themselves have adopted many Jewish food observances, they claim that the Jewish prohibition of camel flesh was abrogated by Jesus, whom they recognize as a prophet.' Frederick J. Simons, *Eat Not This Flesh* (Madison, 1961), p. 89.

11. W. F. Albright, 'Islam and the Religions of the Ancient Orient', *Journal of the American Oriental Society*, Vol. 60 (1940), pp. 283–301; 'Zur Zähmung des Kamels', *Zeitschrift für die alttestamentliche Wissenschaft*, Vol. 62 (1949–50), p. 315; *From the Stone Age to Christianity* (Baltimore, 1957), pp. 149, 164–6; *Archaeology and the Religion of Israel* (Baltimore, 1956), pp. 96–7, 132–3.

12. *See* Reinhard Walz, 'Zum Problem der Domestikation der altweltlichen Cameliden', *Zeitschrift der Deutschen Morgenländischen Gesellschaft*, 101 (1951), pp. 29–51. Note also:
'The lamented H. St. J. B. Philby pointed out to the writer several years ago that the sandy region between el-Hasa and Oman is peculiarly fitted to have been a home of the Arabian camel. Here the Babylonians may have known it early in their history, long before it was successfully domesticated about the third quarter of the second millenium B.C.' W. F. Albright, 'Abram the Hebrew: A New Archaeological Interpretation', *Bulletin of the American Schools of Oriental Research*, No. 163 (Oct., 1961), p. 38.

13. For the geology of Oman see: D. M. Morton, 'The Geology of Oman', *Fifth World Petroleum Congress* (1959); R. G. S. Hudson, R. V. Browne and M. Chatton, 'The Structure and Stratigraphy of the Jebel Qamar Area, Oman', *Proceedings of the Geological Society of London*, No. 1513 (15 June 1954); G. M. Lees, 'The Physical Geography of South Eastern Arabia', *Geographical Journal*, Vol. LXXI (1928), pp. 441–70; G. M. Lees, 'The Geology and Tectonics of Oman and Parts of South-

Eastern Arabia', *Quarterly Journal of the Geological Society of London*, Vol. LXXXIV, No. 336 (1928), pp. 585–670.

14. P. B. Popenoe, *Date Growing* (Los Angeles, 1913), p. 102. *See also* V. H. W. Dowson, 'The Date and the Arab', *Royal Central Asian Journal*, Vol. XXXVI (1949), p. 39.

15. Sir Henry Yule, *The Book of Ser Marco Polo*, Vol. II, 3rd ed. (London, 1903), p. 340.

16. *The Commentaries of the Great Affonso Dalboquerque*, Vol. I (London, 1875), pp. 91–2.

Works also consulted for this chapter

Lt.-Col. S. B. Miles, *Field Notes of November 1875*, Muscat Archives, No. 132/407 (1876).

S. H. Leeder, *The Desert Gateway* (London, 1910), p. 258.

Andre Von Dumreicher, *Trackers and Smugglers in the Deserts of Egypt* (London, 1931), p. 85.

Knut Schmidt-Nielsen, 'The Physiology of the Camel', *Scientific American*, December, 1959, p. 140–51.

Cherry Kearton, *The Shifting Sands of Algeria* (London, 1924), p. 104–5. Andrew Crichton, *History of Arabia*, Vol. I (Edinburgh, 1834), p. 167.

Eyles Irwin, *A Series of Adventures in the Course of a Voyage Up the Red Sea* (London, 1780), p. 303.

C. S. Jarvis, *The Black Garden of Allah* (London, 1949), p. 164.

John Foster Fraser, *The Land of Veiled Women* (London, 1911), p. 38.

Xavierde Planhol, *The World of Islam* (Ithaca, 1959), p. 59.

Desmond Vesey-Fitzgerald, 'From Hasa to Oman by Car', *Geogr. Rev.*, Vol. XLI (1951), pp. 544–60. Alexander Melamid, 'Transportation in Eastern Arabia', *The Geographical Review*, Vol. LII, No. 1 (1962), pp. 122–4.

Frederick Charles Danvers, *The Portuguese in India*, Vol. II (London, 1894), p. 192.

CHAPTER 4: DISEASE AND MEDICINE IN OMAN

1. For a detailed description of an actual digging operation, *see* Anthony Smith, *Blind White Fish* (London, 1953), pp. 92–4. *See also* George B. Cressey, 'Qanats, Karez and Foggarras', *Geographical Review*, XLVIII (1958), pp. 27–44.

2. J. R. Wellsted, *Travels in Arabia*, Vol. I, p. 92.

3. The Persian-appointed governor al-Mukabir established his residence at Jamsetjerd to rule over the two provinces of Oman and Bahrain. Al-Mukabir appears to have confined his troops to the Batinah maritime plain and to have allowed the Julanda princes in Nazwa jurisdiction over the Oman tribes on the payment of tribute and acknowledgement of vassalage to Persia. This name Jamsetjerd may well be Gamastfird or Damastgird. If this governor mentioned was a Sassanian, it is likely that he did not bear the Arab name al-Mukabir, but that this is merely a traditional name coined by the Arabs. Cf. *Kashf al-ghummah*, ed. Hedwig Klein (Hamburg, 1938), p. 23.

4. The carnelian trade of North Western India (now Pakistan) dates back to Roman times. The author of the *Periplus of the Erythraean Sea* mentions that from the port of Barygaza (the modern Broach on the Gulf of Cambay) were exported in his time (the first century of the Christian era) 'agate and carnelian'. The Zimbabwe ruins have also yielded several specimens of red carnelian beads.

5. S. B. Miles, *The Countries and Tribes of the Persian Gulf*, Vol. II (London, 1919), p. 534.

6. See in, e.g. H. St J. B. Philby, *Sheba's Daughters* (London, 1939), pp. 373, 379; D. van der Meulen, *Aden to the Hadhramaut* (London, 1947), pp. 119, 127.

7. *See* Wendell Phillips, 'Recent Discoveries in the Egyptian Faiyum and Sinai', *Science*, Vol. 107, No. 2791 (June 25, 1948); 'Africa from Nubia to Turkana', *Scientific Monthly*, Vol. LXIX, No. 4 (October, 1949); 'Further African Studies', *Scientific Monthly*, Vol. LXX, No. 3 (March, 1950).

8. Ailon Shiloh, 'The System of Medicine in Middle East Culture', *The Middle East Journal*, Vol. 15, No. 3 (Summer, 1961), p. 277.

9. Paul W. Harrison, *Doctor in Arabia* (London, 1943), p. 57. Dr Harrison had once greatly impressed the Arabs of Kuwait by cutting a vein

out of his own arm, and transplanting it into the neck of a dying Arab boy whose father had refused to provide from his own arm, recoiling in horror at the idea. *See* Ann M. Harrison, *A Tool in His Hand* (New York, 1958), pp. 51, 52. Dr Harrison built the Knox Memorial Hospital in Matrah, Oman, in 1932.

10. 'Innoculation for the small-pox has been in use from time immemorial among the Bedouins. Mothers perform this operation on their children, opening the skin of the arm with the prickle of a thorn.' Carsten Niebuhr, *Travels Through Arabia*, Vol. II (Edinburgh, 1792), p. 281.

11. In the latter part of the nineteenth century a schooner was wrecked off the Oman coast and 'the crew taken overland to Muscat by Bedoos [*badu*] who fed them on Camel's milk and dates, which gave them Diarrhœa, as a remedy for which the Bedoos seared them all over with hot irons'. Col. S. B. Miles, *The Countries and Tribes of the Persian Gulf* Vol. II, p. 523.

12. The use of amulets is justified by a saying of Mohammed; 'There is no wrong in using charms and spells so long as you do not associate anything with God.' [Sorcery] 'is fometimes employed, however to feduce a wife from the arms of her husband into thofe of a ftranger, all that is requifte for this is to fix a certain billet on her door. The inhabitants of Oman are peculiarly fkilled in this execrable fcience: Yet they are certainly inferior to our European forcerers; for they know nothing of the art of riding through the air on a broomftich or of nocturnal affemblies under the prefidency of the devil.' Carsten Niebuhr, *Travels Through Arabia*, Vol. II, pp. 286–7.

13. For an account of the animistic beliefs on Arab medicine, *see* Ailon Shiloh, *op. cit.*, p. 279. In the author's opinion Ailon Shiloh's views should be accepted only with considerable reservations.

14. *See*, for an account of med. al advances in Islam, E. G. Browne, *Arabian Medicine* (Cambridge, 1921), pp. 45–46.

15. Ann M. Harrison, *A Tool In His Hand*, p. 118.

16. Wendell Phillips, *Qataban and Sheba* (London, 1955), pp. 76–7.

17. 'The extreme limit of four years after cohabitation is allowed for the birth of a child by the Shafiite and Malikite codes, which within that limit would regard a child as legitimate, provided, of course, that the mother had not in the meantime contracted another marriage. Hanafi law [upon the authority of a tradition reported by Ayisha] makes the limit two years. The Shiites, however, refuse to accept any child as legitimate if born

more than ten months [as under the old Roman law] after the last union of husband and wife.' Ruben Levy, *The Social Structure of Islam* (Cambridge, 1957), pp. 135–6. The present writer's parentheses.

18. The writer wishes to thank Beth Thoms for this graphic account.

Works also consulted for this chapter

De Lacy O'Leary, *How Greek Science Passed to the Arabs* (London, 1949), p. 1.

Luch M. J. Garnett, *The Women of Turkey and Their Folk Lore* (London, 1890), p. 148.

Lt.-Col. P. M. Sykes, *Persian Manners and Customs* (Edinburgh, 1913–14), p. 19.

Hilma Granqvist, *Birth and Childhood Among the Arabs* (Helsingfors, 1947), p. 53.

Reuben Levy, *The Social Structure of Islam* (Cambridge, 1957), pp. 135–6.

Anne Van Sommer and Samuel M. Zwemer, *Our Moslem Sisters* (New York, 1907), p. 150.

Eleanor F. Rathbone, *Child Marriage: The Indian Minotaur* (London, 1924) p. 26.

CHAPTER 5: THE WILL OF ALLAH? FATALISM AND SLAVERY

1. *See* Bertram Thomas, 'The Musadam Peninsula and Its People the Shihuh', *Journal of the Central Asian Society*, XVI (1929), pp. 75–7. The Shihuh correspond to the Ichthyophagoi of Ptolemy. *See* Percy Cox, 'Some Excursions in Oman,' *Geographical Journal*, LXVI (1925), p. 199. *See* Sir Arnold Wilson, *S.W. Persia* (London, 1942), p. 208.

2. G. C. L. Bertram, *The Fisheries of Muscat and Oman* (Revenue Department, Muscat, 1948), p. 5.

3. The word *qadhi* does not have the same meaning all over Arabia. In Yemen it is used as a title bestowed by the Imam upon ministers appointed by him who are not *Saif al-Islam*, sons of the reigning or late Imam. The title is also bestowed in Yemen by the Imam upon commoners who are appointed by his privy council *al-Majlis*, and is adopted by many literate persons who occupy an official position in the country.

4. Muhammad Asad, *The Principles of State and Government in Islam* (Berkeley, 1961), p. 11.

5. *See* Col. S. B. Miles, *op. cit.*, Vol. I, p. 40.

6. Col. (now Sir) Hugh Boustead, famed former Resident Advisor and British Agent, East Aden Protectorate, and distinguished explorer of the South-west Sudan and Mt. Everest; Martin Wynn, an officer in the Indian Police for eighteen years, and former Administrator of Gwader enclave when it was a dependency of Oman (before transfer to Pakistan).

7. Sheikh Mansur, *History of Seyd Said* (London, 1819), p. 117.

8. Taken from Wheeler's *Law of Slavery*, p. 310; *see* William Goodell, *The American Slave Code* (London, 1853), p. 321.

9. 'At Maskat, it is certain, slaves are treated with a degree of humanity that would do honour to our climes. . . . They live at their master's board and sleep under his roof, eating of his dish, and drinking of his cup. . . .' Lieutenant William Heude, *A Voyage up the Persian Gulf and a Journey Overland from India to England in 1817*, p. 25.

10. H. A. R. Gibb and J. H. Kramers, *Shorter Encyclopaedia of Islam* (Leyden and London, 1961), p. 2.

11. In April 1961, the writer and William Terry were introduced to Birkat's equally infamous son Jan Mohammed by Brigadier Pat Waterfield at Bait al-Falaj outside of Matrah. Jan Mohammed was a bandit who had previously preyed on the caramel caravans along the Wadi Aswad, with particular attention given to Baluchis on the Batinah. He was subsequently pardoned by the Sultan and later performed excellent service under Saiyid Tariq during the recent rebellion.

12. Robin Maugham, *The Slaves of Timbuktu* (London, 1961), pp. 4–5, *See also*: *Parliamentary Debates, House of Lords Official Report*, Vol. 225, No. 104 (Thursday, 14 July 1960), pp. 341–3, and Rupert Wilkinson. 'The Slave Trade', *The New Republic*, September 17, 1962, p.11.

13. *Parliamentary Debates, House of Lords Official Report*, Vol. 225, No. 104 (Thursday, 14 July 1960), p. 341.

14. H. St. J. B. Philby, *Forty Years in the Wilderness* (London, 1957), p. 169.

15. C. W. W. Greenidge, Director of Anti-Slavery Society, stated in 1958 with reference to Arabia that 'The most reliable estimate of the slave population would thus be 500,000.' *Slavery* (London, 1958), p. 45. If a number this large is accepted, however, it must be understood

to include many Africans living in Arabia who are not actually owned but who are regarded as members of the slave class.

Works also consulted for this chapter

I. Mendelssohn, *Slavery in the Ancient Near East* (Oxford, 1949), pp. 9, 18.

Bertram Thomas, *Alarms and Excursions in Arabia* (London, 1931), p. 156.

Sir Hamilton Gibb, *Modern Trends in Islam* (Chicago, 1947), p. viii.

Eliot Warburton, *The Crescent and The Cross* (London, 1849), p. 50.

Samuel M. Zwemer, *Childhood in the Muslim World* (New York, 1915), p. 133.

Taha Husain, *Mustaqbal ath-thaqafah fi misr* [The Future of Culture in Egypt] (Cairo, 1938).

James L. Barton, *The Christian Approach to Islam* (Boston, 1918), p. 124.

Gertrude Bell, *Persian Pictures* (London, 1928), pp. 61–2.

Lt.-Col. S. B. Miles, *Field Notes*, Muscat Archives, No. 132/47 (1876).

Syed Ameer Ali, *The Spirit of Islam* (London, 1955), p. 269.

Linda, Incidents In The Life Of A Slave Girl, written by Herself, edited L. Maira Child (Boston, 1861), pp. 75–6, 142.

An Abstract Of The Evidence Delivered Before a Select Committee of the House of Commons In The Years 1790, and 1791: On the Part Of The Petitioners For the Abolition Of The Slave-Trade (London, 1791), pp. 55, 67, 70, 80–1.

William Goodell, *Slavery and Antislavery*, p. 157.

B. M. Palmer, *Slavery a Divine Trust*, pp. 7, 19.

Report on the Anti-Slavery Society of New York (1860), p. 281.

C. Snouck Hurgronje, *Mohammedanism* (New York, 1916), p. 128; also *Mekka* (Leyden, 1931), p. 108.

William Goodall, *The American Slave Code*, pp. 90–1, 120, 229.

Raphael Patai, *Golden River to Golden Road*, p. 87.

Gerald de Gaury, *Arabian Journey and Other Desert Travels* (London, 1950), p. 92.

Aziz S. Atiya, *Crusade, Commerce and Culture* (Bloomington, 1962), p. 30.

S. H. Leeder, *Veiled Mysteries of Egypt* (London, 1915), p. 332.

CHAPTER 6: TRUCIAL OMAN

1. John Marlowe, *The Persian Gulf in the Twentieth Century* (London, 1962), pp. 213–14.

2. 'Seven' could hardly be right – a contract for marriage might be made at that age, but it would be contrary to religious principle to consummate a marriage before physical maturity.

3. J. Robson, *Ian Keith-Falconer of Arabia* (New York), p. 82. In dealing with people in such remote places as Sohar one has to learn a whole new set of weights and measures. The standard weight used here for rice, flour and other foodstuffs is the *kiyas*, which is equivalent to approximately one-half a pound. A larger unit of weight, less commonly employed is the *munn* which is 24 *kiyas* or approximately 12 pounds.
The foot or meter is virtually unknown among the population of Oman. The ancient *shibr*, 'handspan', is used for ordinary linear measurements, along with the *dhira*, 'cubit', i.e. the distance from the elbow to the finger-tips. For larger measurements such as the depth of a well the *ba'a* 'fathom', of approximately six feet is utilized and is the distance between the fingertips with the arms outstretched. These lineal measurements are universal in the Arab world.

4. D. Carruthers, *Arabian Adventure* (London, 1935), p. 28.

5. Sir Hubert Young, *The Independent Arab* (London, 1933), p. 18.

6. The independence of the Sultanate or Kingdom of Oman was affirmed by the Hague Court of Arbitration in the Muscat Doro Case of 1905. *Recueil des Actes et Protocoles concernant le différence entre la France et la Grande Bretagne à propos des boutres de Mascate, soumis au Tribunal D'Arbitage constitué en vertu du Compromis Arbitral conclu à Londres le 13 Octobre 1904 entre les Puissances susmentioneés.* Bureau International de la Cour Permanente D'Arbitrage (La Hague, 1905), *See also* Jasper Y. Brinton, 'The Arabian Peninsula, the protectorates and sheikhdoms'. *Revue Egyptiennes de Droit International*, Vol. III (1947), p. 29; Judge Brinton declares that the rulers of the Sultanate have not alienated either the external or internal sovereignty of the country. Brinton cites the 1862 Anglo-French agreement and the Hague case.

7. *See* Alexander Melamid, 'Political Geography of Trucial Oman and Qatar', *Geographical Review*, Vol. 43 (1953), pp. 194–206; 'Oil and the Evolution of Boundaries in Eastern Arabia', *G.R.*, Vol. 44 (1954), pp.

295–6; 'Boundaries and Petroleum Developments in Southern Arabia', *G.R.*, Vol. 47 (1957), pp. 589–91.

8. *See* G. Bibby, D. H. Gordon and Mortimer Wheeler in *Antiquity*, Vol. 32 (1958), pp. 243–6; also P. V. Glob and G. Bibby, 'A Forgotten Civilization of the Persian Gulf', *Scientific American*, Vol. 203, No. 4 (October 1960), pp. 62–7.

9. Fereydoun Adamiyat, *Bahrein Islands* (New York, 1955), p. 203.

10. *See* Wendell Phillips, 'Recent Discoveries in the Egyptian Faiyum and Sinai', *Science*, Vol. 107, No. 2721, p. 669.

11. 'The Early Arabian Necropolis of Ain Jawan', in *The Bulletin of the American Schools of Oriental Research, Supplementary Studies*, Nos. 7–9 (New Haven, 1950), p. 56.

12. Our classical knowledge of the Persian Gulf comes in the main from the following sources: Megasthenes (about 300 B.C.) whose work has been preserved through quotation by Arrian and Strabo; Eratosthenes of Cyrene (276–194 B.C.) the Alexandrine geographer who knew correctly the general shape of Arabia, testifying to the great trade of the South Arabian states and was the first to call attention to the existence of petroleum in the Gulf region; Polybius (204–122 B.C.); Agatharchides (2nd century B.C.) whose work in five volumes on the Red Sea and southern Arabia has been lost with the exception of a few fragments; Artemidorus of Epheus (about 100 B.C.); Strabo (63 B.C. to A.D. 24) whose Arabian references were mainly taken from Agatharchides, Gallus and Artemidorus; Pliny (A.D. 23–79), a diligent compiler who has left us the most detailed classical description of the Arabian shore of the Persian Gulf; and Ptolemy (middle 2nd century A.D.), the last of the original classical geographical contributors who gave the name of Cape Musandam not incorrectly as Asabon Promontorium'.

13. 'The voyage of Nearchus (326–325 B.C.) from the Indus to the Euphrates is the first event of general importance to mankind, in the history of navigation.' William Vincent, *The Voyage of Nearchus from the Indus to the Euphrates* (London, 1797), p. 1.

14. *See* A. Asher, ed. *The Itinerary of Rabbi Benjamin of Tudela* (2 vols. 1840–1).

15. For general discussion *see* Richard Le Baron Bowen, Jr., 'Marine Industries of Eastern Arabia', *The Geographical Review*, Vol. 41 (1951); 'The Pearl Fisheries of the Persian Gulf', *Middle East Journal*, Vol. 5 (1951), pp. 161–80.

16. For a description of the dhows used in the marine industries of eastern Arabia *see* R. Le B. Bower, Jr., 'Arab Dhows of Eastern Arabia', *American Neptune*, Vol. 9 (1949), pp. 87–132.

'For these Arab dhows were almost the last unspoiled fleet of pure sailing vessels left in the world.' Alan Villiers, *Sons of Sinbad* (London, 1940), p. 3. Large sailing ships in general are very commonly known along the coast of South Arabia as a *sā'iyah* (in agreement with Leo Hirsch's notation of sixty-nine years ago). The largest sailing ship still commonly used is the *būm* or *boom*, which is made in Kuwait and which is frequently seen in the vicinity of Mukalla, Aden, etc. The *sambūq* seems to be a type of sailing vessel built in South Arabia; the 'dhows' made in Aden should be called *sambūqs* (Arabia plural *sanābiq*) if one wants to be accurate. A more colloquial Hadhrami word for large sailing ship is *ẕa'imah*.

17. The Baharna are the original inhabitants of Bahrain and are thought to be the descendants of Arabs taken by Nebuchadnezzar around 550 B.C.

Works also consulted for this chapter

J. S. Buckingham, *Travels in Assyria, Media and Persia* (London, 1830), Vol. II.

C. R. Low, *History of the Indian Navy* (London, 1877), Vol. I, pp. 333–4.

Sheikh Mansur, *History of Seyd Said* (London, 1819), pp. 62–3.

Lieutenant Richard Blakeney, *The Journal of an Oriental Voyage in His Majesty's Ship Africaine* (London, 1841), p. 202.

S. M. Zwemer, *Arabia: The Cradle of Islam* (New York, 1900), p. 108.

George B. Cressey, *Crossroads, Land and Life in Southwest Asia* (New York, 1960), p. 334.

Bombay Government Selections, No. XXIV (Bombay, 1856), p. 544.

S. A. Rao, 'A "Persian Gulf" Seal from Lothal', *Antiquity*, Vol. 37 (1963), pp. 96–9.

Sir Mortimer Wheeler, *The Indus Civilization*, 2nd ed. (Cambridge, 1960), p. 84.

S. N. Kramer, 'Quest for Paradise', *Antiquity*, Vol. 37 (1963), pp. 111–12.

Alan Villiers, *The Indian Ocean* (London, 1952), p. 37.

Admiral G. A. Ballard, 'The War of the Arabian Sea', *The Mariner's Mirror*, Vol. XI, No. 1 (January 1952), pp. 30–1.

CHAPTER 7: DUBAI TO BURAIMI

1. Lady Anne Blunt, *Bedouin Tribes of the Euphrates*, Vol. II (London, 1879), p. 210.

2. J. L. Burckhardt, *Notes on the Bedouins and Wahabys* (London, 1830), p. 102.

3. J. R. Wellsted, *Travels in Arabia*, Vol. I, p. 223.

4. The first report of Adolf von Wrede's remarkable journey appeared in the *Journal of the Royal Geographical Society*, XIV (1844), p. 107; a letter of Wrede's subsequently appeared in the *Bulletin de la Société de Géographie*, Ser. III (1845), p. 41.

5. T. Bent (Mr & Mrs), *Southern Arabia* (London, 1900), p. 106.

6. Wendell Phillips, *Qataban and Sheba* (London, 1955), p. 196.

7. J. R. Wellsted, *Travels in Arabia*, Vol. II (London, 1838), p. 72.

8. C. Raswan, *The Black Tents of Arabia*, p. 185.

9. *See* Atkins Hamerton, *Bahrain Archives*, Book 123 (1840), pp. 84–106. This report is the earliest known first-hand account of Buraimi by a European. *See also* Lt.-Col. S. B. Miles, 'Field Notes of November 1875', *Muscat Archives*, No. 132/47 (1876); S. M. Zwemer, 'Three Journeys in Northern Oman', *The Geographical Journal*, XIX (1902), p. 62; Major Percy Cox, 'Overland Journey to Maskat from the Persian Gulf', *The Geographical Journal*, Vol. XX (1902), p. 452.

Works also consulted for this chapter

Carlo Guarmani, *Northern Najd* (London, 1938), p. 19.

Lt.-Col. S. B. Miles, *Field Notes of December 1885*, Muscat Archives (1886).

E. W. Lane, *Manners and Customs of the Modern Egyptians* (London, 1954), p. 297.

D. van der Meulen, *Faces in Shem* (London, 1961), pp. 101–2.

G. W. Murray, *Sons of Ismael* (London, 1935), p. 85.

A. Locker, *With Star and Crescent* (Philadelphia, 1890), p. 171.

Gerald De Gaury, *Arabia Phoenix* (London, 1946), p. 82.

Alois Musil, *In the Arabian Desert* (London, 1931), p. 186.

E. C. Ross, 'Annals of Oman', in *Journal of the Asiatic Society of Bengal,* Vol. XLIII, Part I (1874), p. 116.

James Morris, *Sultan in Oman* (London, 1957), p. 122.

Richard Hilton, *The Thirteenth Power: The Middle East and the World Situation* (London, 1958), p. 180.

David Harrison, *Footsteps in the Sand* (London, 1959), pp. 163–164.

D. van der Meulen, *The Wells of Ibn Saud* (London, 1957), p. 186.

CHAPTER 8: WOMEN IN OMAN

1. J. R. Mott, Ed. *The Moslem World Today* (London, 1925), pp. 220–21.

2. *Islam and the Modern Age* (New York, 1958), p. 48.

3. Edward Westermarck, *Marriage Ceremonies in Morocco* (London, 1914), p. 54.

4. *See* A. Musil, *The Manners and Customs of the Rwala Bedouins* (New York, 1928), p. 137.

5. J. L. Burckhardt, *Notes on the Bedouins and Wahabys* (London, 1830), p. 65.

6. Carlo Guarmani, *Northern Najd* (London, 1938), p. 57.

7. 'The dipilatory much used by Egyptian women is a kind of resin, called liban shamee, applied in a melted state; but this, they pretend, is not always necessary: by applying the blood of a bat to the skin of a newly-born female infant, on the parts where they wish no hair to grow, they assert that they accomplish this desire.' E. W. Lane, *Manners and Customs of the Modern Egyptians*, p. 42.

8. Fulanain, *Haji Rikkan Marsh Arabs* (London, 1927), p. 170.

9. An unknown author quoted by al-Ishaqi relative to the Khalifa al-Mutawakkil, taken in its present form from E. W. Lane, *Arabian Society in the Middle Ages* (London, 1883), pp. 215–16.

10. Carlo Guarmani, *Northern Najd*, p. 21.

11. W. G. Palgrave, *Central and Eastern Arabia* (London, 1869), pp. 366–367.

12. Major David Price, *Essay Towards the History of Arabia* (London, 1824), p. 57.

T

13. Ailon Shiloh, 'The System of Medicine in Middle East Culture', *The Middle East Journal* Vol. XV (1961), p. 282.

14. G. A. Wilken, *Das Matriarchat (Das Mutterrecht) bei den alten Araben* (Leipzig, 1884), pp. 23, 25.

15. W. H. Ingrams, 'Hadhramaut: A Journey to the Sei'ar Country and Through the Wadi Maseila', *The Geographical Journal*, Vol. 88 (July–December 1936), p. 537.

16. The Arabic word *harim* has the basic meaning 'inviolable' or 'forbidden' and is used as the plural of *hurmah*, wife. In Mesopotamia, excavations at Tello, 3000 B.C., suggest that the *harim* was already an institution. Sargon, King of Assyria, who was murdered in 705 B.C., had a harem in his palace.

17. A. Musil, *The Manners and Customs of the Ruala Bedouins* (New York, 1928), p. 240.

18. Taken with modifications by the writer from Paul W. Harrison, *Doctor in Arabia* (London, 1943), pp. 98–9.

19. Fornication and homosexuality are not common sexual deviations of Arabs as are adultery – in our sense (in the Arab view there can be no male adultery comparable to female adultery) – and bestiality. Although not widely known, the latter is extremely common among young males in most parts of Arabia and throughout the Near East in all probability. Except among the effete and idle upper class in the towns, taking part in a homosexual act, even as the active partner, destroys absolutely the individual's reputation as a 'man' in most badawi tribes, and such an action, if known, is about the greatest disgrace that can be brought down upon the tribe. Bestiality, in contrast is less serious – and less frequently known, as a ewe or female donkey cannot talk. In general, bestiality is socially ignored quite unlike homosexuality which is vigorously condemned (it is expressly forbidden, of course, in the Quran).

20. *See* Caroline M. Galt, 'Veiled Ladies', *American Journal of Archaeology*, Vol. XXXV (1931), p. 393.

21. W. G. Palgrave, *Central and Eastern Arabia* (London, 1869), p. 401.

Works also consulted for this chapter

Farouk Luqman, 'Love Matrimony and Mental Health in Aden', *Aden Chronicle* (Aden, 1962), pp. 19–21, 28, 39.

E. W. Lane, *Arabian Society in the Middle Ages* (London, 1883), p. 215.

Raphael Patai, *Sex and Family in the Bible and the Middle East* (New York, 1959), pp. 69, 250.

Omar El-Barghuthi, 'Judicial Courts among the Bedouin of Palestine', *Journal of the Palestine Oriental Society*, Vol. II (1922), p. 58.

G. Wyman Bury, *The Land of Uz* (London, 1911), p. 278.

The Life and Travels of Mungo Park (Edinburgh, 1838), p. 35.

The Chevalier De Hesse-Wartegg, *Tunis: The Land and The People* (London, 1882), p. 95.

Harry E. Wedeck, *Dictionary of Aphrodisiacs*, p. 164.

Leo Africanus, *The History and Description of Africa*, Vol. II (London, 1896). p. 450.

Iver Lissner, *The Living Past* (London, 1957), p. 79.

Felix Bryk, *Dark Rapture* (Forrest Hills, N.Y., 1944), p. 100.

P. C. Remondina, *History of Circumcision* (Philadelphia, 1891), p. 51.

H. R. P. Dickson, *The Arab of the Desert* (London, 1949), p. 163.

Burgo Partridge, *A History of Orgies* (London, 1960), p. 230.

J. L. Burckhardt, *Notes on the Bedouins and Wahabys* (London, 1830), pp. 63, 150.

D'Arvieux, *Travels in Arabia the Desert* (London, 1718), p. 235.

Claudia de Lys, *To Be or Not To Be a Virgin* (New York, 1960), p. 59.

David and Vera Mace, *Marriage East and West* (London, 1960), pp. 215, 297.

William J. Robinson, *Woman* (New York, 1944), p. 20.

Paolo Mantegazza, *Sexual Relations of Mankind* (New York, 1932), p. 57.

G. Mouette, *The Travels of Sieur Mouette in the Kingdoms of Fez and Morocco, etc.* (London, 1710), p. 43.

Morroe Berger, *The Arab World Today* (New York, 1962), pp. 122–3.

Lt.-General Sir George MacMunn, *Slavery Through the Ages* (London, 1938), p. 257.

C. Snouck Hurgronje, *Mekka* (London, 1931), pp. 86, 107–8.

Edward Podolsky's *Sex Today in Wedded Life* (New York, 1943), p. 64, 115–17.

Bronislaw Malinowski, *The Sexual Life of Savages* (New York, 1929), p. 169.

W. H. Ingrams, *Zanzibar* (London, 1931). p. 215.

Philip K. Hitti, *The Near East in History* (Princeton, 1960), p. 522.

James Cleugh, *Ladies of the Harem* (London, 1955), p. 19.

Bayle St. John, *Village Life in Egypt* (Boston, 1853), Vol. I, pp. 42–3.

Raphael Patai, *Golden River to Golden Road*, p. 106.

H. R. P. Dickson, *Kuwait and Her Neighbours* (London, 1956), pp. 84–6.

Sir Charles Belgrave, *Personal Column* (London, 1960), p. 62.

Charles M. Doughty, *Wanderings in Arabia* (London, 1908), Vol. I, p. 88.

Edward B. Pollard, *Oriental Women* (Philadelphia, 1907), Vol. IV, p. 51.

William Nassau Senior, *Conversations and Journals in Egypt and Malta* (London, 1882), Vol. II, p. 198.

C. M. Doughty, *Arabia Deserta* (Cambridge, 1888), Vol. I, p. 238.

Sheikh Mansur, *History of Seyd Said*, p. 125.

C. Colliver Rice, *Persian Women and Their Ways* (London, 1923), p. 52.

D. van der Meulen, *The Wells of Ibn Saud* (London, 1957), p. 77.

Harold Jacobs, *Perfumes of Araby* (London, 1915), p. 29.

Sheikh M. H. Kidwai of Gadia, 'Woman,' *Islamic Review* (Woking, 1917), p. 24–5.

Humayum Kabir, *Science Democracy and Islam* (London, 1955), pp. 21–2.

Ilse Lichtenstader, *Women in the Aiyam Al-Arab* (London, 1935), pp. 81, 85–6.

Reynold A. Nicholson, *A Literary History of the Arabs* (London, 1907), pp. 87–8.

Dorothy Van Ess, *Fatima and her Sisters* (New York, 1961), p. 178.

W. Robert Smith, *Kinship and Marriage in Early Arabia* (Cambridge, 1885), pp. 279–80.

Captain Sir Richard Burton, *First Footsteps in East Africa* (London, 1894), Vol. II, p. 38.

Mohammed Ali Al-Haj Salmin, *The Holy Prophet Mohammed Through Different Lights* (Bombay, 1954), p. 280.

Carsten Niebuhr, *Travels Through Arabia* (Edinburgh, 1792), Vol. I, p. 118.

Sir Richard Burton, *The Sotadic Zone of Sexual Inversion* (Falstaff Press, N.Y.), p. 35.

H. I. Katibah, *The New Spirit In Arab Lands* (New York, 1940), p. 215.

Walter M. Gallichan, *Woman Under Polygamy* (London, 1914), p. 72.

Captain Sir Richard Burton, *Pilgrimage to Al Madinah and Meccah*, Vol. I (London, 1893), p. 229.

H.H. Nawab Sultan Jehan Begun Saheba, *Al Hijab (or) Why Purdah is Necessary* (Calcutta, 1922), pp. 164, 194.

Zeyneb Hanoum, *A Turkish Woman's European Impressions* (Philadelphia, 1913), pp. 89, 91.

Milton Stauffer, *Voices from the Near East* (New York, 1927), p. 52.

CHAPTER 9: THE BADU

1. P. K. Hitti, *The Arabs: A Short History* (London, 1960), p. 14.

2. Abu-Tammam, *Ash'ar al-Hamasah*, ed. Freytag (Bonn, 1828), p. 171.

3. 'There was a reason for this; for to abuse any woman in ghazzu would be for the raider to jeopardize the safety of his own family under a system whereby he might end up in defeat the next day.' Harry B. Ellis, *Heritage of the Desert* (New York, 1956), p. 21.

4. Abu-Dawud, *Sunan* (Cairo, A.H. 1280), Vol. I, p. 89.

5. Sir Tom Hickinbotham, *Aden* (London, 1958), p. 207.

6. The Bani Hilal are considered descendants of Hilal, one of the four sons of Amir bin Sa'asa'ah (A.D. 381) of Adnan origin. They were a northern Qais tribal confederation who left the Yemen – 'Asir region of Arabia in the ninth or tenth century, invaded Egypt and spread all over North Africa. *See*, concerning the *badu* in early times, Ibn Khaldun, *The Muqaddimah, An Introduction to History*, Vol. I (New York, 1958), pp. 302–3.

7. The notion abroad that some veritable deserts of the Near East 'bloomed' in the past is not literally true, with the one exception of Mesopotamia, where ancient irrigation systems, built and maintained by strong central governments, made the difference between wind-swept desert plain and endless gardens, fields and orchards. The introduction of great quantities of fresh water is the *sine qua non* for making a true desert bloom; the development of an economical method of converting sea water or other mineral water is the only possibility for transforming a

significant area of Arabia from desert to garden – and engineers appear far from a practical solution to this problem, though it is to be hoped that an unexpected break-through comes soon.

8. P. Cox, 'Some Excursions in Oman', *Geographical Journal*, Vol. LXVI (1925), p. 201.

9. In the *Memorial of the Government of Saudi Arabia*, Vol. I (1955), pp. 46–7, occurs the following: 'Wadi-al Jizy, the direct route through the mountains of al-Hajar connecting Buraimi with al-Batinah, has been blockaded by its inhabitants so that the Sultan's people cannot use it.' A great deal of this *Memorial* is impressive in direct proportion to one's ignorance of the areas and problems involved.

Works also consulted for this chapter

Lt.-Col. S. B. Miles, *Field Notes of Nov. 1875*, Muscat Archives, No. 132/47 (1876).

Raphael Patai, *Golden River to Golden Road*, p. 26.

Bertram Thomas, *Alarms and Excursions in Arabia* (London, 1931), p. 165.

Captain G. J. Eccles, 'The Sultanate of Muscat and Oman', *Journal of the Central Asia Society*, Vol. XIV (1927), p. 36.

Samuel M. Zwemer, *Arabia: The Cradle of Islam* (New York, 1900), pp. 156, 264.

Captain G. Forster Sadlier, *Diary of a Journey Across Arabia* (Bombay, 1866), p. 40.

Muhammad Abdullah Enan, *Decisive Moments in the History of Islam* (Lahore, 1949), pp. 193–4.

W. G. Browne, *Travels in Africa, Egypt and Syria, from the year 1792 to 1798* (London, 1799), p. 427.

George Sale, *The Koran* (London, 1734), Preliminary Discourse, pp. 21–2.

Bosworth R. Smith, *Mohammed and Mohammedanism* (London, 1889), p. 76.

Bertram Thomas, *Arabia Felix* (London, 1932), pp. 219–20.

Samuel M. and Amy E. Zwemer, *Zigzag Journeys In the Camel Country* (New York, 1911), p. 93.

Reuben Levy, *The Social Structure of Islam* (Cambridge, 1957), p. 201.

Lt.-Col. Lewis Pelley, 'A Visit to the Wahabee Capital Central Arabia', *Journal of the Royal Geographical Society*, Vol. XXXV (1865), p. 171.

Pierre Ponafidine, *Life in the Moslem East* (London, 1911), p. 126.

CHAPTER 10: SOHAR TO DHOFAR

1. See *Ars Islamica*, Vols. XI–XII (1946), pp. 203–4.

1a. R. Ettinghausen, 'The Uses of Sphero-conical Vessels in the Muslim East', *Journal of Near Eastern Studies*, Vol. XXIV (1965), pp. 218–229.

2. For a more detailed summary of the archaeological work at Sohar refer to Ray L. Cleveland, 'Preliminary Report on the Archaeological Soundings at Sohar (Oman)', *Bulletin of the American Schools of Oriental Research*, No. 153 (February, 1959), pp. 11–19.

3. Sir Cyril S. Fox, *The Geology and Mineral Resources of Dhofar Province, Muscat and Oman* (1947), p. 12. (Obtainable – Director of Revenues to Oman, Muscat, S.E. Arabia).

4. Qara (Shahari), Sahara (Shahari), Barahama (Shahari), found in the Qara Mountains; Bait ash-Shaikh (Shahari), found N.E. of Qara Mountains in the Steppe; Batahir (Bathari), found in the Kuria Muria district; (Harasis Harsusi), found N.E. of Qara Mountains in the Steppe; Mahrah (Mahri); Afar (Shahari) found N.E. of Qara Mountains in the Steppe; Bil Haf (Mahri), found in Dhofar and to the west.

5. *Ancient and Modern Man in Southwestern Asia* (Miami, 1956), p. 113. The physical characteristics of the South Arabians have been studied by C. G. Seligman, Bertram Thomas, Sir Arthur Keith, W. M. Krogman, Carleton Coon and Henry Field.

6. See 'Correspondence', *Journal of the Royal Central Asian Society*, XX (1933), pp. 488–91.

7. According to Dr Ray Cleveland (personal communication) the Shahari (Gabbali) language is very closely related (but with distinct phonetic variations) to the speech of the Mahrah people; Mahri and Gabbali are probably dialects of the same language.

8. For example, the Beit Shuyukh inhabit a certain area to the east while the Beit Said are to the west of Salalah, the Beit Mashini are at Darbat.

9. Bertram Thomas, 'Among Some Unknown Tribes of South Arabia', *Journal of the Royal Anthropological Institute*, Vol. LIX (1929), p. 102.

10. A very ceremonial circumcision used to be performed in Yemen, which seems to be getting out of vogue as fewer cases are now coming to the Queen Elizabeth Hospital in Aden for repair surgery, reports Dr Mohammed Mazhar to this writer.

The circumcision used to be performed when the boy was of marriageable age. The womenfolk used to watch the performance. The circumcision was done without any anaesthesia. The operator with a sharp instrument cuts the foreskin and then with a long sweep takes away the skin of the dorsum of the penis. Sometimes the cut is so deep that a permanent urethral fistula takes place.

11. 'The origin of the Dhofar cattle is not known but they are similar in conformation and colour to the early Spanish and Portuguese cattle. They are very small. Adult females stand about 3′ 4″ at the shoulder and weigh approximately 300 pounds. Bulls are somewhat larger. When slaughtered the animals yield from 150–240 pounds of boned meat. A mature animal ready for slaughter sells for MT60.

'They have a short fine coat which is predominantly black in colour but can be varying in shades of black, brown, tan, fawn or dun with or without white markings. Pure red or white cattle are rare.' V. C. Peterson, *Extracts From a Report On the Agriculture of Dhofar*, Food and Agriculture Officer USOM/Somali Republic (1960), p. 4.

12. The Al Kathir and Mahrah of the Qara Mountains also prohibit their women from milking cows and camels; in the rest of Oman the reverse holds, for an Arab male would lose face by milking cows.

13. B. Thomas, *Arabia Felix* (London, 1932), p. 59.

Works also consulted for this chapter

Carlo Guarmani, *Northern Najd* (London, 1938), p. 115.

Alexander Hamilton, *A New Account of the East Indies*, Vol. I (London, 1930), p. 47.

Andrew Crichton, *History of Arabia*, Vol. I (Edinburgh, 1843), p. 40.

Bertram Thomas, 'The South-Eastern Borderlands of Rub' Al Khali, *The Geographical Journal*, Vol. LXXIII (1929), p. 206.

Ameen Rihani, *Around the Coasts of Arabia* (London, 1930), p. 209.

Wilfred Thesiger, 'A Journey Through the Tihama, the Asir and the Hijaz Mountains', *The Geographical Journal*, Vol. CX (1947), p. 193.

P. C. Remondino, *History of Circumcision*, p. 35.

Carsten Niebuhr, *Travels Through Arabia*, Vol. II (Edinburgh, 1792), p. 249.

Raphael Patai, *Golden River to Golden Road*, pp. 138, 251, 259.

H. St. John B. Philby, *The Empty Quarter* (New York, 1933), p. 81.

Reuben Levy, *The Social Structure of Islam* (Cambridge, 1957), p. 102f.

Women of All Nations, ed. by T. Athol Joyce and N. W. Thomas (New York, 1912), Vol. II, p. 260.

Frederick J. Simons, *Eat Not This Flesh*, pp. 55, 73–4.

Bertram Thomas, *Arabia Felix*, p. 42.

CHAPTER 11: FRANKINCENSE FROM DHOFAR

1. Gus W. Van Beek, 'Frankincense and Myrrh in Ancient South Arabia', *Journal of the American Oriental Society*, Vol. 78 (1958), p. 146.

2. Ibn Battuta noted that at Hasik the frankincense trees were not tapped by slashing the trunk but by cutting the leaves. This was confirmed by recent observations of Eric Macro.

3. *See* Frank P. Albright, 'Explorations in Dhofar, Oman', *Antiquity*, No. 113 (March, 1955), pp. 37–9. *Also* Wendell Phillips, *Qataban and Sheba* (London, 1955), pp. 300ff.

4. In 1846, Dr H. J. Carter described his visit to the ruins and noted: 'Whether El Balad, "the city" par excellence, was in reality the ancient name of this place, or whether the real name has been lost, and the most modern one of El Balad has been found the most convenient term to supply the deficiency, I was unable to determine.' 'A Descriptive Account of the Ruins of El Balad', *Transactions of the Bombay Geographical Society*, Art. XIV, Vol. VII (December, 1846), p. 25.

5. Early in 1960, Homer P. Brannon found an irregularly shaped bronze coin on the sandy beach at Ras Raisut. Subsequent study of the coin at the Johns Hopkins University by Dr Ray Cleveland and comparison with types in the catalogue of Byzantine coins in the British Museum disclosed that it is a coin of Justinian I (reigned A.D. 527 to 565) of a full face type minted from A.D. 538 until the end of his reign. For a full description of this coin, the first published Byzantine coin from Dhofar, *see* Ray L. Cleveland, 'The 1960 American Archaeological Expedition to Dhofar', *Bulletin of the American Schools of Oriental Research*, No. 159 (October 1960), p. 15. According to the authority of al-Hamdani, in his time (tenth

century) a portion of the tribe of Judaid, a branch of the Azd of Oman, were driven out of their stronghold at Ras Raisut (by the local inhabitants) and had eventually returned and retaken the area; this tribe had been the first to migrate to Ras Raisut and settle among the original Bayasira. Another authority, Ibn al-Mujawir, who was in Zafar (Dhofar) about 1221, says that (Ras) Raisut was a large town and that from Baghdad to Ras Raisut there was a highway or road used by caravans to bring Baghdad fabrics and return with Indian brass, cinnabar, rosewater and silver.

6. *See* Frank P. Albright, 'The Himyaritic Temple at Khor Rory (Dhofar, Oman)', *Orientalia*, Vol. 22 (1953), pp. 284–7. Trade with the East was demonstrated by our discovery at Khor Rori (Dhofar) of a second century A.D. bronze statuette of an Indian dancing girl; this was our first proof of trade between South Arabia and India; *see* F. P. Albright, 'From South Arabia', *Archaeology*, Vol. 7 (1954), p. 254; also Hermann Goetz, 'An Indian Bronze from South Arabia', *Archaeology*, Vol. 16 (1963), pp. 187–9; 'A Unique Indian Bronze from South Arabia', *Journal of the Baroda Oriental Institute*, Vol. XII (1963), pp. 241–3.

7. *See* A. Jamme, 'Une inscription hadramoutique en bronze', *Orientalia*, Vol. 22 (1953), pp. 158–65.

8. The authors of the *Aramco Handbook* (Arabian American Oil Company, 1960), are inaccurate relative to Hadhramaut when they state on page 257 'Frankincense and myrrh . . . still grow wild in the region of Dhofar and Hadhramaut'. Marco Polo who had not visited Shihr himself was likewise mistaken in saying that the district of the town of Shihr (now located in the former Eastern Aden Protectorate) produced frankincense; he must have meant Dhofar. From the middle of the thirteenth century (approximately a century before Marco Polo) we have this description from the Chinese writer Chu Ju-Kua, 'Ju-hiang (milk incense) or Hüm-lu-hiang, comes from the three Ta-shi [Arab] countries of Ma-lo-pa [Murbat], Shi-ho [Shihr] and Nu-fa [Dhofar] from the depths of the remotest mountain valleys. The tree which yields this drug may, on the whole, be compared to the sung (pine). Its trunk is notched with a hatchet, upon which the resin flows out, and when hardened, turns into incense, which is gathered and made into lumps. It is transported on elephants to the Tas-shi [Arabs] (on the coast); the Ta-shi [Arabs] load it upon their ships for barter against other goods in San-fo-ts'i [N.E. coast of Sumatra]', Chou Ju-Kua, *Chu-fanchi*, trans. from the Chinese by Freidrich Hirth and W. W. Rockwell (St. Petersburg, 1911), p. 195.

It is possible, in accordance with a suggestion by Gus Van Beek, that the repeated references to Shihr, as a centre of frankincense production are based on the false assumption that a product famed in such quantities *must* be of local origin. Shihr was, of course, an important port town in Islamic times, and perhaps the explanation is that frankincense was brought from Dhofar to Shihr for marketing, just as in the late centuries B.C. and the early centuries A.D., frankincense was brought to Cana, the principal port on the southern coast of Arabia at that period.

The eminent historian Prof. Philip K. Hitti writes, 'On the highlands parallel to the southern coast, and particularly in Mahrah, the frankincense tree, which figures prominently in the early commercial life of South Arabia, still flourishes.' *History of the Arabs* (New York, 1951), p. 19. The word 'Mahrah' should be replaced with Dhofar and 'highlands' limited to the Qara Mountains, as frankincense bushes grow mainly in Dhofar and the Qara Mountains, but only at the edge of Mahrah country.

This same error relative to Mahrah occurs in the *Encyclopaedia of Islam*, New Edition, Vol. I (Leiden, 1960), p. 540, where we read 'Frankincense ... and other aromatics ... still grow in the south, especially in the land of Mahra'.

'As regards Islamic history up to the 14th century, it should be noted that any distinctive name that may have been used for the province [Dhofar] does not appear to be mentioned by the Arab historians or geographers. The coast of South Arabia from a point opposite Hadramaut to another about the same distance from Masqat [Muscat] as the first is from Aden, was known as the coast (bilad) of Mahra or Esh-Shihr [according to Ibn Hauqal]. Masudi, indeed, extends the coast (ard) of Esh-Shihr farther East to the extremity, Ras el-Hadd.' R. Guest, 'Zufar in the Middle Ages', *Islamic Culture*, Vol. IX (1953), p. 402.

As regards the western limit of the frankincense area, Gus Van Beek communicated the following statement to me shortly before this book went to press: 'It is possible, I suppose, that frankincense grew and grows in Mahra country between Hadhramaut and Dhofar. We simply have no reliable information on this area. I have very grave doubts if frankincense ever grew in Hadhramaut, having recently spent a few months there. The climate, which differs considerably from that of Dhofar, is almost certainly not right for it. As I've noted in articles, when Hadhramaut is referred to in ancient sources as a frankincense producing area, we must not automatically take it that "Hadhramaut" then meant the same geographical area that it does today. We must interpret the term as a political one describing the area controlled or dominated by the Kingdom of Hadhramaut, which then included Dhofar, as shown by inscriptions from Khor Rori'.

In Professor Hitti's most recent book, *The Near East in History: A 5000 Year Story*, he states that Yemen's 'products and those of its neighbour Hadhramaut – including spices, myrrh, and frankincense – were from earliest times in great demand in Egypt and the Fertile Crescent and later in the Greco-Roman world' (p. 458) and that 'Hadhramaut, of ancient renown as a source of spices, frankincense and other tropical products, covers an extensive area in the eastern part of the protectorate' (p. 471). While it is true that these items were in great demand in ancient times and while we have no reasons to dispute Hitti's location of Hadhramaut, it is simply unsupportable on the basis of trustworthy ancient and modern sources to say that frankincense is a product of Yemen and Hadhramaut. Myrrh probably grows in both places, though there is some doubt about its presence in Yemen. What Hitti means by 'spices' completely eludes the writer.

9. The Bents have, in their pioneer contribution, 'Exploration of the Frankincense Country, Southern Arabia', *The Geographical Journal*, Vol. VI, (1895), pp. 116, 123, and *Southern Arabia* (London, 1900), p. 266, identified the 'hole' of Ghaur Fazl as Ptolemy's *Dianae Oraculum*. On p. 265, *Southern Arabia*, the Bents refer to this 'natural hole' as being '150 feet deep and about 50 feet in diameter'. My expedition members, Dr Frank Albright and George Farrier reached bottom at approximately 75 feet; due to dangerous sloping sides it is impossible to view the lower portion of the hole from the surface.

10. This was assuredly an exceptional instance, for in this writer's wide experience the R.A.F. universally produces the most gallant of the gallant.

11. In 1962, Major Mohammed Sakhi Raja was seconded from the Frontier Force Regiment of Pakistan to serve as Commandant of the Dhofar Force. This forty-six-year-old Muslim officer had won six decorations during the famous World War II battle when the Japanese had surrounded a whole Indian Army Division; eventually the Indian Army won.

At present the Dhofar Force consists of a rifle company, supported by armoured cars and 3-inch mortars. In addition to the Commandant, now Colonel Raja, there are three other Pakistani officers. The force consists of three types of soldiers – the Jabbali or hill people, the *Hadhar* or town people, and the Bait Kathir from the steppe and desert.

A recruit receives 39 M.T. dollars a month, and after six months training becomes a Young Soldier and receives 34 M.T. dollars. After serving one year and passing his firing classification he receives 3 M.T. dollars more or a total 37 dollars a month. In addition he receives long-service and good-conduct allowances of 2 M.T. dollars a month if he successfully completes three years good service and undertakes to serve another three years. During the third, fourth and fifth years he receives 2 M.T. dollars more a month for each year. After completing six years he receives a lump sum bonus of 100 M.T. dollars.

Thus 43 M.T. dollars a month, plus rations and clothing, is the maximum a Dhofar soldier (Private) can draw plus an education allowance of 2 M.T. dollars a month for passing the third-class Arabic examinations, 3 M.T. dollars a month for the second class, and 4 M.T. dollars a month for the first-class examinations.

The objectives of the Dhofar Forces are as follows:

(a) To act as a striking force in the defence of Dhofar as and when ordered by the Sultan.

(b) To act in support of civil authority when required.

(c) To provide fighting patrols as and when ordered by the Sultan.

12. See H. Comfort, 'Some Imported Pottery at Khor Rori (Dhofar)', *Bulletin of the American Schools of Oriental Research*, No. 160 (December, 1960), pp. 15–20.

13. See Bertram Thomas, 'The South-Eastern Borderlands of Rubʿ Al Khali', *The Geographical Journal*, Vol. LXXIII (1929), p. 205; and by the same author, *Arabia Felix*, pp. 128–37.

See Wilfred Thesiger, 'A New Journey in Southern Arabia', *The Geographical Journal*, Vol. CVIII (1946), p. 138; and by the same author, *Arabian Sands*, pp. 163, 174–5.

By the time Thesiger and his *badu* reached the pool of Hanum on the northern slopes of the Qara Mountains they had been travelling for forty-four days, having covered some 700 miles by camel.

14. Erosion had cut deeply into the Tertiary sediments forming good surface exposures of grey, nodular, weathered, massive limestone of Middle Eocene age (the Dammam Formation).

15. Ray L. Cleveland, 'The 1960 American Archaeological Expedition to

Dhofar', *Bulletin of the American Schools of Oriental Research*, No. 159 (October, 1960), p. 26.

Works also consulted for this chapter

G. W. Van Beek and A. Jamme, 'An Inscribed South Arabian Clay Stamp from Bethel', *Bulletin of the American Schools of Oriental Research*, No. 151 (October, 1958), pp. 9–16. A. Jamme and G. W. Van Beek, 'The South-Arabian Clay Stamp from Bethel Again', *B.A.S.O.R.*, No. 163 (October, 1961), pp. 15–18.

James H. Breasted, *A History of Egypt* (New York, 1954), p. 127.

De Lacy O'Leary, *How Greek Science Passed to the Arabs* (London, 1948), p. 99.

Mustafa Amer 'The Ancient Trans-Peninsular Routes of Arabia', *Compte rendue du Congres International de Geographie* (Le Caire, 1925), Vol. V., p. 129.

The latest edition of the Periplus is H. Frisk, *Le Périple de la mer Erythrée* (Goteborg, 1927). This work is out of print and obtainable only in large libraries. An earlier translation is W. Schoff, *The Periplus of the Erythraean Sea* (London, 1912). Dr. A. G. Matthew and Dr. G. S. P. Freeman-Grenville are making a new edition and translation of the Periplus.

J. H. Breasted, *Ancient Records of Egypt*. II (Chicago, 1906), p. 113.

Gus W. Van Beek, 'Frankincense and Myrrh', *The Biblical Archaeologist*, Vol. XXIII (1960), p. 85.

Jean Aubin, 'Les princes d'Ormuz [Hormuz] du XIIIe and XVe siecle', *Journal Asiatique*, Vol. 241 (1953), pp. 84–5.

Alawi bin Tahir, *Djanyal Shamarikh* (Aden, A.H. 1369), p. 31.

Sir Henry Yule, *The Book of Ser Marco Polo the Venetian* (London, 1903), Vol. II, pp. 444–5.

H. A. R. Gibb, *Ibn Batuta: Travels in Asia and Africa, 1325–1354* (London, 1929), p. 113.

The Commentaries of the Great Affonso Dalboquerque, Vol. I, p. 84.

C. F. Beckingham, 'Some Early Travels in Arabia', *Journal of the Royal Asiatic Society* (October 1949).

The Itinerary of Ludovico di Varthema of Bologna from 1502 to 1508. Translated from the original Italian Edition of 1510 by John Winter Jones in 1863 for the Hakluyt Society (London, 1928), p. 38.

R. B. Serjeant, *The Portuguese off the South Arabian Coast* (Oxford, 1963), p. 29.

C. F. Beckingham and R. B. Serjeant, 'A Journey by Two Jesuits from Dhofar to Sana in 1590', *The Geographical Journal*, Vol. CXV (1950), pp. 194–207.

R. Meinertzhagen, *Birds of Arabia* (Edinburgh, 1945), p. 3.

CHAPTER 12: SALALAH TO SHABWAH

1. V. C. Peterson, *Extracts from a Report on the Agriculture of Dhofar*, Food and Agriculture Officer USOM/Somali Republic (1960), pp. 1–2.

2. Approximately one mile from Murbat is the tomb of a Mohammed Ali bearing the date A.H. 556 (A.D. 1160). Not long after, Yaqut (1179–1229) observed in his *Geographical Dictionary* as to the good people of Mirbat that 'Every night their women go outside their town and spend the evening in conversation with the men who are not forbidden to them and they play with them and they sit beside them until most of the night passes; [there is no sexual intercourse implied in this] and the man passes by his wife or sister or mother or paternal aunt, and if she is playing and conversing with him he turns away from her and goes on to another woman and sits with her as was being done with his own wife. . . .'
In the middle of the thirteenth century the Chinese writer Chou Ju-Kua wrote, 'There is the country of Ma-li-pa [Murbat]; ships leaving Kuang Chou during or after the eleventh moon (December) and sailing with a northerly wind, can make the country called Lan-li (N.W. Sumatra) in forty days. Here they trade buying sapan-wood, tin and long white rattans. The following year, in winter, they set to sea again and, with a north-easterly wind favouring them they make the voyage to this country of Ma-li-pa [Murbat] in some sixty days'. Chou Ju-Kua, *Chu-fanchi*, pp. 119–20.

3. In the Dependency of Dhofar a slightly different coinage system exists from the rest of Oman, with special Dhofari coins issued by the Sultan in denominations of half-*riyal*, fifty-*baisah* (*baisah* is an Indian word, 'pice'; it is spelt with s on Dhofar coinage though with ẓ, *baiẓah*, in the rest of Oman) twenty-*baisah*, and ten-*baisah* coins. One-*baisah* coins (actually inscribed '¼ anna'), of which there are 208 to the riyal, are also in circulation. They are worn coppers about the size of a nickel bearing the name of Faisal bin Turki, grandfather of the present Sultan. All of the other Dhofar coins bear the name of Said bin Taimur in artistic script. The

Sultan has recently introduced a new bronze three-*baisah* coin in Dhofar bearing his name. The replacement of copper by bronze will make it impossible to melt up this coin for coffee pots, etc. In December of 1958 the Sultan minted in London the first 500,000 impressive new silver Saʿidi Riyals, each bearing the name Saʿid bin Taimur and the date A.H. 1378. This Saʿidi Riyal is valued at one dollar USA or seven shillings and contains 300 *baisahs*.

4. The 19th-century war dhow carried up to fifty guns and four hundred men; Wellsted measured one 140 feet long. According to Sheikh Sirhan bin Said, the first ruler of Oman who constructed vessels and employed them in naval warfare was the Imam Ghassan bin Abdullah who died of illness in A.D. 822. 'Those were the days when the kingdom was in its prime and in the fullness of its power, and learning at its height.' *Annals of Oman*, pp. 124–5.

5. S. B. Haines, 'Memoir of the South and East Coasts of Arabia', Part II, *The Journal of the Royal Geographical Society*, Vol. 15 (1845), p. 130.

6. The late Col. S. B. Miles mentions visiting Hasik in 1883 in Vol. II of *Countries and Tribes of the Persian Gulf* (London, 1919), p. 321. 'The Joasmees now in 1815, turned their attention to the Red Sea; having raided Hasik and Dhofar, etc. . . . . The town was sacked by the pirates, who carried off the women and children into slavery.' If this reference is correct, Hasik must have been occupied in the early nineteenth century.

7. Nabih Amin Faris, 'Derivation and Orthography of al-Rubʿ al-Khali', *Royal Central Asian Journal*, Vol. XLIV (1957), pp. 28–30.
Refer also for discussion and meaning and use of term *ar-rubʿ al-khali* to C. D. Matthews, 'Bedouin Life in Contemporary Arabia', *Revista degli studi orientali*, Vol. XXXV (Roma, 1960), pp. 38–9.
The area is called *ar-rubʿ al-khali* in one of Ibn Majid's texts of the sixteenth century published by G. Ferrand as *Instructions Nautiques*, I (Paris, 1921–3), which shows that the name was known to literary circles by that time. The interesting point, according to Prof. R. B. Serjeant, is that it is *khali* not *khāli*, the usual name given, and he would not call *khali* so much 'empty' as 'open', as one says 'open country-side'.

8. Captain Sir Richard Burton, *Pilgrimage to Al-Madinah and Meccah*, Vol. I, p. 3.

9. Colonel S. B. Miles, *The Countries and Tribes of the Persian Gulf*, Vol. II, p. 348.

10. H. St. J. B. Philby, *Forty Years in the Wilderness*, p. 180.

11. *See* H. St. John B. Philby, 'Rub' al Khali', *The Geographical Journal*, Vol. LXXXI, January (1933), pp. 1–26; *see also* Philby, *The Empty Quarter*. For Thomas the longest space between wells was 335 miles; for Philby 375 to 400 miles, an astonishing feat for men and camels.

12. T. E. Lawrence, 'Foreword' *Arabia Felix* (London, 1932), p. xvii.

13. R. A. Bagnold, 'Sand Formations in Southern Arabia', *Geographical Journal*, January–March 1951, p. 78.

14. George B. Cressey, *Crossroads: Land and Life in Southwest Asia*, p. 86.

15. R. E. Cheesman, *In Unknown Arabia* (London, 1926), p. 228.

16. Wilfred Thesiger, *Arabian Sands*, p. 37.

17. C. D. Matthews, 'Bedouin Life in Contemporary Arabia', *Revista Degli Studi Orientali*, Vol. XXXV (Roma, 1960), p. 40.

18. Bertram Thomas, 'The South-Eastern Borderlands of Rub' Al Khali', *The Geographical Journal*, Vol. LXXIII (1929), p. 210.

19. Wilfred Thesiger, 'A New Journey In Southern Arabia', *The Geographical Journal*, Vol. CVIII (1946), p. 133.

20. 'No stratified sites are so far known from the great interior desert of the Arabian Peninsula, the Rub' al Khali, and until some are found our knowledge of the pre-history of this land mass will remain in the amorphous condition which characterizes it today.' Philip E. L. Smith and George Maranjian, 'Two "Neolithic" Collections from Saudi Arabia', *Man*, Vol. LXII (1962), p. 21.

21. John Lewis Burckhardt, *Notes on the Bedouins and Wahabys*, p. 61.

22. Snouck Hurgronje, *Mekkamische Sprichwörter* (The Hague, 1886), p. 17.

23. Wilfred Thesiger, *Arabian Sands*, p. 168.

24. Bertram Thomas, *Arabia Felix*, pp. 161–2.

25. St. John B. Philby, *The Empty Quarter* (New York, 1933), p. 160.

26. None of the writer's *badu* had ever heard of Wabar but they were all familiar with Ubar. In London during July, 1960, Philby explained to the writer that he believes Wabar and Ubar (with slight differences of pronunciation) both refer to the same ancient city of tradition which still remains to be discovered.

27. H. R. P. Dickson, *Kuwait and her Neighbours* (London, 1956), p. 502.

28. There are three species of Arabian gazelle; the most prevalent is the

agile faun-coloured *Gazella arabica*; the *Gazella saudiya* is smaller and lighter in colour with longer horns in the female; the *Gazella marica* possesses massive lyrate horns and is usually confined to the edges of *ar-rub' al-khali*.

29. In 1503, Ludovico di Varthema, while entering the temple precinct of Mecca noted: 'In another part of the said temple is an enclosed place in which there are two live unicorns, and these are shown as very remarkable objects, which they certainly are'. Di Varthema describes the unicorns (in reality two captive oryx) as if he had actually seen them as resembling a dark bay horse with a stag's head, slender legs like a goat's and cloven hoofs. 'These two animals were presented to the Sultan of Mecca as the finest things that could be found in the world at the present day, and as the richest treasure ever sent by a King of Ethiopia, that is, by a Moorish King.' *The Itinerary of Ludovico di Varthema of Bologna from 1502 to 1508* (Hakluyt Society, London, 1928), p. 22.

30. When later analysed in the laboratory, the presence of the marine micro-fossil *Orbitolina concava* in the pottery fragments indicated that the clay used could not have been found within *ar-rub' al-khali* and was likely obtained from the coast of Dhofar.

31. *See* L. Hirsch, *Reisen in Süd-Arabien, Mahra-Land und Hadramut* (Leyden, 1897).

32. When Arab kills Arab, in a no-quarter raid, the life of the slave is spared, for like the camel, the slave has a commercial value; the slave also had an advantage over the free tribesman, for he is not involved in blood feuds.

33. *See Journal of the Royal Asiatic Society*, Vol. 34, pp. 231–41 for his 'Land of the Mahra'.

34. According to Wilfred Thesiger, *Arabian Sands*, p. 182, 'The Mahra are descended from the ancient Habasha, who colonized Ethiopia as long ago as the first millenium [*sic*] B.C. and gave their name to the Abyssinians'; whereas Philby believes there is no evidence for a date as early as the first millennium B.C., but there is evidence from Sabaean inscriptions of the Habasha coming in the third century A.D. (Personal communication).

35. Wendell Phillips, *Qataban and Sheba* (London, 1955), p. 152.

36. William H. Schoff, *The Periplus of the Erythraean Sea* (London, 1912), p. 32.

37. D. van der Meulen, *Aden to the Hadramaut* (London, 1947), p. 99.

38. Richard H. Sanger, *The Arabian Peninsula* (Ithaca, 1954), p. 238.

39. Wendell Phillips, *op. cit.*, p. 50.

40. The writer wishes to express his gratitude and appreciation to Arthur Watts, Resident at Mukalla for the Eastern Aden Protectorate, Alastair J. McIntosh, Principal Adviser to the High Commissioner's Office, Aden, and Colonel J. W. G. ('Pat') Gray, Commander of the Hadhrami Bedouin Legion, for making this reconnaissance expedition a reality.

41. Wendell Phillips, *op. cit.*, p. 48.

42. Although at the time of his visit in 1936, Philby imagined himself as the first European to lay eyes on Shabwah – he was not. The year before when the intrepid Miss Freya Stark, *The Southern Gates of Arabia*, pp. 243–5, lay seriously ill at Shibam in Hadhramaut (frustrated in her own objective to be the first to reach Shabwah), she wrote, 'I have given up Shabwa because I am not really strong enough to face such an arduous waterless journey before the heat – so am sadly renouncing it. It doesn't seem worth so great a risk. . . . I am awfully sad at my failure', *The Coast of Incense* (London, 1953), p. 87. It was a young German, Hans Helfritz, who won the victor's laurels as the first foreigner to enter the ancient city of Shabwah. He published an account of his adventures in Germany entitled *Geheimnis um Schobua* (Berlin, 1935).

There is only one possible challenger to Helfritz priority and that is the claim of Baron Adolf von Wrede to have reached Shabwah in the course of a journey made in 1843 from the Wadi Amd. [Von Wrede] 'then bore to the west again across high tableland beyond which in four days he reached Shabwa on the Wadi Rasha'. R. H. Kiernan, *The Unveiling of Arabia* (London, 1937), p. 208.

43. H. St. John B. Philby, *Sheba's Daughters*, p. 80.

44. 'The history of the saintly house of Shabwa is a little obscure. Buraik, the eponynous ancestor of the Buraiki (or ahl Buraik) clan, was the father of Muhammad, the patron saint, who may have been the first settler on the ruins of Shabwa.' Philby, *Sheba's Daughters*, p. 95.

'The Bareiki are poor in everything but alliances, have a large number of protective treaties with their neighbours as far afield as Ma'in itself. Their principal protectors are the nomadic Karab, who own two-thirds of so-called Bareiki land . . . the Bareiki claim that their first progenitor was one seil al leil, the "Night Flood". They have probably been keepers of sacred places from centuries before Islam.' A. Hamilton, *The Kingdom of Melchior* (London, 1949), pp. 131–2.

'Al-Karab, of the confederation of Bal-'Ubaid, are based upon Wadi 'Irma and the contiguous areas west and east of the town bearing the historic name of Shabwah. After good rains have enlivened the varied smaller vegetation, sections of al-Karab move north through the territory of their neighbors and friends al-Sai'ar to penetrate into the southwestern Sands as far as al-Qa'āmīyāt and Shiqāq al Ma'ātif.' C. D. Matthews, 'Bedouin Life in Contemporary Arabia', *Revista degli studi orientali*, Vol. XXXV (Roma, 1960), p. 53.

45. *Sheba's Daughters*, pp. 88–90.

Two years later, Hamilton commenting on the same temple stated: 'The temple is sacred to Ithtar (the Son of Sin, the male moon and of Shams, the female sun), who is the male equivalent of Ishtar of Babylon and of the Phoenician goddess Astarte. The curving horns of the bull and the ibex were symbolical of the horned moon. I am inclined to think that the statues were of the kneeling ibex for I found lying in the rubble a baked clay model. . . . This ibex is in a crouching posture, its head bent low to the ground, and thus portrayed, its tall, curved horns bending forward, it might well be imagined to be in worship, bowing to the moon.

'Here was the ruin of an Arabian city, small in area and overflowing with rubble of costly stone, with walls useless to defence, containing no wells, without a water cistern, with a small temple on a hill overlooking fields with their sluice gates of polished alabaster; this was a city famous in the ancient world, a cause of contention among modern kingdoms, still venerated by the neighbouring Arabs and the desire of the explorer. The Hidden City, hidden no longer, had become the enigma of the sands.

'I went once more to the north gateway and looked up the rubble filled street between the massive building to the ruined temple of Ihtar and I suddenly understood for these buildings, with their massive stone fronts had neither doors or windows. They were not built for living men. No children were born behind these white walls, or played in the dust outside them. They were the dwellings of the dead and Shabwa was a holy place and a city of tombs [this conclusion does not seem at all likely to the writer].' A. Hamilton, *The Kingdom of Melchior*, pp. 160–1.

Works also consulted for this chapter

R. H. Kiernan, *The Unveiling of Arabia* (London, 1937), p. 18.

Lt.-Col. Lewis Pelly, 'A visit to the Wahabee Capital, Central Arabia', *Journal of the Royal Geographical Society*, Vol. 35 (1865), p. 183.

E. W. Lane, *Manners and Customs of the Modern Egyptians* (London, 1954), p. 432.

Zakariya bin Muhammad bin Maḥmud al-Qazwini, *Athar al-bilad wa-akhbar al-'ibad* (Beirut, 1380/1960), pp. 63–65.

G. W. Murray, *Sons of Ishmael* (London, 1935), pp. 120–1.

Sir Richard F. Burton, *Pilgrimage to Al-Madinah and Mecca*, Vol. II, p. 106.

H. St. John B. Philby, *Forty Years in the Wilderness*, p. 37.

Wilfred Thesiger, 'A New Journey in Southern Arabia', *The Geographical Journal*, Vol. CVIII (1946), p. 134.

A. Hamilton, *The Kingdom of Melchior* (London, 1949), pp. 54, 144.

D. van der Meulen, *Aden to the Hadhramaut*, p. 100.

Harold Ingrams, *Arabia and the Isles* (London, 1952), p. 344.

INDEX

DATE